Unionists & Separatists

TSEHAI
Publishers & Distributors

Printed on acid-free, recycled paper.

Unionists & Separatists

THE VAGARIES OF ETHIO-ERITREAN RELATION 1941-1991

Shumet Sishagne

TSEHAI
Publishers & Distributors

WWW.TSEHAIPUBLISHERS.COM

Unionists and Separatists: The Vagaries of Ethio-Eritrean Relation
Copyright © 2007 by Shumet Sishagne

All rights reserved. Apart from any fair dealing for the purpose of private study, research, criticism or review, as permitted under the Copyright Act, no part of this publication may be reproduced in any form, stored in a retrieval system or transmitted in any form by any means — electronic, mechanical, photocopy, recording or otherwise — without the prior permission of the publisher.
Enquiries should be sent to the under mentioned address.

Tsehai books may be purchased for educational, business, or sales promotional use. Please contact our Marketing and Special Sales Department.

Tsehai Publishers and Distributors
P. O. Box: 1881, Hollywood, CA 90078

www.tsehaipublishers.com
info@tsehaipublishers.com

ISBN: 10: 1-59907-023-5 | 13: 978-1-59907-023-0

First Edition 2007

Publisher: Elias Wondimu
Cover Design: Yoseph Gezahegne
Cover Art by www.artmesk.com

Library of Congress Cataloging in Publication Data.
A catalog record for this book is available from the Library of Congress.

British Library Cataloguing in Publication Data.
A catalogue record for this book is available from the British Library.

10 9 8 7 6 5 4 3 2 1

Printed in the United States of America

To
Tarik Shumet
(1981-1998)

CONTENTS

Preface ix

CHAPTER ONE
Introduction 1

CHAPTER TWO
The Establishment of British Military Administration and the Beginning of Organized Political Expression 15
- 22 The Establishment of the *Mahbär Feqri Hagär* (Love of Country Association)
- 29 British Military Administration: Objectives in Eritrea and Response to the Irredentist Challenge

CHAPTER THREE
Fission and Fusion in Eritrean Politics: Internal Actors and External Patrons, 1945-1951 51
- 54 The Anti-Unionist Movement
- 64 The Italian Factor in Eritrean Politics
- 70 The Ethiopian Government on the Eritrea Issue

CHAPTER FOUR
Federation, 1952-1962 91
- 100 The Eritrean Constitution and the Establishment of an Autonomous Administration
- 106 The Vicissitudes of the Federation

CHAPTER FIVE
The Beginning of Armed Opposition 127
- 130 The Arab Factor in Promoting and Sustaining the Eritrean Insurgency
- 133 Government Mishandling of the Insurgency
- 135 Discord in the Secessionist Movement

CHAPTER SIX
Split and Civil War 153
  159   The Period of Uneasy Truce, 1975-1979
  165   The War of Liquidation, 1980-1981

Epilogue 175

Bibliography 179

Notes 191

Preface

This book is written at a time of considerable uncertainty regarding the future direction of Eritrean politics and its relation with Ethiopia. The euphoria and optimism that was generated by the birth of a new Eritrean state after a spectacular victory over the Ethiopian army is now tempered by the growing realization that battle field victory does not necessary complete the making of a nation. The reappearance of the fissures that had characterized the Eritrean body-politic over the last half century has led to some reflection and reassessment of the genesis of the Eritrean struggle for independence.

This work offers readers a critical appraisal of the history of the Eritrean nationalist movement. It is intended to cover the broad political history of Eritrea and its relation with Ethiopia from 1941 to 1991. It highlights crucial developments in Ethio-Eritrean politics including the struggle over the future of Eritrea after the end of Italian colonial rule, the vicissitudes of the Ethio-Eritrean federation, the birth and development of the Eritrean insurgency, the course of the bitter civil war between rival Eritrean guerrilla factions, and the process through which the Eritrean People's Liberation Front (EPLF) succeeded in imposing its hegemony over the Eritrean political arena.

The data for this study came mainly from archival sources. I was able to fully utilize consular reports and diplomatic papers in the National Archives in Washington, D.C.; the Public Records Office in England; and the Archivio Storico del Ministero degli Affari Esteri and the Archivio Storico del Ministero dell'Africa Italiana in Rome. I have also made extensive use of the published materials found at the Library of the Istituto Italo-Africano in Rome. In addition, I was able to consult various private papers of ex-British officials in Eritrea, especially at the Bodleian Library in Oxford.

The most valuable source, which I believe distinguishes my work from many like it, however, came from Ethiopia. I was fortunate to get access to the documents of the Ethiopian Liaison Office in Eritrea. This rich collection of official and private papers, which has not previously been used by any researcher, provides valuable insight into Eritrean politics in the 1940s and early 1950s.

I have also made extensive use of the archives of the Governorate General of Eritrea Province in Asmara, which contain useful materials for the period from the end of the federation to the beginning of the 1970s. In addition, I was able to consult a number of documents from the archives of the former Ministry of the Pen.

I was able to gather a wealth of both oral and written information from individuals who were intimately connected with events in Eritrea over the last fifty years. These included persons with varied experiences ranging from those who played prominent roles in the politics of the 1940s to guerrilla fighters of the 1980s. Specially useful are some of the manuscripts written by ex-members of the liberation fronts. I have also attempted to consult as many of the publications of the liberation movements as possible.

The breadth and depth of the sources I have utilized, have, I believe, enabled me to present a work that is based on comprehensive documentation. Researchers on modern Eritrea have so far paid scant regard to the internal sources. This has left them at the mercy of consular reports, which are mostly incomplete, and far too often based on an inaccurate understanding of the situations on which they are reporting. In societies where open political expression is restricted, most consular officials tend to depend for their information on disgruntled elements. This was quite evident in Eritrea where the American, British, and Italian consuls in Asmara, surrounded themselves with dissident elements who sought their support and fed them with their version of developments inside the country. These sources need to be carefully scrutinized, and cross-checked with other independent evidence.

I have attempted to maintain the coherence and integrity of the subject through a chronological presentation. The main section of the book starts, in Chapter Two, with a description of the replacement of Italian rule in Eritrea by the British Military Administration and the beginning of the first organized political expression in the territory. It analyses the character of the irredentist movement and the British reaction to it.

Chapter Three which deals with the period from 1945 to 1951, discusses the interests of external powers in Eritrea and explores the circumstances under which various political factions emerged in the territory. This chapter also delves into the connection between external interference and the polarization of local differences.

Chapter Four continues the discussion on the relative position of the various external powers on the future settlement in Eritrea and the changes in alignment among the political forces in Eritrea. This section outlines the major factors which lay behind the international decision to resolve the Eritrean case through a federation with Ethiopia. A large portion of this chapter is devoted to analyzing the underlying causes which undermined the federal arrangement and finally led to the annexation of the territory.

The final chapter covers the period from the birth of the armed secessionist movement in 1961 to its triumph in 1991. This section considers the sociopolitical base of the insurgency and its impact on the character of the movement. It provides an assessment of the role of foreign support in fostering and sustaining the Eritrean insurgency. The chapter also follows the factional strife within the secessionist movement and discusses how this led to the fragmentation of the Eritrean Liberation Front (ELF) and the growth of the EPLF as a powerful contender. It concludes with an investigation of the stages which led to the emergence of the Eritrean Peoples Liberation Front (EPLF) as the sole power in the Eritrean arena.

This book has benefited immensely from the support of many people. I was fortunate to interview several extraordinary individuals who were intimately acquainted with the subject of my research. I am greatly indebted to them. I also owe a special debt of gratitude to my former teachers and colleagues at Addis Ababa University: Merid Wolde Aregay, Taddesse Tamirat, David Chapple, and Bahiru Zewde for their unfailing support during the early stage of my career as a historian. Thanks are also due to my mentor and friend Donald Crummey of the University of Illinois, and my colleague James M. Morris of Christopher Newport University, for reading successive drafts of this work and offering valuable suggestions, and correcting grammatical and syntactical errors.

My wife Mulu Tefera and our daughter Meheret Shumet deserve mention for their patience and support. I also want to acknowledge the friendship and support of Mulugeta Petros, Eliane Petros and Gizaw Zewdu. Finally, I want to give special thanks to Elias Wondimu of Tsehai Publishers for the dedication he showed in the preparation of this work.

CHAPTER ONE

INTRODUCTION

In August 1981, some 5,000 fighters of the Eritrean Liberation Front (ELF), the survivors of a once formidable army of over 20,000 men which had been decimated in a bloody war between contending guerrilla forces in Eritrea, crossed the border in to the Sudan, abandoning the field to their rival, the Eritrean People's Liberation Front (EPLF). This event marked the culmination of four decades of political fermentation during which attempts to forge an Eritrean national consensus were continually frustrated by the weak historical foundations on which the territory's unity rested and by the deep seated socio-cultural differences which divided its diverse ethnic and religious communities which appeared to have more in common with groups and traditions outside of Eritrea than with each other.

Neither the political parties that mushroomed briefly in the 1940s, nor the various guerrilla forces which had emerged since the 1960s had been able to create a political consensus based on a coherent national identity. Ethnic, religious, and regional rivalries were more potent than the desire to establish a unified Eritrean nation.

By waging a successful war of liquidation against rival forces in Eritrea, the victorious EPLF had managed by 1981 to impose a degree of political cohesion which had eluded its predecessors. Yet how deeply this has taken root in Eritrea remains to be seen, for it required naked power under a rigidly centralized organization to establish even the semblance of political cohesion in the territory.

This work examines closely the evolution in Eritrea politics from 1941 to 1991. It explores the circumstances under which the Eritrean urban and rural elites were politicized following the Italian defeat in 1941 and the main political trends which emerged at that time. It investigates in detail the role of traditional loyalties in the mobilization of both the urban and rural masses and the survival of precolonial sentiments in determining political affiliation. Special effort is made to identify the major forces which shaped the Eritrean political landscape in the forty years with which this study is concerned.

Few territories have been as intensely affected by foreign intervention as Eritrea. A major gateway to the extensive commercial contacts of the Axumite Kingdom in the first six centuries of the Christian era, the Eritrean coastline came under increasing pressure first from Arab expansion and later from the Ottoman Empire, which culminated in the seizure of the port of Massawa in 1557.

The revival of Egyptian power under Mohammed Ali in the nineteenth century ushered in another era of contention over the territory we now call Eritrea. This led to several decades of confrontation between the Egyptians and the Ethiopian state, which culminated in two major battles in 1875 and 1876 in which the Ethiopian Emperor, Yohannes IV, defeated the Egyptian offensive.

Less than a decade after Yohannes's defeat of the Egyptians, a new threat introduced itself to the region in the form of Italian colonialism. Although its further expansion into the remainder of Ethiopia was arrested by Emperor Menilek's victory at the Battle of Adwa in 1896, Italian power managed to entrench itself over this northernmost portion of Ethiopia, which it named Eritrea, until it was ejected by British forces in 1941 during World War II.

The British seized the colony as an occupied enemy territory and administered it for a decade. The final settlement of the territory's future was left, first, to the Big Four Powers (USA, USSR, Great Britain and France). When they failed to reach an agreement, it was transferred to the General Assembly of the United Nations in 1949, where it became an issue of contention between forces marked by varied and competing interests and loyalties.

No study of Eritrea would, therefore, be complete without due regard for the influence of external factors on internal developments. This study underscores the scope and nature of the external involvement, the respective interests of the various forces at play in Eritrean politics, and the underlying motives behind the issues which they raised. Eritrea's modern political history can be understood only through a meticulous unraveling of the web of complex interests which entangled themselves in the struggle to determine the political future of the territory.

Once this task is achieved it becomes comparatively easy to assess the dynamics of the various internal political forces and the issues around which they congregated. Based on this approach, my study demonstrates that no viable separate Eritrean identity existed in 1941 to promote the growth of a cohesive political movement. Available evidence illustrates that what transpired in Eritrean politics in the decade following 1941 negated the existence of a territorially based Eritrean identity.

This book argues that Italian colonialism, which created Eritrea as a separate territorial unit was neither long enough in its duration nor sufficiently intense to promote socio-economic changes which could override pre-existing loyalties and shape new identities.[1] Pre-colonial identities, in the form of allegiance to the Ethiopian state or to other ethnic, linguistic, and religious affiliations remained the most potent mobilizing forces rather than loyalty to "Eritreanism." The notion of constructing an Eritrean nation appealed to few people in the territory, and it was firmly resisted particularly by a great majority of the highland population. In this the Eritrean experience followed a different pattern from the path pursued by other colonial communities.

In most parts of Africa and Asia nationalism principally arose as a result of and in reaction to Western imperialism. European colonialism unwittingly created the conditions which favored the rise of nationalist forces. The establishment of viable political units and infrastructural expansion, including the development of indigenous intelligentsias which were capable of imitating the Western model of nationalism, were crucial factors which stimulated the national movements in the colonies.[2]

Estranged from their white masters by their exclusion from positions of power, Africa's intelligentsia developed a brand of nationalism which emphasized solidarity based on Africanness, and, by extension, on their opposition to the colonial domination they all shared.

African nationalist leaders presented the struggle as one between the colonial power and its subject peoples. According to Amilcar Cabral the issue was one between the colonized people who constitute a "nation-class" and the colonial state. He wrote: "as a dominated people we only present one ensemble vis-à-vis the oppressor."[3] This strategy of focusing on combating alien rule enabled the nationalist movement to build broad alliances among various sectors of the indigenous society. Although these coalitions were short lived and did not fare well in the post-independence period, they were largely instrumental in bringing a number of independent African states into existence.

The nationalist movement which arose in Eritrea in the 1940s showed similar patterns of broad mobilization based on opposition to colonial domination. However, the Eritrean case significantly differs from those of many other African territories in that it arose to undo the territorial demarcation imposed by the Italian colonial regime. The largest nationalist force (and the first organized political body in Eritrea), the Mahbär Feqri Hagär (Love of Country Association), pursued irredentist goals which aspired to unify the territory with Ethiopia and fought against attempts to create a separate political entity based on the frontiers created by the Italians.

The handful of Eritrea's modern intelligentsia in the 1940s, who also happened to be dominantly from the Christian section of the population,[4] championed the cause of Ethiopian irredentism and was averse to the creation of a separate Eritrean nation. Thus, the first organized anticolonial movement in Eritrea distinctly manifested a powerful Ethiopian irredentism. This Eritrean intelligentsia was able to mobilize first the urban population,[5] and later the countryside, behind its bid for independence and unity with Ethiopia.

By opting for irredentism rather than the creation of a separate Eritrean state, the Eritrean intelligentsia class of the 1940s reaffirmed a long-standing goal of its predecessors. Most Eritreans with some education had been the leading champions of Ethiopian nationalism throughout the colonial period. This group was acutely aware of the need to build a strong Ethiopia, thereby to end colonial domination in Eritrea.

One of the earliest representatives of this group of Eritrean intelligentsia and a noted articulator of Ethiopian nationalism was Blatta Gäbräegziabhér Gilamaryam (ca. 1860-1914). He acquired his political enlightenment while serving the Italians in the 1890s, and turned into a fierce anticolonialist and a staunch propagandist of Ethiopian nationalism. In a manuscript completed in 1897, Gäbräegziabhér regretted "the degradation and distress that befell the beautiful and great Ethiopia," and entreated his readers "to feel sorry for her [Ethiopia] and try as much as you can to pull her out of her distress and tribulation."[6] Regarding his motive for expressing such sentiments, he said, "I wrote these...because I witnessed my countrymen, my brothers, my sisters and my religion daily being chained and thrown into the jaws of a python [Italians] far more rapacious than the earlier one. And I wrote this commentary so that you would lament for their plight and so that ways could be found to redeem them from their distress."[7]

In a separate letter Gäbräegziabhér reminded the Emperor Menilek that the Italians were ruling over "the cradle lands of Ethiopia" and that they had reduced "the sons of Ethiopia to a state of slavery far worse than that experienced by the people of Israel."[8] His advice to Ethiopians was to "remain united as sons of a single Mother Ethiopia against European encirclement."[9]

Succeeding generations of Eritreans who acquired their education either from the Italian or mission schools in Eritrea expressed their anticolonial sentiments through a strong assertion of Ethiopian identity. A good number of them migrated to Ethiopia. Here they constituted a significant proportion of the Ethiopian bureaucracy and were generally in the forefront in the advancement of Ethiopian nationalism.

The Italian authorities were aware of the special attachment of politically articulate Eritreans to Ethiopia. In a dispatch to the Ministry of Colonies the Eritrean Governor, Jacopo Gasparini, noted in 1924 that "students from the Swedish mission demonstrated a major attachment to Ethiopia rather than to Eritrea."[10] Lamenting the Italian failure to arrest the continued growth of Ethiopian irredentism in Eritrea, Governor Zoli wrote in 1930, "We must admit that we find ourselves in a situation that has changed little over the last forty years. We have not even benefited from the small changes in the traditional institutions and we, therefore, find ourselves at a much inferior position compared to Ethiopia."[11]

Indeed, the factors which could have encouraged the growth of a separate Eritrean identity under Italian colonialism were extremely limited. Colonialism had scarcely affected the close socio-cultural relations which existed between the highland communities of Eritrea and the rest of northern Ethiopia. Inter-marriage between important families on both sides of the Märäb river, supported by the common language, Tegreñña, and common social customs, continued as in the old days. Additionally, traditional trade links were maintained, and the Ethiopian Orthodox Church continued to influence the Christian population. Ambitious students from Eritrea seeking church education went to monasteries in Ethiopia; in turn, many students from northern and central Ethiopia journeyed to Eritrea to be educated at such famous monasteries as Däbrä Bizän. One Italian governor in Eritrea went as far as to call the churches in Eritrea the "hotbed of Ethiopian nationalism."[12]

The Italians also maintained many of the political institutions inherited from Ethiopia, especially at the local level. The structures of government, the names of the various offices, and the titles of the local officials all dated from Ethiopian times. It is perhaps significant that during the initial period of their rule the Italians followed their Ethiopian predecessors as rulers in the area in using Amharic rather than the local Tegreñña side-by-side with Italian, in issuing decrees and various government instructions to the indigenous population.[13] The Italians also continued to refer to the highland Christian population as Abyssinians. They began using the term "Eritrean" in 1937,[14] a scant three years before the end of their rule.

The later period of Italian rule was also marked by increasing racist policies which were designed to strengthen white supremacy and keep the indigenous population in a state of perpetual subjugation. In his statement justifying the 1937 law which banned inter-racial cohabitation, Martino Moreno, the director of the Political Affairs in the Ministry of the Colonies, said,

> He who studies the history of the African people should recognise that they have created nothing universal ... All those that are permanent, from the Obelisks of Aksum to the Castles

of Gondar are ... products of foreign civilizations. It is thus utopian to think that Africans could be elevated quickly to the level of the Westerner ... We are dealing with people who will never reach the age of maturity.[15]

Eritrea's modern intelligentsia reacted against European racism and its efforts to relegate Ethiopian civilization by consciously upholding the cause of Greater Ethiopian nationalism. Considering the survival of the many links which connected highland Eritreans with the rest of Ethiopia and the powerful motives which pulled the Eritrean intelligentsia towards Ethiopia, it is not surprising that the first organized nationalist manifestation in Eritrea should assume an Ethiopian irredentist character. In fact, sentiments of irredentism and nationalism were used synonymously in Eritrea. Official sources of the British Administration in Eritrea referred to the Unionist movement as a nationalist movement,[16] and irredentist forces were invariably called "nationalists."

It should, however, be pointed out that not all sectors of Eritrean society shared the enthusiasm for union with Ethiopia. A great majority of the Muslim lowland communities, which accounted for almost half of the Eritrean population, had little desire to associate themselves either with Ethiopia or, for that matter, with the Tegreñña-speaking Christians in Eritrea.[17]

Political consciousness had been slow to develop among the nomadic population of the lowlands, and when it did it arose in reaction to Christian irredentism. But none of the opposition forces were able to build a coherent political program which envisaged the creation of an independent Eritrean political unit. The strongest party which arose in opposition to the Unionists, the Muslim League of Eritrea, was exclusively Muslim and openly championed Muslim interests only. In later days it split into two factions, with one group, the Muslim League of the Western Province, advocating the creation of a separate political unit in the western lowland.

Other smaller political groups which emerged in the late 1940s developed an autonomous political strategy which aspired to create a unified Eritrean state. Most of them arose as splinters from the larger groups or were created through the sponsorship of foreign patrons.

Considering the circumstances under which Eritrea was created as a single political unit and the lack of an appreciable degree of socio-economic change under colonialism, the fragmentation of opinion which characterized Eritrean politics at the end of Italian rule came as no surprise. As a territorial unit Eritrea had been formally created by the Italians, as G.K.N. Trevaskis remarked, "by an act of surgery: by severing its different peoples from those with whom their past had been linked and by grafting the amputated remnants to each other under the title of Eritrea."[18]

The largely Christian population in the Eritrean highlands of Hamasén, Seraé and Akälä-Guzai were separated from their Tegreñña-speaking kinsmen to the south of the Märäb river with whom they also shared a very high degree of material culture. This was also true of the mainly pastoral population of eastern Eritrea, the Saho and Afar, of whom the majority resided in Ethiopia. To the west, the Beja tribes were partitioned between the Sudan and the new Italian colony.

It is clear from the evidence, then, that the fifty years of colonial rule had not created the necessary conditions for the grafted parts to grow into one integrated body. No major social and economic transformation was brought by the Italians save for a brief period in the 1930s when the highland areas experienced a boom created by the Fascist war preparation against Ethiopia.

Many of the Eritrean communities remained socially and economically unaffected throughout the four-decade colonial period. In most of the lowland areas, the Italians simply recognized pre-existing tribal groupings and formalized their institution. Although their hold over the highland regions was relatively firm, here, too, the Italians integrated many of the old Ethiopian institutions into their new administrative apparatus especially at the village level.

During the occupation of Ethiopia (1936-1940), the Italians merged their Eritrean colony with the rest of Ethiopia. Combined with the province of Tegray, Eritrea constituted one administrative region in the new Italian East African Empire ruled from Addis Ababa.

To sum up, neither relations during the pre-colonial period nor the experience under Italian rule warranted the growth of a new national feeling among the population which inhabited the territory of Eritrea.

Rather, comprehensive investigation of the records of the 1940s lends credence to the conclusion that the initiative to create an all-inclusive Eritrean identity came largely from interested foreign patrons rather than from the indigenous elite of the territory. First British and later Italian efforts to promote Eritrean separatism, the former as part of its effort to secure a strategic position along the Red Sea, and the latter to reestablish its lost position in Eritrea in the postwar period bear out this conclusion, challenging several assumptions made about political developments in modern Eritrea. The issue of the origins of Eritrean nationalism is a contentious topic characterized by intense passion and partisanship. This has inevitably led to gross factual distortions and misleading interpretations. In the last few decades a considerable literature has developed to lend legitimacy to the struggle for Eritrean separation from Ethiopia.[19]

An often repeated assertion, usually emanating from the various Eritrean liberation movements, presents Eritrea as having existed as a separate and distinct political entity for centuries. This line of argument denies any political association with Ethiopia, and views the subsequent relation with the latter as a colonial imposition.[20]

In these and other studies, the resilience of the separatist demand is taken as convincing proof of the existence of an all-encompassing Eritrean national sentiment dating at least from the end of Italian rule. The proponents of this view assume that a powerful desire for the creation of an Eritrean national state was frustrated by Ethiopian intervention in the post World War II period in collusion with the Western powers.[21]

This study questions most of the basic theses of these works and challenges the premise which forms the basis for many of the recent conclusions and reinterpretations of modern Eritrean history. It demonstrates that Eritrean nationalism was non-existent in the first two decades following the end of Italian rule and that the decisive forces in Eritrean politics were not those that were inclined to build an Eritrean nation but, rather, those that negated the existence of a separate Eritrean entity.

This work illustrates that contrary to widely spread assumptions, Ethiopian irredentism in Eritrea was largely the work of Eritrean Christian highlanders and not of the newly restored Ethiopian government, which was itself fighting for its life.[22]

Irredentist forces which aspired to unite with Ethiopia were first on the scene following the Italian defeat in 1941, and they remained by far the largest and the best organized political force in the territory, commanding the loyalty of the predominantly Christian highlanders of Eritrea. The major opposition group which emerged later to challenge the irredentist demand, the Muslim League of Eritrea, was based entirely on religious affiliation and had no single Christian members. Later attempts to build a coalition between a small Christian minority group opposed to unconditional union with Ethiopia and the Muslim League of Eritrea failed for lack of common ground between them.

This study also attempts to clarify the role of foreign powers in the decision to create the Ethio-Eritrean federation. It questions the widely held view that the West in general, and the United States in particular, handed over Eritrea to Ethiopia on a silver platter. It concludes that the European powers in general were not enthusiastic over seeing a unified and strong Ethiopia, fearing its potential influence on their respective colonies in Africa. Each of the Great Powers also had vested interests that were opposed to Ethiopia's claims to Eritrea.

Britain was adamantly opposed to passing over the whole of Eritrea to Ethiopia because it wanted to annex the western portion of the territory to its colony in the Sudan and sought to merge the remaining parts with the Ethiopian province of Tegray and place it under its trusteeship. To achieve these objectives the British fostered the creation of anti-Ethiopian forces in Eritrea.

The French were interested in preventing Ethiopia from having its own access to the sea so that it would remain dependent on the port of Djibouti, which they then controlled. United States policy wavered for a long time between supporting Britain's objectives in the region and returning the territory to Italy. Western support for a federal formula came after the realization that no other solution could break the international deadlock created over the future settlement of Eritrea.

The most crucial issue in modern Eritrean history is the birth and development of the armed insurgency for the creation of a separate Eritrean state. In fact, its success in defeating the Ethiopian army and declaring an independent Eritrean state seems to cast doubt on the thesis that no viable sense of Eritrean nationhood existed at the time that the future of Eritrea was being discussed in the 1940s. It may even appear presumptuous to argue, after the separatist forces have triumphed in the battle field, that secessionism was not the choice of the great majority of Eritreans when the insurgency started in the early 1960s.

The secessionist war began as an exclusively Muslim affair, confined to the pastoral regions of the western lowlands. Throughout the 1960s the forces of the Eritrean Liberation Front spent as much time fighting Christian Eritrean peasants as they did the government forces. The handful of Christian fighters who joined them in the mid-1960s were mostly eliminated, and the few dozen survivors had to break away and seek shelter in the highlands at the end of the decade. But the Muslim forces coming from the various regions of the territory were unable to stay together under one organization. The splintering of the ELF into four separate organizations in 1970 signaled that Eritrean nationalism had yet a long way to go before it could marshal significant loyalty among the various sections of the population.

That the Eritrean insurgency managed to survive regardless of these vicissitudes for a decade and half during Emperor Haile Selassie's regime, can be best explained by the political failure of the Ethiopian state, the gross incompetence with which the rebellion was handled, and the massive socio-economic and political disaffection (dating back to the early years of the 1940s) which continued to smolder in the province.

In subsequent years the secessionist movement was able to feed on a growing disillusionment with the Ethiopian government and to expand its hold over areas that had hitherto remained closed to it. The crisis which accompanied the 1974 revolution in Ethiopia gave the insurgency a tremendous impetus. Brutal repressions by the military regime, especially in the highland towns, drove thousands of Eritrean youth into the camps of the secessionist forces. The Christian highlands, which had been the bastions of Ethiopian nationalism only a few decades before, provided a base for one of the most successful of the guerrilla forces, the EPLF.

Three decades of sustained struggle to create an Eritrean identity could not fail to leave its impact. After all, national identity is not something fixed. Given the right combination of forces it could be created, or invented, as some say.[23] What is crucial in understanding the whole phenomenon is not the end product, i.e., the success of the armed rebellion in fostering a separate Eritrean identity, but the process which brought it about. Undue emphasis on the national or colonial character of the insurgency in Eritrea has greatly confused the issue and may have distracted social scientists from unraveling the basic causes that lay at the root of the horrendous conflict which has ravaged the whole region for over four decades.[24] While this work does not pretend to fulfill this task, it attempts to make the job easier for future researchers by presenting a coherent account of the events and identifying the principal actors on the Eritrean political stage.

Notes

[1] For a useful discussion of the limitations of Italian colonialism in creating an integrated colony, see Tekeste Negash, *Italian Colonialism in Eritrea, 1882-1941: Policies, Praxis and Impact* (Uppsala: Acta Universitatis Upsaliensis), 1987.

[2] As J. Plamentaz put it, this was a claim "against the West the right to imitate the West:" J. Plamentaz, *On Alien Rule and Self-Government* (London: Longmans, 1960), 2.

[3] Amilcar Cabral, *Revolution in Guinea* (London: Stage One, 1969), 56.

[4] Italian colonialism had little impact on the predominantly Muslim pastoralists of the western and eastern lowlands. Satisfied with exercising indirect control through their traditional chiefs, the Italians left most of the traditional institutions intact and did little to economically integrate these areas with the center. The few schools (including the mission schools) in the territory were largely concentrated in the highland, Christian areas.

[5] Asmara, the largest urban center in the territory, became the hotbed of Ethiopian irredentism from the first days of the British occupation.

⁶ Quoted in Tekeste Negash, *No Medicine for the Bite of a White Snake: Notes on Nationalism and Resistance in Eritrea, 1890-1940* (Uppsala: University of Uppsala, 1986), 4.

⁷ Ibid., 8.

⁸ Draft of a letter to Emperor Menilek, 19 May 1899, cited in ibid.

⁹ Ibid., 15.

¹⁰ Archivio storico del Ministero degli Affari Esteri [here after ASMAE], paco 1025, Gasparini to Ministry of Colonies, 6 June 1924. According to a missionary survey published in 1927, the Italians complained that the type of instruction given by the Protestant missionaries does not appear "to educate the people to become obedient Italian subjects:" World Dominion Press, *Light and Darkness in East Africa: A Missionary Survey of Uganda, Anglo-Egyptian Sudan, Abyssinia, Eritrea, and the Three Somalilands* (London, 1927), 184-85. Since the Eritreans were prohibited from advancing after grade four in the government schools, the Swedish mission schools played an important role in producing the few educated Eritreans. The colonial government closed these schools and expelled the Swedish missionaries in 1932. Many prominent Eritreans who played leading roles in the political movements of the 1940s were products of the Swedish mission schools.

¹¹ ASMAE, pacco 1015, Zoli to Ministry of Colonies, 30 June 1930.

¹² Zoli to Ministry of Colonies, Asmara, 15 July 1929, cited in Tekeste Negash, *Italian Colonialism in Eritrea*, p. 128. In an attempt to undermine the connection with the Ethiopian Church, the Italian government managed to get the Eritrean churches placed under the direct authority of the Patriarchate of Alexandria in 1930, thereby eliminating the authority of Addis Ababa.

¹³ Several files containing official decrees in Amharic, including some from General Oreste Baratieri, military governor of Eritrea (1892-96), and the governor of Kärän district, as well as assorted petititions from locals, also written in Amharic are found in Archivio Eritrea located in the Archivio Storico del Ministero degli Affari Esteri.

¹⁴ In 1937, the Italians issued a directive in which they granted a few privileges to their Somali and Eritrean subjects in recognition of the contribution of the askaris recruited from these colonies in the conquest of Ethiopia. Among the privileges granted was the right to be called Eritreans and Somalis instead of natives and subjects. They were also allowed to own and operate small businesses: Archivio Storico del Ministero dell'Africa Italiana, Rome [hereafter ASMAI], position 181/46, Lessona (Minister of Colonies) to General Graziani, 7 October 1937.

¹⁵ Martino M. Moreno, "Politica di Razza e la Politica Coloniale Italiana," *Gli Annalidell' Africa Italians*, 2, 2 (1939).

¹⁶ See for instance, G.K.N. Trevaskis, *Eritrea: A Colony in Transition* (Oxford: Oxford University Press, 1960), pp. 59-69. Trevaskis, a senior official of the British Military Administration in Eritrea wrote: "By the time of Mussolini's fall in July 1943 the Nationalist movement had won over most of the Christian Abyssinians of Asmara and the other Plateau towns."

¹⁷ Concerning the conflicting loyalties of the various population groups in Eritrea, Tekeste Negash underscores peoples' perceptions of their pre-colonial history in shaping their subsequent political affiliation. He argues:

While the Tigrinyans maintained throughout the colonial period a clearly discernible notion of Ethiopian nationalism, the non-Tigrnyans appeared to align themselves with the colonial rule ...Dispersed widely in the regions of the colony that were of least importance to colonial economic and political exploitation, the non-Tigrinyans, who were mostly Muslims, rated the colonial system as more favourable than the Ethiopian system.

[18] Trevaskis, Eritrea, pp. 19-21.

[19] See for instance, F. Houtart, *Social Analysis of the Eritrean Revolution* (1979); ELF, The Eritrean Revolution (Beirut, 1979); Bereket Habte Selassie, *Conflict and Intervention in the Horn of Africa* (New York: Monthly Review Press, 1980); David Pool, *Eritrea: Africa's Longest War* (London: Anti-Slavery Society, 1980); Richard Sherman, *Eritrea: The Unfinished Revolution* (New York: Praeger, 1980); Basil Davidson, Lionel Cliffe and Bereket Habte Selassie, eds., *Behind the War in Eritrea* (London: Spokesman, 1980); Research and Information Center on Eritrea, *Revolution in Eritrea: Eyewitness Reports* (1980); Dan Connell, "The Birth of the Eritrean Nation," *Horn of Africa*, III, 1 (1980); J. Firebrace and S. Holland, *Eritrea Never Kneel Down* (Trenton, N.J.: The Red Sea Press, 1985); Cahsai Berhane and E.C. Williamson, *Erythrée: Un peuple en marche* (L'harmattan, 1985); Jordan Gebre-Medhin, *Peasants and Nationalism in Eritrea* (Trenton, N.J.: The Red Sea Press, 1989; Araia Tseggai, *The Economic Viability of an Independent Eritrea* (Ph.D. dissertation, Lincoln, Nebraska, 1981; Stefano Poscia, *Eritrea Colonia Tradita* (Roma: Edizioni Associate, 1989).

[20] See for instance, Eritrean People's Liberation Front, *Memorandum* (August 1978); R.I.C.E., *The Eritrean Case: Proceedings of the Permanent People's Tribunal* (Rome: Research and Information Center on Eritrea, 1982), 17-31; Eritrean Liberation Front, *Eritrea, the National Democratic Revolution Versus Ethiopian Expansion* (Beirut, 1979); Bereket Habte Selassie, a one time senior official of the Ethiopian government and later a prominent propagandist of the EPLF, wrote that Eritrea was "a colony of a neo-colony," see his "From British Rule to Federation and Annexation," in *Behind the War in Eritrea*, 45.

[21] Abdul Rahaman Babu, "The Future That Works," in *Adulis*, III, 1(1986); Dan Connell, "Eritrea and Self-Determination," *Guardian* (New York), Feb. 21, 1979; Okbazghi Yohannes, *Eritrea a Pawn in World Politics* (Gainesville: University of Florida Press, 1991); Roy Pateman, *Eritrea: Even the Stones are Burning* (Trenton, N.J.: The Red Sea Press, 1990); Bereket Habte Selassie, *Eritrea and the United Nations* (Trenton, N.J.: The Red Sea Press, 1989); Ruth Iyob, *The Eritrean Struggle for Independence: Domination, Resistance, Nationalism*, 1942-1993 (Cambridge: Cambridge University Press, 1995).

[22] Emperor Haile Selassie's government, which was restored in 1941 after five years of devastating Fascist occupation, remained weak, disorganized, and highly dependent on British political and financial support until the mid-1940s. It was even unable to get the British government to agree to the appointment of an Ethiopian representative in Eritrea until 1946.

[23] Ernest Gellner, a noted scholar on nationalism, wrote: "Nationalism is not the awakening of nations to self-consciousness: it invents nations where they do not exist," Thought and Change (London: Weidenfeld and Nicholson, 1964), 169.

²⁴ A good beginning in seeking alternative explanations is made by Christopher Clapham who draws a connection between the growth of opposition to the modern Ethiopian state in the north, which had formed the core of the old Ethiopian empire, and both the increasing political and economic marginalization of the elites of the region, and the total destitution of the local population: Christopher Clapham, *Transformation and Continuity in Revolutionary Ethiopia* (Cambridge: Cambridge University Press, 1988); and idem., "The Structure of Regional Conflict in Northern Ethiopia," in *Henock: Journal of Historical and Philosophical Thought*, I (August 1990), 77-89. Another attempt to explain the intense crisis in the Horn in terms of the material deterioration of society is made by Frederick C. Gamst, "The Horn of Africa as a Problem Area in Anthropological Perspective," *XIth International Congress of Anthropological and Ethnological Sciences* (Harrison Hot Springs, British Colombia, August 1983).

CHAPTER TWO

THE ESTABLISHMENT OF BRITISH MILITARY ADMINISTRATION AND THE BEGINNING OF ORGANIZED POLITICAL EXPRESSION

Britain's hopes of appeasing Benito Mussolini by recognizing his conquest and annexation of Ethiopia to the Italian crown were shattered when, on June 10, 1940, he declared war on her. Fascist forces from Tripolitania and Cyrenaica pushed east towards Cairo. The Italians from Eritrea overran British defense lines at Kassala, Gallabat, and Kurmuk in the Sudan. In the east, British Somaliland fell into Italian hands. Similar advances were also made in the south on British positions on the Kenyan side bordering Ethiopia. These swift offensives imperiled Britain's interests and possessions in the Middle East and East Africa and threatened to block her line of communication to the Far East via the Suez Canal.

The British launched their counteroffensive against the Italian threat in North and East Africa from three bases. The main front from Cairo moved westwards to drive the Italians out of their new positions in Egypt and to capture Cyrenaica and Tripolitania. Simultaneous campaigns were opened from Khartoum and Nairobi to deal with the Italian forces in Eritrea, Ethiopia, and Somaliland. And the British commands in Khartoum and Nairobi established liaison with the resistance movements inside Ethiopia. Together with Emperor Haile Selassie, who was hastily brought back from his exile in England early in July, 1940, British forces rolled back the Italian army in several directions.

Less than a year after Mussolini's declaration of war on Britain, the Italian African Empire had collapsed, leaving Britain with her hands full of a conglomeration of territories in East and North Africa. Not expecting such a rapid disintegration of its adversary, the War Office was unprepared to take over the administration of the newly conquered territories. There were few precedents to follow. The breakup of the Turkish empire in the Near East and the occupation of German colonies in Africa during the First World War were the most recent, if useful, examples to which they could turn. It was perhaps significant that the two major architects of the administration of the newly occupied territories, General Earl Wavell, commander-in-chief of the Middle East, and Sir Philip Mitchell, the chief political officer, both had some experience in administering conquered territories at the end of the First World War, Wavell in the Near East and Mitchell in Tanganyika. They improvised an on-the-spot structure called Occupied Enemy Territory Administration (O.E.T.A.). It set up military administrations for Eritrea, Italian Somaliland, and Cyrenaica and Tripolitania under the authority of the Commander-in-Chief, Middle East, who, in turn, assigned the chief political officer, who assumed much the same role as Colonial Office appointees played in the regular British colonies. In each of the ex-Italian colonies the chief political officer delegated his authority to a chief military administrator.

With regard to Ethiopia, the arrangements grudgingly recognized the Emperor's power and the country's sovereignty, but under the rather uneasy and ill-defined supervision of the British military. This, in effect, threatened to make Ethiopia a protectorate.

With most of its attention focused on the rapid escalation of the war on the European front, the British government at first saw little use for the new territories beyond the more effective prosecution of the war. The new administrations were designed to function with minimum cost to Great Britain. In the face of war-time shortages of material resources and trained personnel, British officials opted to maintain as much of the Italian administrative machinery as possible: its functionaries, laws and various institutions.[1]

At a time when the Italians' national prestige had diminished in the eyes of the indigenous population, maintaining the status quo was also seen as a step necessary to guarantee the safety and privileges of the many Italians now living under British rule.[2] This meant retaining some of the Fascist racial laws designed to hold down the local population. With their judges still on their benches, backed by the Carbinieri and the Polizia Africana Italiana (Mussolini's version of the Gestapo which exercised unlimited power to ensure compliance with the Fascist system), the Italian position vis-à-vis their former subjects remained dominant.

Italian officials serving the British Military Administration (BMA) worked hard to ensure that the indigenous population was kept in the "old manners," lest, they feared, it acquire new ambitions and become unmanageable should Eritrea be handed back to Italy.[3] Some Italians openly admitted that they had to cooperate with the British authorities because they were "in the midst of a primitive native population whose instincts against the whites have been encouraged by the recent war."[4]

Italian officials, especially in the police force and the judiciary, used their positions to combat any manifestation of anti-Italian feelings in the guise of maintaining public security. According to British intelligence reports, Chief Prosecutor Montefusco Emanuele, who was a member of the Fascist Council of Discipline, used his office under the BMA to settle scores with anti-Fascists. Lauro Angelo, the Fascist Commissario of the Hamasén before the British occupation, was allowed to remain in his post fulfilling the same functions. Spiccacci, another ardent Fascist official in Adi Ugri, ruled with an iron hand, and prevented the local population from making complaints to the British senior political officer.[5]

Fascist speculators, who had made fortunes under the old administration, continued to employ their skills by bribing O.E.T.A. officials to gain government concessions and other benefits. Some of the very prominent businessmen, like Barattolo, Filippinni, and Patrignani, who had acquired their fortunes through manipulating the Fascist system, used their skills once again to win the favour of the BMA[6] In the words of a BMA intelligence officer, the new administration extended almost the complete range of commercial facilities to "the same sharks who had flourished under the Fascist Regime."[7]

To the inhabitants of Eritrea the Italian defeat and the establishment of a British Military Administration seemed to bring little change in the system of government or in their relation with their former masters. A contemporary official observed that the transfer of power "looked little different to all but the more perceptive."[8]

But the British success in buying the cooperation of Italian residents in Eritrea was achieved at the cost of alienating a large section of the Eritrean population, particularly in the towns. Italy had been defeated in war, and there appeared no legitimate reason why its citizens should enjoy unfair advantages over Eritreans. British propaganda against Fascism and the promises they had made at the beginning of the war aroused great expectations for the collapse of Italian power. Disappointments were, therefore, immediate when the local population saw quick fraternization between British and Italian soldiers and the exclusive preoccupation of British authorities with Italian welfare.[9]

The British did little to remove the color segregation imposed by the Italians and in many instances appeared officially to condone it. An official report of the Civil Affairs Branch of the Middle East advised: "Many of the native inhabitants are of low type with whom free association by Europeans can hardly be imagined....It is highly doubtful if any sweeping change would be advisable in present circumstances."[10]

Both the British officials and Italian residents in Eritrea failed to appreciate the rapid change which occurred in the political attitudes of important sections of the Eritrean population during the fighting and in the few months that followed the British victory. The Italians in Eritrea lost not only the war but also the psychological advantage that they had enjoyed over the local population. This humiliating defeats on the battlefield had broken the myth of Italy's might and Roman superiority that had so carefully been built up by Fascist propaganda. In the eyes of the local population, Italian officials no longer commanded the moral authority to rule. Foreign domination, which they had grudgingly accepted in the past, suddenly appeared intolerable. The harsh economic situation that followed the Italian defeat further accelerated the sentiment of resistance to foreign rule.

While preparing for the invasion of Ethiopia, Mussolini had built an artificial prosperity in Eritrea. To secure the total obedience of Eritreans and to mobilize them for the campaign against Ethiopia, the Italians had provided them with generous economic benefits. Taxation was light, state subsidies kept prices for consumer products imported from Italy and other countries low, and wartime requirements created a number of jobs offering relatively good wages and salaries. In addition, generous largesse, titles, and salaries secured the support of prominent Eritreans.

However, the collapse of the Italian Empire in 1941 replaced the Fascist boom with a severe slump. Money stopped pouring in from Italy and subsidized Italian imports ceased. The disintegration of the Italian army left tens of thousands of demobilized Eritrean soldiers without a livelihood. Thousands more were thrown out of their jobs as more and more subsidized Italian enterprises closed down.[11]

The situation was further aggravated by the policy of the British Military Administration which aimed more at saving additional expenses rather than at easing the deteriorating economic condition of Eritrea. Immediately upon taking over, the British authorities sharply devalued the lira. They argued that Britain should not run the risk of buying a currency which could turn worthless any moment, and, therefore, they not only ran down the lira but also limited its usage to within the boundaries of the territory. According to Sir Philip Mitchell, the Chief Political Affairs Officer, O.E.T.A., the object was "to make the lira like poker chips, valid only in the grounds of the casino."[12] The conversion was fixed at the rate of 480 lire to the pound sterling, as against the 1940 rate of 83.65 lire. This suddenly left Italian residents and Eritreans with their savings greatly diminished from their pre-April 1941 value.[13]

An increase in taxes, an alarming rise in the cost of living, strict wartime rationing and controls, and the general economic and political insecurity created by so many drastic changes all accelerated the downhill trend in the Eritrean economy.

The urban population, which had more than quadrupled since 1935, was especially hard hit by the economic and financial crisis that gripped the territory. Much of it was unemployed, and the few who managed to keep their jobs could hardly survive on the wages they were paid. The resulting feeling of deprivation was more acute, considering the rather high standard of living that the urban population had come to enjoy during the boom years of the second half of the 1930s.

The growing misery in the towns led to large-scale migration towards the countryside. This reversed the trend of the last few years, which had seen many highland peasants attracted to the towns by the job opportunities created by immense recruitment of askaris into the Italian army and the rapid expansion of Eritrea's infrastructure in preparation for the invasion of Ethiopia. The Italian colonial army alone absorbed some 40 percent of the Eritrean male population of military age.[14]

The earlier movement from the rural areas could not have come at a better time. Rural Eritrea, especially Hamasén, Akälä Guzay, and Särae were beset by land shortage. The absorption of its surplus population in the towns had significantly eased the problem. Many rural families had also supplemented their meager farm income with cash repatriated by their urban relatives. However, all this ended with the Italian defeat. More and more askaris and jobless urban residents began to trek back to their former villages, overcrowding an already crowded countryside.

Many of the returnees entered into desperate competition with their kin as they staked their claims to highly fragmented and strongly contested plots of land. Litigation over land, already a chronic problem in the villages of the Eritrean plateau, became even more acute.[15] Making the situation worse, the British saddled the peasantry with an increase in the land tax from 10 lire to 90 lire.[16] When added to the soaring prices in consumer products, this made life in the countryside increasingly precarious.

These adverse economic developments fell on a population that was already showing signs of increased political consciousness. Wartime British propaganda had focused on causing large-scale desertions in the Italian army by agitating Eritreans with the prospect that the days of their subjugation were over and promising that they would soon be reunited with their motherland, Ethiopia. Leaflets carrying the Emperor's pictures, his messages to Eritreans (approved by the Foreign Office), and the Ethiopian flag were showered by the Royal Air Force over much of Eritrea.[17]

This propaganda work had been carried out on a colossal scale. Over half a million flags had been dropped on a front not more than ten miles long in the Keren area.[18] Its results had been instantaneous. According to George Steer, the British officer in charge of the operation, "Eritreans were seen to kiss the seal, press it to their foreheads and weep."[19] Sir Douglas Newbold, Civil Secretary of the Sudan government, also wrote in March 1941 that the propaganda managed by Steer "have worked wonders,"[20] a judgement perhaps confirmed by the fact that the Italians instituted the death penalty for anyone discovered with these papers. This stiff penalty did not, however, restrain the exodus of Eritrean askari into the British camp. Some 6,000 of them passed over to the British side on the Keren front alone, "waving pamphlets as a passport."[21]

Later accounts by individuals and groups in Eritrea indicate that the agitation to drive out the Italians and the prospects of reunion with Ethiopia had aroused the political consciousness of a large section of the population. Many date their conversion to the idea of active irredentism to this period.[22]

There appears to have been a general perception that, as in the rest of Ethiopia, the British were in Eritrea as caretakers for the Emperor.[23] Some of the leaflets contained messages from the Emperor which reminded the people of Eritrea that their "destiny is strictly bound with that of the rest of Ethiopia," and telling them, "I have brought you the aid of the government of Great Britain."[24] The more credulous elements in the countryside believed that the British were simply hired by the Emperor to drive the Italians from Eritrea.[25]

Although the Italians had brought into existence a separate territorial unit out of the ethnic and linguistic conglomeration of northern Ethiopia, their half century of colonial rule had not loosened the bonds of kinship between the population on both sides of the Märäb river. In particular, to the highland Christian population, who had maintained their ties with the rest of Ethiopia through various institutional affiliations and economic bonds, it seemed to be in the normal order of things that with the demise of Italian power the territory should revert to its pre-colonial status, which, in effect, meant joining with the rest of Ethiopia. One Unionist memorandum later described the prevailing view in 1941 as "a simple and natural desire for things to return as they used to be in the not-so-far past. It was like saying: I WANT TO GO HOME."[26]

The colonial experience was neither intense nor long enough to dim the memory of most Eritrean highlanders of their identity with their kin to the south. Many elders still remembered when the territory had been under the

Ethiopian crown. A 1944 survey in the Hamasén district made by the British Administration concluded: "one and all confirm that Ras Alula [the last Ethiopian appointed governor before the Italian occupation of Eritrea] was a just ruler, well loved by the people, and that at no time in its history has the Hamasén been so tranquil or free from the interminable disputes which are today the characteristic features of its daily life."[27] A few chiefs in office traced their appointment to Ethiopian times,[28] and some Eritrean veterans who had fought against the Italians at the Battle of Adwa in 1896 still lived.

Some Eritreans maintained an identification with Ethiopia as a spiritual weapon against the degrading effects of colonial domination. The Italian invasion of Ethiopia was remembered with regret even by those who were not enthusiastic about reunion with that country.[29] Some Eritreans later expressed how deeply they felt the loss of hope and inspiration during the years of the Italian occupation.[30] The significant role played by some members of the highland Eritrean elite during the five years of patriotic resistance in Ethiopia from 1936-1941 is a further indication of their strength of the continued attachment to Ethiopia.[31]

In addition, it had been a common practice for Eritreans who fell out with the Italians to seek a new opportunity in Ethiopia. This was especially true of those with some education who found their advancement severely restricted by Italian racial laws and practices, which did not permit education beyond the fourth grade, and which envisaged no career for the indigenous elite beyond serving as interpreters and low level clerks.

Most Eritreans with some education had gone to Addis Ababa for further studies.[32] The Täfäri Mäkonnen School in Addis Ababa had had a large enrollment of students from Eritrea before the Fascist invasion. Most of these students ended up serving the Ethiopian government.[33] A number of Eritreans were also recruited into the new military academy at Holäta which opened in 1932. These groups of Eritreans had been quite keen to see the reunification of Eritrea with the rest of Ethiopia even before the Italo-Ethiopian war. Major E.A. Chapman Andrews, a British intelligence officer who had a fair grasp of conditions in Ethiopia, wrote in 1942:

> Before the Italo-Ethiopian War perhaps the keenest, most nationalistic and most patriotic among the growing band of educated young men round the Emperor were Tigreans, while many of his best advisers and loyal servants were Eritreans; and it will be recalled that two Eritrean battalions deserted to him during the Italo-Ethiopian war.[34]

Old loyalties now combined with newly aroused expectations to create a political atmosphere which militated against the British effort to legitimize their authority in Eritrea. The breakup of Italian power and the dramatic liberation of Ethiopia, as well as the generous promises made by the British to facilitate victory, had engendered a feverish desire for change. What Eritreans experienced following the Italian defeat fell far short of their expectations.

To all appearances the British were not eager to leave Eritrea or to administer it any differently from the Italians. Nor did the Italians seem to have lost much of their grip. Worse still, the standard of living had deteriorated substantially in the short period since the war. These grievances produced visible changes in the territory's political landscape. Above all, since the effects were felt by many sections of the Eritrean population, there appeared, perhaps for the first time since the beginning of colonial rule, a relatively broad political consensus.

The Establishment of the *Mahbär Feqri Hagär* (Love of Country Association)

Eritrean political awakening first expressed itself in a general movement of resistance to the survival of Italian colonial laws and of opposition to the British policy of maintaining former Fascist officials in power. Protest against the latter started almost from the establishment of the British Military Administration in April 1941. The determination of Italian residents in Eritrea to maintain a status quo which favoured their privileged positions, on the one hand, and the unwillingness of British officials to undermine Italian interests vis-à-vis Eritreans on the other, led the indigenous population to suspect collusion among whites to keep their black subjects in subjection.

Irritation was particularly noticeable among Eritreans living in Asmara, where the recently created economic deprivation was most acute, and relations between the Italians, who numbered over 50,000, and the Eritreans, was marked by undisguised hostility. Fear and mutual suspicion led the two communities to consider more sinister methods of attack against each other.

Italian officials in the service of the British Military Administration did not hesitate to use their power to the full to suppress what they perceived as Eritrean insubordination. They dealt harshly with any manifestation of public grievance. A delegation of 20 ex-askaris who went to the BMA office to present a petition was met, on the orders of an Italian captain, by a volley of fire which killed two of them and wounded others.[35] Former members of the Carabinieri and the Polizia Africa Italiana used every pretext to harass Eritreans. Italian soldiers living in Däqemehara were reported to have killed a number of the local residents.[36]

Mutual distrust between Italians and Eritreans reached such a stage that the latter believed that the former were deliberately cutting off the water supply to Asmara's indigenous quarters and that they were planning to poison them. They also complained that Italian officials in the courts and prisons were using their power to maltreat Eritreans and requested their immediate removal.[37] Similar stories of Italian atrocities, whether true or fabricated, further embittered the Eritreans.

The youth in Asmara, the target of many of the repressive measures, developed a political militancy not seen in the past. Acts of revenge on Italians became frequent. These measures, in turn, bred further insecurity among the Italian residents, widening the rift between the two communities. Italian suppression combined with British acquiescence heightened a spirit of solidarity among the urban youth united in a common identity, of which color consciousness was an important component. Although they lacked any form of organization, the bond established by their common aspirations and grievances, as well as by the prevailing suspicion of a white conspiracy to keep them under the colonial yoke, prompted the youth to come out openly and in great strength in demonstrations against Italians and the BMA especially in Asmara. A contemporary account by an Eritrean youth describes the movement of those days as a veritable revolution:

> [I]rredentist sentiment was intensified during the war when manifestos heralding the impending union with our mother country rained over our city from British airoplanes ...The fall of Italy brought a complete change in the relation between the people of Eritrea and Italians. Italian soldiers transferred from the colonial army to the Police Force began to spread death and grief among Eritreans. This... created the famous Revolution. The Asmara youth picked any weapon they found and rose up against the Italians and their likes.[38]

One of the demonstrations held in Asmara at the end of April 1941, which attracted over 4,000 people, and which was dispersed only after the intervention of a contingent of the Indian Army supported by armed carriers, had a special significance in shaping the events soon to follow. The BMA took drastic action to discourage further resistance. Several of the leading participants were arrested, and a new regulation forbidding Eritreans to assemble in groups of more than three and to carry the Ethiopian flag was issued by the Chief Administrator.[39]

The intensification of the conflict as well as the growing militancy of the youth seem to have embarassed the elders in Asmara because significant developments were taking place without their participation and leadership. Although most of them appeared to favor a wait-and-see attitude in their relations with the BMA, they soon realized that events were moving at a much faster pace than they had anticipated and that they would have to take a more active role if they were to avoid being swept away by events.[40] Hence, some of the town notables began to act in consort with the young educated elite to represent local grievances to the British Military Administration.

At the end of April 1941, when Brigadier Brian Kennedy-Cooke, the first chief military administrator, called on community leaders to discuss the continued ferment in Asmara a body of representatives was already in existence to respond to his call. In succeeding days this informal body took steps to set up an organization. It held secret meetings, elected a committee of organizers, and decided to recruit followers.[41]

The founding date of the organization, which they named the Mahbär Feqri Hagär (Love of Country Association), has yet to be definitely established. Most oral sources and the scant documentary evidence remain vague on this point. A majority view holds that it occurred following the big demonstration at the end of April, 1941.[42] Others hold that it coincided with the Emperor's entry into Addis Ababa a few days later on May 5.[43]

The composition of the new association's central committee reflected careful attempts to create an acceptable balance among Eritrea's diverse communities. While the organizational initiative had been taken largely by Christians, its leadership had a significant Muslim representation. Equally noteworthy was the attempt by its founders to accommodate both the old guard in the Christian community and the emerging radical youth, most of whom were products of mission education. The election of Fitawrari Gäbrämäsqäl Wäldu, a fiery nationalist and one of the leading radicals, was an indication of how far the organization was prepared to go.[44]

The Mahbär Feqri Hagär adopted the prevailing demand for union with Ethiopia as its primary objective and built its membership around this idea. Unionism became one of the major forces around which Asmara residents rallied. At least in the first two years of the British period, there appears to have been no competition to this movement. Even its later opponents admit that the organization's aspiration was principally the incorporation of the territory into Ethiopia.[45]

Increased friction with the white community produced stronger assertions of Ethiopian nationalism and increased the appeal of Mahbär Feqri Hagär's irredentist agitation. As one contemporary observer put it, "the spirit of Ethiopianism was nurtured by the hatred for foreigners."[46]

Union with Ethiopia made an emotional appeal to traditional and historical ties. Many of its promoters boosted it as a magic formula which would resolve the economic and political malaise which confronted Eritrean society and restore self-respect. One leaflet distributed in 1943 said,

Eritreans...Remember your mother Ethiopia! Your mother will not deny you and you, her sons, must not deny her. She will feed you. The Italians beat you and dishonoured your women. The British starve you and fatten the foreigners. Have you seen how the Italians and Arabs grow rich while you go naked? Have you seen how the British protect them and despise you?... You will find no help except from your mother Ethiopia. Fight the foreigner and prepare to die for your country. Long live Haile Selassie! Long live Ethiopia![47]

The more educated elements among the irredentists envisaged the vindication of the black race through the establishment of a stronger Ethiopia. The example of Japan had aroused intense interest among pre-war intellectuals in Ethiopia and appears to have now caught hold of the Eritrean intelligentsia. They drew analogies between Japan and Ethiopia and concluded that Ethiopia could play in Africa a role similar to that played by Japan in Asia. Proponents of the idea of Greater Ethiopia argued that if the latter were unified and strengthened it would be better able to lead a pan-African struggle against the "tyranny of the white race."[48]

Stories, factual and fictional, of how the European powers exposed Ethiopia to Mussolini's depredations by putting an arms embargo on her were cited to strengthen the argument of a white conspiracy against the blacks. It was also said that fighter aircraft donated by the black community in the United States to help their Ethiopian brothers during the Italo-Ethiopian war had been confiscated by the French government at the port of Djibouti.[49]

Winning the allegiance of the elite of Asmara promoted the rapid expansion of the irredentist movement. Within a year of its establishment the Mahbär Feqri Hagär had the overwhelming majority of the Asmara intelligentsia on its side and could count on the support of a great many of the elders and other prominent personalities in the town. The British officials found out that the Native Advisory Council, composed of prominent persons who enjoyed popular support and established in early 1942 to serve as a vehicle of local opinion for the Administration, was "a hot bed of irredentism."[50]

Irredentist feelings were also high among Eritreans working in the civil service and the police force.[51] Members of the latter group in particular attained notoriety among their employers for their exploits in distributing irredentist propaganda in Asmara. They were known to spend much of their nightly police duty in painting the walls and electricity poles in Asmara with the Ethiopian colors and posting pictures of the Emperor.[52] At one time Brigadier Longrigg, the Chief Administrator, found a picture of Emperor Haile Selassie wrapped in the Ethiopian flag lying on his desk.[53]

Although the BMA dismissed some two hundred Eritrean police constables[54] to stamp out sedition in the very body which it had established to enforce its authority, most local recruits remained loyal to the Unionist cause. They organized a strike in February 1944 which drew the participation not only of the 3,000 Eritrean members of the police force, but also the sympathy and active support of much of the indigenous population of Asmara town.[55] In the end the BMA was forced to rely on a contingent of the Sudanese Defense Force for much of the police work in the territory.

By 1943 the irredentist movement had won over most of the Christian population of Asmara and was making rapid headway in other towns and in the highland countryside among the predominantly Christian peasantry. An American observer reported to President Roosevelt from Gura in March 1943 that even those living far north of the frontier regarded themselves as Ethiopians and that "shop-keepers in Asmara, Massawa, Keren, and other cities displayed the photographs of Haile Selassie on their walls."[56] The mass exodus of disbanded askari and other urban dwellers back to the countryside since the collapse of Italian power had been important in carrying the ideas of the irredentist movement into the countryside.

The success of the Mahbär Feqri Hagär in reaching the peasantry and in welding it into a force that could affect the political process in Eritrea owed a great deal to the Orthodox Church. The Orthodox Church in Eritrea was a part of the Ethiopian Orthodox Church, with which it had maintained relations throughout the colonial period. It provided a major forum for rallying the peasantry to the Unionist cause. In each village the church was central to organizing most social functions, its compound the most important place for transacting business whether communal or private.

Although in many respects the village clergy in the villages differed very little from the rest of the peasantry, by virtue of their religious training they were relatively better equipped to articulate nationalistic ideals. Many of them would also have received part of their education in a monastery in Ethiopia and consequently needed little persuasion to convert to the ideas of unionism. As the sole literate group in the countryside, the clergy was also important in transmitting messages from the towns and in organizing signatures for petitions in support of union with Ethiopia.

Important as it was, however, the role of the Church should be placed in correct perspective. British officials, challenged with growing irredentism among the Eritrean peasantry, tended to attribute much of the movement's inspiration and leadership to the Church. In March 1943, Brigadier S. Longrigg, the Chief Military Administrator of Eritrea, reported to the Foreign Office that the religious influence which the Abun (bishop) in Eritrea "wields among superstitious, priest-ridden peasants may well tend to make them politically conscious."⁵⁷ One of the sermons of Abunä Marqos, the bishop in question, was frequently mentioned to illustrate the powerfully irredentist message of the clergy. During the celebration of Epiphany, in January 1942, the Abun had said,

> A male child is brought into the Church forty days after it has been born and a female child is brought eighty days after birth. Names are then given to them. When the child cries, its mother gives it milk and it stops crying as soon as she lifts it to her breast. But you my people, have you a name? Yes, you have a mother and you must come to know her as she already knows you.⁵⁸

Although by this time more powerful, highly assertive irredentist speeches and writings had become frequent in almost all walks of life in Eritrea, administrative officials continued to emphasize the role of the Church. Because religious celebrations provided many of the occasions for manifestations of irredentist sentiment, this might have led British officials to suspect instigation by the priesthood. In actual fact, the church was a kind of civic center, the one place where people congregated. Religious celebrations provided the occasion for collective activities ranging from effecting reconciliation among feuding groups to discussing strategies on handling the demands of their rulers. All outstanding issues in the village were brought up during gatherings in the church. It was not, therefore, surprising to see the highland peasantry using the church and church-related celebrations as a forum for manifesting their Unionist sentiments.

It appears that BMA officials used the excuse of the church to explain away their failure to create loyalty for British rule in Eritrea. They could claim, as did the chief administrator, that they were dealing with "superstitious, priest-ridden peasants."⁵⁹ One is reminded of the complaints of Marshal De Bono, the Fascist Commander who led the conquest of Ethiopia in 1935-36, who accused the priests in Eritrea of confusing the minds of his new recruits by spreading news of the immense power of the Ethiopian Emperor.⁶⁰ In this way actual Eritrean grievances and concrete aspirations could be conveniently dismissed and the implication of the movement, the rejection of British authority, could be ignored.

The British officials' exaggerated assessment of the clergy's role in Eritrean politics seems to have influenced subsequent writers on Eritrea. Most accounts of Eritrean political movements during the 1940s tend to place the central leadership in the hands of the Church.⁶¹

The mistaken tendency to attribute the mass conversion of the Eritrean peasantry to the Unionist cause to the work of the clergy results from a misperception of the type of relation which existed between the peasantry and the clergy. Peasant receptiveness to the worldly messages brought by the priests was due largely to the appeal of the idea rather than to blind obedience. The priests did not possess a sufficiently independent authority to, nor had they any mechanism with which they could, force an unpopular idea on to a reluctant peasantry. Relations between the peasantry and their priests were essentially based on mutually beneficial arrangement between them.

Further more, while a few monasteries and prominent churches (*däber*) had been generously endowed by rulers in former times, most village churches were supported by land set aside by the villagers. This made the clergy dependent on their parishoners[62] and the authority they enjoyed was essentially based on respect for their services to the community. Besides, the hierarchical organization of the Ethiopian Church has traditionally been very loose. Few structural devices allowed the Church to impose its will at the village level. Once a priest was ordained by his bishop, very little went on between his parish and higher ecclesiastical bodies.

As regards the higher ecclesiastical authorities, their relations with the land-hungry peasants of highland Eritrea were not such as to allow them to bring the latter under their influence. In actual fact, as land shortage became desperate in the 1940s, relations between the peasantry and many of the land-rich monasteries were marked by constant friction. A 1944 study indicated that the holdings of the monasteries were being reduced

> by the will of the people, whose respect for the Church is more than offset by their land-hunger. Indeed the respect for the Church must not be exaggerated....Disputes between chiefs and abbots, villages and priests are common. It happens more and more often nowadays, that the peasants refuse to work on the land of the monasteries, thus breaking away from the old feudal obligation.[63]

Emphasis on the Church has led many commentators to overlook the most important agent in the politicization of the Eritrean countryside. This was the large number of urban dwellers who returned to their villages since the beginning of 1941. These elements formed a vital link between the countryside and the towns. Demobilized askaris and others who had lost their jobs were among the first recruits into the Mahbär Feqri Hagär. In most instances, they constituted the first committee members of the organization at the village level.[64] They were able to follow political developments closely and were crucial in laying the groundwork which finally brought the countryside under urban influence.

By 1943 the British Military Administration had to contend with an irredentist force, the Mahber Feqri Hager, which not only had won the loyalty of most of the Christians of Asmara and other towns but also was spreading rapidly in the countryside. Its following was diverse, its motives powerful. The chief administrator reported early in 1944 that Unionism "commands a fairly strong following." He wrote that the urban notables were favorable to it and "the younger Intelligentsia are nearly all Irredentists." Besides members of the Ethiopian Church, he also included Catholics and Protestants, who form "a very large part of the educated youth of the Territory," and merchants, "who hope for better and freer trade under a united Territory."[65]

Besides gaining a much wider constituency, the movement was also able to benefit from the relatively free arena which the countryside provided. The rural areas were comparatively free from close scrutiny by the officials. Unlike the towns where the apparatus of control was strong and few activities went unnoticed, the government's presence was relatively weak in the countryside. Once it had rooted itself the movement was able to expand with fewer restrictions than was the case in the towns.

At the end of 1943, the Mahbär Feqri Hagär decided to test its strength by openly petitioning the British government for an immediate and direct union with Ethiopia. Suspicions that the BMA was trying to influence Eritrean chiefs to demand a British protectorate caused Unionist leaders to counter with direct appeals to the people. Accordingly, Unionists campaigned to secure mass signatures for the petition demanding immediate union with Ethiopia. The petition asserted: "we the people on this side of the Märäb believe that Ethiopia is our foundation, our mother and proof of our very being" and demanded that "the name Eritrea should be abolished and one Ethiopia should prevail."[66] Such assertions and the political ferment which they created were more than the British authorities were prepared to entertain at this stage.[67] They took steps to dampen irredentist enthusiasm and intimidated its leaders into suspending their canvassing.

British Military Administration: Objectives in Eritrea and Response to the Irredentist Challenge

Having come on to the Eritrean scene by a sudden turn of events at the beginning of the war, the British government, as we have seen, took control of the territory without a clearly formulated policy. Complications created by strategic necessities during the war, considerations of the post-war international order, and the difficulty of determining the status of an enemy-occupied territory while the war was still in progress kept the government from drawing up a final and concrete position concerning the territory. The absence of a clearly defined policy gave rise to confusion and led different branches of the government to pursue different, and sometimes mutually contradictory, objectives.

As a territory under military control Eritrea mainly involved the War Office. However, the Colonial Office, which provided much of the personnel and many of the guidelines for the administration, was also involved intimately. The Foreign Office also had a hand in many Eritrean issues. The positions adopted by each of these bodies was influenced by the specific agendas they had in the region.

The military was basically interested in Eritrea's capacity to satisfy Britain's strategic requirements in the Middle East and East Africa. The western and northern portions of Eritrea were to be used to beef up the British colony of the Sudan, a prized territory whose importance had increased during the War.

The port of Massawa was considered strategic to the protection of the Red Sea and the highlands of the Asmara plateau were deemed essential for air bases to protect Massawa.[68] Out of these elements grew a plan to create a more viable unit under British protection, a "Greater Tigray," which would include the Tegreñña-speaking Eritrean highland region and the Ethiopian province of Tegray. The military invisaged the incorporation of this unit into an East African bloc.[69] An initial attempt to implement this plan was made immediately following the Italian defeat in northern Ethiopia. The British officers appointed Ras Seyum, a descendent of Emperor Yohannes, as governor of the whole region without even taking the trouble of informing the Emperor. The scheme failed when Ras Seyum rejected the offer and chose instead to make his peace with Addis Ababa.[70]

Central to certain British imperial defense concepts was the creation of an East African bloc, which, besides ensuring continued British dominance over central and southern Africa, could also be used to guard her interests in the east. The soldiers' master plan envisaged the formation of some kind of union of the British East African territories of Kenya, Uganda, and Tanganyika. A "Greater Somaliland" was to be carved out of the former Italian Somaliland, British Somaliland, parts of the Ogaden (which was taken from Ethiopia for the duration of the war), and the Northern Frontier District of Kenya. "Greater Tigrai" was to be linked with "Greater Somalia" by securing a connecting corridor west of Jibouti from Ethiopia, or by trading Jibouti for Gambia with the French.[71]

The more enthusiastic elements in the Middle East and East Africa Commands sought to incorporate Ethiopia within this vast East African scheme. This openly manifested its opposition to the restoration of an independent

Ethiopia while the war against Italy was in progress. When asked in October 1940 what part the Emperor would play in the liberation of Ethiopia, General Platt, the Commander in Chief of East African Forces, reportedly replied, "Haile Selassie will enter Abyssinia by the grace of William Platt, and with his baggage."[72] General Platt continued to insist that Britain should maintain her presence in Ethiopia to control the waters of the Blue Nile on which the Sudan and Egypt depended.[73] A project by the military at the beginning of the war to send a British mission into southern Ethiopia to arouse the Oromo in the name of an independent Oromo state was dropped only under strenuous opposition from Emperor Haile Selassie and such British political advisers as Brigadier Sandford, Major Orde Wingate, Major R.E. Cheesman, and E.A. Chapman-Andrews.[74]

In spite of repeated reassurance from the Foreign Office to the Emperor, the soldiers continued to treat the country as an occupied enemy territory. Field-Marshal Smuts, Commander-in-Chief of the British Imperial forces in enemy territory, expressed the South African dislike of the appearance of an "independent barbaric state" in Africa.[75] Even Anthony Eden had to admit that what the military leaders visualized was in fact a virtual protectorate of Ethiopia.[76]

The British East African Command reserved to itself the right to establish military control over any part of Ethiopia and its Military Mission in the country enjoyed wide ranging powers. The military showed its hand clearly in the negotiations leading to the treaties signed in 1942 and 1944 between Ethiopia and Great Britain. To maintain sufficient control over Ethiopia the agreement provided that British advisers be assigned to all government departments and that the Emperor and his subordinates agree "to abide in all matters touching the Government of Ethiopia by the advice of His Majesty's Government."[77] Sir Reginald Wingate, a former governor of Egypt, commented at the time that the whole exercise had many features in common with what had happened in Egypt in 1882-1983 when British power under Lord Cromer had been established behind the facade of an Egyptian government under the Khedive.[78]

The idea of creating a chain of dependent territories stretching over the whole of the eastern half of Africa became even more appealing after the end of the war when Britain's positions in Egypt and India appeared to be tenuous. Its forces in the latter countries could be easily withdrawn into the Sudan and East Africa thereby leaving Britain's defence capacities in the region largely unaffected.[79]

While not differing substantially from the goals of the military, the diplomats in the Foreign Office were in favor of toning down the soldiers' demand for immediate overhauling of the region. In the Eritrean case they had to contend with the possibility of protracted international negotiations to determine its future. They opted to pursue a strategy which would maintain Britain's presence in the region, and, at the same time, use parts of the territory to settle outstanding border issues with Ethiopia. They supported the annexation of the western and northern parts of Eritrea into the Sudan.

Although it favored the creation of a "Greater Tegray,"[80] the Foreign Office shied away from the inevitable dispute with Ethiopia which it would entail. Its representatives in Addis Ababa were in a better position than either the military or their colleagues in London to assess the strength of Ethiopian resistance to British tutelage and recommended caution.[81]

Those in the Foreign Office who were familiar with Ethiopian affairs were particularly wary of the military's frequent predictions of the impending disintegration of Ethiopia and their tendency to oversimplify the task of erecting a protectorate over the country. R.E. Cheesman, who was called "an Ethiopian encyclopaedia" by Sir Douglas Newbold (Civil Secretary of the Sudan government),[82] in his capacity as adviser to the British Minister, warned:

> The crazy structure, which best describes the Ethiopian Empire, is held together by a mysterious magnetism, which is incomprehensible by one who has no more than a superficial knowledge of Ethiopia... It is little understood by those who have many years' experience in Ethiopia...During the reign of Menelik, and since then, the foreign policies of England, France and Italy in regard to Ethiopia have been based on the assumption that she must break up, yet she did nothing of the sort.... In 1940, although scattered, the Ethiopians returned, welded together by adversity as never before, and rallied to the Emperor under the banner of "Our Flag, Our Empire." After the Emperor has been re-established... the [British] military view could not realise that a national unity existed in Ethiopia and that a government that was not visible to them and was so differently constituted from their own could possibly last more than a few months.[83]

Aware of the serious complications which would follow, the Foreign Office tried to avoid involving Britain in a headlong clash with the Ethiopian government. On the Eritrean issue it sought to soften Ethiopian opposition by recognizing the Emperor's sovereignty over a "Greater Tegray" which would be administered for him by the British. What they had in mind was a kind of Anglo-Ethiopian condominium in Eritrea, similar to the Anglo-Egyptian one erected in the Sudan.[84] If this did not work out, the Foreign Office was also willing to trade off the Tegreñña-speaking parts of Eritrea for the Ogaden province to realize its "Greater Somalia" project and make certain frontier adjustments in the western and southern parts of Ethiopia.[85]

The somewhat vague and periodically shifting signals coming from above about Britain's position on the occupied territories created fertile ground in which those directly involved in the administration of the territories could make assumptions and speculations. Taking their cue from bits and pieces of position statements made by the various branches of government, the BMA personnel on the ground largely pursued a line which they thought would strengthen Britain's hand in any eventual decision regarding the future of the territory.

Besides considerations of national interest, there were more personal and immediate reasons which influenced the Administration towards a more permanent hold over Eritrea. The perpetuation of British rule there had implications for the careers of many of the British staff in the territory. As one of the Chief Administrators admitted, army officers and civilian officials "have remained in Eritrea in the hope that His Majesty's government might take over this territory and that they might look to permanent employment here and get in on the ground floor of any permanent Colonial Office Administration to be set up."[86] Many of them could not have relished the prospect of looking for a new career in a war devastated England.

The desire for a permanent hold over Eritrea led the administration to try to consolidate its control and to find ways to legitimize Britain's rule. Any activity which hampered these efforts was considered a threat. This meant a headlong clash with the Unionist movement. Irredentism posed a serious challenge to the legitimization of British power over Eritrea. Its radical preachings against European domination and its frequent outcry against alleged prejudice and corruption in the Administration were irritating to BMA officials, who could not overlook the keen nationalist awareness it aroused or the large number of adherents it had won over in a short time. Unionists made no secret of the fact that their objective was to end British presence in Eritrea in the shortest time possible. The authorities considered this subversive and dealt with it accordingly.[87]

The British Military Administration took various measures to discourage the growing influence of Unionism. It banned demonstrations and strikes and imposed a rigid censorship. The British press law forbade the publication of "articles or cartoons which were defamatory of the BMA, His Majesty's Government, the British Information Service, or any individual or official of the existing government."[88] The chief administrator promised firm measures would be taken against actions that "inevitably lead to conditions of excitement among irresponsible persons." Included in these category of actions were public meetings, street demonstrations, secret publications, and the display of flags and badges.[89]

Both published and unpublished materials originating in Ethiopia were not allowed to enter Eritrea without first passing through the censorship office. All letters coming from Ethiopia had to be sent through postal channels. The Censorship Regulation imposed stiff penalties on lorry drivers found carrying letters from Ethiopia to Eritrea.[90] *The Voice of Hamassien* (*Yä Hamasén Dems'e*), a Unionist Paper published by Eritreans living in Addis Ababa, was banned in Eritrea in spite of repeated protests from the Ethiopian government.[91]

It also passed tough laws to discourage Eritreans working in the civil service and the police force from joining the Unionist movement. Following the strike of the Eritrean police in February, 1944, which was suspected to have been Unionist inspired, the Administration took firm measures to purge irredentism in the police force and to discourage any similar recurrence. It decreed that,

> Any person who aids, abets, or is accessory to any sedition in the Force, or maliciously endeavours to seduce any member of the Force from his allegiance or duty, shall on conviction by a Military court be liable to be punished by death or imprisonment.[92]

The BMA made it understood that those on the side of irredentism would be viewed with disfavor. Appointments and largesses were withdrawn from chiefs and other employees in the service of the Administration who identified themselves with the Mahbär Feqri Hagär. Some prominent notables who showed open sympathy for the Unionist cause were relieved of their positions, and a few were exiled to the lowlands in western Eritrea, away from their followers.[93]

Drastic measures were also taken against Mahbär Feqri Hagär leaders suspected of organizing the canvassing of signatures for the petition demanding immediate union with Ethiopia and instigating the strike in the police force in February 1944. Five prominent members were detained, and a number of Eritrean inspectors in the police force, who were believed to be partisans to the Unionist cause were imprisoned and dismissed.[94]

Violent reaction in Asmara against the detention of the leaders of the Mahbär Feqri Hagär prompted the Administration to further action against irredentist forces.[95] The chief administrator issued a notice warning the public that speeches and actions "likely to disturb the peace and good order won't be tolerated." He also instructed influential members of the community, such as the bishop of the Ethiopian Church in Eritrea, to desist from preaching irredentism.⁹⁶ These tough measures drove Unionist forces into hibernation for more than a year.

Brigadier Longrigg, the chief administrator in Eritrea since 1942, described by one of his colleagues as "the author of British policy and the architect of the Administration itself,"⁹⁷ believed that it would take much more than stiff regulations to combat irredentism. He envisaged the creation of a force as an alternative to the Mahbär Feqri Hagär which would support British authority in Eritrea. His first step was to foster a rival ideology to end the dominance of Unionist opinion throughout the country.

Various plans were devised to encourage the expression of non-irredentist ideas. The Administration provided forums in which those who believed that their interests might not be served best by union with Ethiopia could express their wishes publicly. The weekly Tegreñña newspaper, *Nay Eritrea Semunawi Gazetta*, published by the British Ministry of Information in Asmara, became an important vehicle in countering Unionist propaganda and in promoting rival ideas.⁹⁸

The Administration also sought to counter the publicity which the Unionists had gained at the international level through a concerted campaign agaist them. The British Information Office in Asmara was instructed to prepare articles contradicting writings which were sympathetic to the Unionist cause. An Overseas Planning Committee was established to coordinate the progaganda. This body suggested ways by which the information services of the Admininstration could take the initiative. It also proposed to enlarge the *Eritrean Weekly News* in order "to capture the literate Eritreans." Civil Affairs officers were urged to contact the outlying tribes to detach them from Unionist politics.⁹⁹

On the international front special attention was given to combating Sylvia Pankhurst's agitation for the union of Eritrea and Ethiopia. This indomitable fighter for the Ethiopian cause had established liaison with some of the Eritrean youth and had recruited English sympathisers who supplied her with reports of the Administration's hostile activity against Unionists.¹⁰⁰ Her newspaper, *New Times and Ethiopia News*, which served as the major forum for exposing the Administration's designs was a constant source of irritation to BMA officials.

Major Mumford, the Public Information Officer in Eritrea, mentions a decision made after a discussion by the authorities at the end of 1944 to prepare articles on Ethiopia and irredentism specially written with a view to publication in the *Manchester Guardian*, the *New Statesman*, and other major newspapers. Mumford wrote, "This may take the wind out of her [S. Pankhurst's] sails."¹⁰¹

The Administration in Eritrea was so wary of Miss Pankhurst's work that they suggested to London during her visit to the territory in 1944, that "she should not be allowed any further opportunity of meeting Eritreans at her own discretion" and that they should look for some way of getting her out of Eritrea within twenty-four hours.[102]

Arrangements were also made between the Foreign Office and Margery Perham, a reader of colonial administration at Oxford, by which the latter would author a book to counter Pankhurst's agitation. Perham concurred with the British officials in Eritrea that "the hysterical propaganda of Miss Pankhurst has gone further….and the need for such a book is even more urgent."[103]

Brigadier Longrigg himself participated directly in much of the publicity work. Besides the numerous memoranda which he presented to the various branches of the British government, he also authored a number of newspaper and journal articles propounding the idea of "Greater Tigray" and the need for a `civilized' European power to administer the region.[104]

Within Eritrea itself the chief administrator took the initiative in manufacturing pro-British opinion. The first significant article in Tegreñña, one which opened the discussion on the future of Eritrea in the *Nay Eritrea Semunawi Gazetta*, although signed "by an Eritrean," was in fact authored by Longrigg. Wäldä'ab Wäldämaryam, the editor of the newspaper, recently revealed that he was ordered to translate Longrigg's article into Tegreñña.[105] The article was full of praise for British achievements and warned against precipitous demands for immediate union with Ethiopia. It suggested that the best future of Eritrea lay in a union with Tegray under British trusteeship. This article set the theme for most subsequent articles on the subject which appeared in the weekly newspaper.[106]

Longrigg regretted the absence of a dynastic or social figure whom the Administration could use to counterpoise irredentism.[107] He was aware of the difficulty of bringing the diverse communities of Eritrea under a common banner that excluded union with Ethiopia. In his own words, Eritrea "is no ethnic, no geographic, no cultural unit; it represents the unplanned residue of Italy's grab at Africa."[108] He believed that "there is no `typical Eritrea', and no `typical Eritrean.'"[109]

The chief administrator hoped that his efforts would find a receptive ear among the Muslim half of the Eritrean population who would presumably find no attraction in union with a Christian-dominated Ethiopia. However, Muslims constituted a small minority in the highly agitated high-lands of Eritrea and could not be expected to influence strongly political developments there. In addition, some urban Muslims, who were essentially engaged in commerce, were not negatively disposed towards a union with Ethiopia, which, they believed, might open a larger trading forum to them.

The bulk of the Eritrean Muslim population lived in the Western Lowlands and in the eastern and northern parts of the territory and was predominantly nomadic. Although the Administration was interested in mobilizing this group as a pro-British force, its scattered and highly mobile way of life, as well as its fragmented political institutions, precluded immediate results.

The limitations which existed in the lowlands convinced the Administration to act more vigorously to create support in the highlands. Longrigg resorted to the idea of "Greater Tegray," which he hoped would invoke some shared memories among the highland population of a political and cultural unit. He devoted a good deal of his own time and the Administration's resources to popularizing this plan and building it into a viable movement.[110]

Longrigg calculated that the "Greater Tegray" scheme might appeal to some of the Eritrean chiefs. In any case, since most of them depended on the Administration for their positions and salaries they were expected to be more amenable to official suggestion. Since much of the urban elite had apparently gone to the Unionist camp, the hope of the Administration to create a pro-British constituency in Eritrea depended very much on its success with the chiefs.

Although a number of the highland notables were initially irredentists, their support was by no means unqualified. Some of them were not happy to see the growing influence of the urban elite in the movement. When asked to sign a petition for union with Ethiopia which many in Asmara had already signed, some of the Akälä Guzai and Säraé chiefs reportedly refused to associate themselves with a "crowd of Asmara nonentities" and argued that only chiefs were entitled to speak for the people.[111] One of the most important chiefs in Eritrea, Däjazmach (later Ras) Täsämma Asbärom (1870-1964)[112] of Akälä Guzai, is said to have been driven into opposition out of resentment at not having been consulted when the organization was established.[113]

The dominant role of people from Hamasén in the Mahbär Feqri Hagär was another cause of anxiety and resentment for some of the nobility in Akälä Guzai and Säraé. With the bulk of its membership coming from Asmara and surrounding districts,[114] the Unionist organization initially appeared to be a Hamasén affair. Considering the traditionally dominant position of the Hamasén ruling families over the rest of the highland, the development within the Unionist movement did not fail to arouse suspicion and fear among those who were removed from the center of activity in Asmara.

Although a few of the chiefs in Eritrea could trace their positions to precolonial times, they were able to maintain them through service rendered first to the Italian colonial government and later to the British Military Administration. They were paid officials and were required to conform to BMA policies. This dependence on the Administration drove most of them into an alliance with the authorities.[115] Although a number of them openly flirted with irredentism, the crackdown on potential Unionist leaders which started in 1943 had persuaded many to sit on the fence rather than risk antagonizing the British.

The Administration fully utilized its leverage over the chiefs to advance its agenda in Eritrea. It generously rewarded and increased the powers of chiefs who proved their loyalty. This proved to be helpful in challenging the Unionist movement. In March 1943, Longrigg wrote that "the policy adopted by the Administration of increasing the power of chiefs cannot but have the beneficial results in the deflation of irredentism."[116]

In addition, a number of the chiefs needed no persuasion to oppose the irredentist movement. Those who had been heavily compromised on the Italian side during the invasion of Ethiopia feared retribution should they come under the Emperor's authority. For those who had already attained the highest position which they could expect, Unionism had nothing to offer but an uncertain future.[117]

Some of the old families in the Eritrean highland also did not relish the idea of becoming junior partners in an Ethiopian government which they believed was dominated by the Shäwan aristocracy. This idea was particularly strong among chiefs who were connected to the Tegréan nobility across the Märäb. Quite a number of notables, especially in Akälä Guzai, entertained the idea of reviving Tegréan ascendancy under Däjazmach (made Ras by the Italians) Hayläsellasé Gugsa,[118] a great-grandson of the Emperor Yohannes, then living in exile in the Seychelles. Dejazmach Täsämma Asbärom, his son Abreha Täsämma (1901-1967), both related by marriage to the latter; Däjazmach Dämoz, his ex-secretary, appointed chief of Sänafé district by the British; and a number of others who had similar interests and connections found the British plan of a "Greater Tegray" appealing on this ground.[119]

In time British officials built this group into a significant force which was able to challenge among the highland communities the irredentist assertion of undivided loyalty to union with Ethiopia. They generously rewarded its members with titles and other privileges. Däjazmach Täsämma Asbärom, the principal figure on the pro-British side, was made a Ras, the highest title that could be conferred to a non-royal member of the Ethiopian aristocracy. His son, Fitawrari Abreha Täsämma, was elevated to the rank of Däjazmach. Four other chiefs also in Akälä Guzai, known for their support for the British, received the title of Däjazmach at the same time.[120]

Chiefs who continued to espouse the cause of Unionism were gradually dropped from official functions and their districts were given to partisans of the British Administration. Prospects of rewards and fear of official retribution from the Administration brought a steady flow of adherents to the pro-British side. Those who had been sitting on the fence for fear of making a wrong move finally made their choice. Colonel Trevaskis, then a senior civil affairs officer in Eritrea, wrote, "The majority of chiefs, believing that the British had at last shown their hand, began to intimate their separatist sympathies."[121]

Notes

[1] In a general memorandum of 8 February 1941, the Chief Political Officer, Middle East, instructed that Italian law and regulation should be maintained and Italian judges and magistrates retained as far as possible. See, Lord Rennell of Rodd, *British Military Administration of Occupied Territories in Africa during the year 1941 - 1947* (London: His Majesty's Stationary Office, 1948), 51-52.

[2] The British showed serious concern for the protection of Italians against revenge from the indigenous population even while the war was going on. They prevented the Emperor and the Ethiopian forces from entering large towns including Addis Ababa for fear that the `natives' might endanger Italian lives and property. Whereever possible they made sure that Italian garrisons surrendered only to British forces. See Christopher Sykes, *Orde Wingate: A Biography* (Cleveland: The World Publishing Company, 1959), 301: on the unfounded British fear of Ethiopian retaliation against Italians and the controversy over the Emperor's entry into Addis Ababa; and Anthony Mockler, *Haile Selassie's War: The Italian Ethiopian Campaign, 1935-1941* (New York: Random House, 1984), 372. Finally the Emperor disregarded General Cunningham's decision to delay his entry and went ahead to Addis Ababa.

[3] British Government, Ministry of Information, *The First to be Freed: The Records of British Military Administration in Eritrea and Somalia, 1941-1943* (London: His Majesty's Stationary Office, 1944), 25.

[4] Imperial Ethiopian government, Papers of the Liaison Office to the British Military Administration in Eritrea [hereafter Liaison Office Papers], Un Italiano qualunque, "Cosa Vuole ancora l'Autorita Inglese dell'Eritrea?" [n.d.].

[5] Eritrea Intelligence Bureau, "Public Opinion and Reaction, Relations with the Italian Civil Population in Eritrea," 2.4.1942, in Liaison Office Papers. See also Wäldä'ab Wäldämaryam's account in his forward to Stefano Poscia, *Eritrea Colonia Tradita* (Roma: Edizioni Associate, 1989), 8.

[6] Liaison Office Papers, "General Situation," 9 March 1942.

[7] Liaison Office Papers, "The General Situation in Eritrea," 30 September 1942.

[8] Trevaskis, *Eritrea*, 29.

[9] See *The Times* (London: 2 August, 1941), on the harmonious social contact established between Italian and British officers, who, among other things held frequent football matches.

[10] Foreign Office Archive (Great Britain), Public Records Office, [hereafter FO], 371/35655, Civil Affairs Branch G.H.Q., M.E.F. "Color Bar in Eritrea," 6 Oct. 1943; see also Alazar Tesfa Michael, *Eritrea Today: Fascist Occupation Under the Nose of British Military*, (Essex: New Times Book Department, n.d.) fora description of how the British authorities condoned the victimization of the indigenous population. The author was employed as an interpreter in the Civil Police Authority Section at Gura

[11] Gilbert Mackereth, a Foreign Office official in the Africa Department, commented in regard to this transition from boom to slump, "Eritrea is doomed to decay. Its revival during the Italian occupation of Ethiopia, itself uneconomic, was a false dawn." FO 371/27582, 13 August 1941. Mackereth had published a work on the Ethiopian economy before the Italian invasion: G. Mackereth, *Economic Conditions in Ethiopia*, Department of Overseas Trade, No. 507, 1932.

[12] Sir Philip Mitchell, *African Afterthoughts* (London: Hutchinson, 1954), 198-99.

[13] Ethiopian government, Documentation and Information Service of the Central Committee of the Workers' Party of Ethiopia, "Yä Qeññ Gezat Astädadär Bä Eretra, 1941-52" [an unpublished compilation of documents from various government archives including the Archives of the Ministry of the Pen relating to Eritrea], 25; see also S.H. Longrigg, "Some Problems of Administration in Eritrea," March 1944, 11, in FO 371/4116 for the Chief Administrator's report on the problems created by the heavy devaluation of the lira currency.

[14] FO 371/7973, cited in James C. McCann, "A Dura Revolution and Frontier Agriculture in Northwest Ethiopia, 1898-1920", *Journal of African History*, 31(1990), 125.

[15] See Papers of John Morley, Acting Senior Civil Affairs Officer, Rhodes Library, MSS. British Empire, S.27, for a description of the desperate shortages of land in Hamasén created by returning demobilized soldiers and others who had been in the service of the Italian administration.

[16] Sylvia Pankhurst, *British Policy in Eritrea and Northern Ethiopia* (Essex, 1946), 9.

[17] FO 371/31608.

[18] George Steer, *Sealed and Delivered: A Book on the Abyssinian Campaign* (London: Hodder and Stoughton, 1942), 172. One of the leaflets said, "The time has come for you to fight for your own King and your own Flag, because people without a flag have no life at all." Steer was special war correspondent for *The Times* in Addis Ababa during the Italo-Ethiopian War of 1935-36, and for the *Daily Telegraph* in Africa in 1938-39.

[19] Ibid., 33.

[20] K.D.D. Henderson, *The Making of the Modern Sudan: the Life and Letters of Sir Douglas Newbold* (London: Faber and Faber, 1953), 198.

[21] Ibid., 175. Ato Heywot Hedaru, a former employee of the British Consulate in South Western Ethiopia, who talked to several ex-askari in Täsänay and Barantu shortly after the defeat of the Italians in Eritrea, reported that many of them defected from the Italians and surrendered to the British in response to the call made by the Emperor: Heywot Hedaru, *Yachi Qän Täräsach: Kätemehert Bét Wädä Qonsela Sera, 1925-1933* (Addis Ababa: Berhanena Sälam Printing Press, 1967 [E.C.]), 420-422.

[22] Edward Ullendorff, who was then working for the censorship department of the BMA in Eritrea, later wrote, "The genii of democracy and of self-determination which had been so powerfully evoked by our war aims and the concomitant propaganda efforts refused to return to the bottle.": Edward Ullendorff, *The Two Zions: Reminiscences of Jerusalem and Ethiopia* (Oxford: Oxford University Press, 1988), 180

[23] Azmach Barakhi Habtä'ezgi, a chief of S'ena Däglé exiled to Tässänäy by the BMA for his irredentist activities, spoke on the occasion of the Sixth Anniversary of Ethiopia's liberation from Fascist occupation: "When the British told us that they were bringing our Emperor for us we said, `Grazie! Grazie! Mr. English get us our Emperor... and we received them with open arms. From what they said in those days it did not seem as if they would stay in Eritrea even for a year," Liaison Office Papers, Azmach Barakhi Habtä'ezgi.

[24] Leaflets of 8 July 1940 and 20 January 1941, reproduced in Steer, *Sealed and Delivered*, 121 and 231-34.

[25] Interview, Qäññazmach Gäbräsellasé Barakhi, Rome, June 1990; Ato S'ägay Abreha, Addis Ababa, December 1989.

[26] "Patriotic Association - Eritrea With Ethiopia - One Ethiopia," 18 August 1947, in Liaison Office Papers.

[27] "The Hamasien: A Social Survey," 1944, p. 139, in Trevaskis Papers, Rhodes Library, MSS Brit.Emp. S 367, Box 1.

[28] See for instance, Richard Caulk, "Ethiopia and the Horn," in A. Roberts (ed.), *The Cambridge History of Africa*, Vol. VII, who mentions that "many families who had been prominent in the 19th century were still powerful in 1941."

[29] Liaison Office Papers, Wäldä'ab Wäldämaryam, letter to the Emperor, 29 April 1947, in which he claims to have spent the five years in prayers for the restoration of Ethiopia's dignity, and how he vowed to forsake worldly pursuits until the liberation.

[30] A petition submitted by a number of Eritrean personalities sometime in 1943 to Brigadier Longrigg, the Chief Military Administrator, says "although we were unfortunate in being subjected to a life of degradation under the Italians, we were able to hold our heads high because of our pride in the existence of Ethiopia," Liaison Office Papers, "Petition to the Chief Administrator Brigadier Stephen Longrigg" [Tegreñña], Asmara, n.d.

[31] The patriotic force led by Col. Belay, himself an Eritrean, had several Eritreans including askaris who defected from the Italian Army, see Tadässä Méça, *Tequr Anbässa Bä Me'erab Ethiopia* (Asmara, n.d.) 15. Eritreans predominated in Ras Emeru's army. 600 Eritreans who had fled to Kenya later joined the Emperor.

[32] Regarding this exodus, Richard Caulk wrote that "Those who wished to continue their education, or to seek careers other than as interpreters or junior clerks, looked to Addis." R.A. Caulk, "Ethiopia and the Horn," 726.

[33] Several prominent positions in the restored government of Emperor Haile Selassie were held by Eritreans. Lorénzo Ta'ezaz (Minister in Moscow), Blata Efrém Täwoldämädhen (Minister in Washington), Blatta Dawit Oqbazghi (Vice Minister), Ato Gäbrämäsqäl Habtämaryam (Director of Posts and Telecommunication), Ato Gäbrämäsqäl Kefläzgi (Secretary General of the Ministry of Interior), Mälässe

Andom (First Secretary at New Delhi); see also, Imperial Ethiopian government, "The Ethiopian Memoranda" (1945), presented to the London meeting of the Council of Ministers of Foreign Affairs of the four great powers, for a list of some 1600 Eritreans serving in the Ethiopian government. In a statement to the United Nations Commission for Eritrea Aklilu Habtäwäld, the Ethiopian Foreign Minister, said that there were more than two hundred thousand Eritreans permanently residing in Ethiopia: United Nations, Report of the United Nations Commission for Eritrea, General Assembly Official Records: Fifth Session, Supplement No. 8 (A/1285), Annex 6, 1950, 46.

[34] FO 371/31608, E.A. Chapman Andrews, "Memorandum on Eritrea," 18 April, 1942. General Duncan Cumming, Chief Secretary of the British Military Administration in Eritrea in 1941, and Chief Administrator in 1951-1952, also observed: "Not infrequently the young Eritrean who acquired some education, but who saw little prospect of advancement in competition with Italian officials crossed the frontier into Ethiopia where he became an ardent advocate of the union of Eritrea with Ethiopia:" Duncan Cameron Cumming, "The Disposal of Eritrea," *The Middle East Journal*, VII, 1(Winter 1953), 22.

[35] "Yä Qeñññ Gezat Astädadär Bä Eretra," 7.

[36] Ibid.

[37] Ibid. 9. A contemporary witness later recounted: "Since feelings between Eritreans and Italians had deteriorated British and Indian troops had to be called out to come to the aid of the Italian police:" J.A. Baker, *Eritrea* 1941 (London: Faber and Faber, 1966), 183.

[38] Mezhiet [pen name], "Relazione Approssimativa dei Partiti Politici - Attuali Affiliati al Partito Centrale (Mahber Fikri' Hagher)," Asmara, March, 1947, p. 1. in Liaison Office Papers.

[39] "Yä Qeñññ Gezat Astädadär Bä Eretra," 8.

[40] Mezhiet (see note 36) says that, "the elders came out of their hiding because they knew that if they continued to shirk responsibilities, they would lose the respect they had among the youth."

[41] The most important secret meeting in which the need for organization was discussed and an organizing committee set up is said to have been held in the house of Fitawrari Abära Hagos some time in the early days of May 1941. "Yä Qeñññ Gezat Astädadär Bä Eretra"; see also Mamo Wudeneh, *Yä Eretra Tarik*, 123. He puts the number of participants at this meeting at about one hundred.

[42] Ibid., 40; Trevaskis, "The Former Italian Colony of Eritrea," 44, in Trevaskis Papers, Rhodes Library, S 367; see also U.S. National Archive, State Department Papers, [hereafter State], Office of Intelligence Research, "Affinities of the Western Provinces of Eritrea with Adjacent Areas" (O.I.R. Report No. 4996), September 1949, 10: This source claims that the Mahbär Feqri Hagär was formed in Asmara shortly after the British occupation in 1941. Ato Heywot Hedaru (see above note 22), who visited Asmara shortly after its occupation by the British, wrote in June 1941, "in spite of the repression following the demonstration and the ban on meetings, their [Eritreans] commitment to their country and their Emperor was such that they founded an association called Yä Hagär Feqer." Ato Heywot Hedaru mentioned this in a note he submitted to S'ähafi Taezaz Wäldä-Giyorgis, the Minister of Pen, on 8 June 1941. See Heywot Hedaru, *Yachi Qän Täräsach*, 422.

⁴³ Mohammed Omar Qadi, one of the founders and a central committee member in the Mahbär Feqri Hagär, gives May 5 as the date of foundation: Mohammed Omar Qadi, "Promemoria Della Lega Musulman Independente Dell'Eritrea, Con Sede a Massawa," in Liaison Office Papers ; another leading personality in the organization mentioned in 1947 that it was founded on May 5, 1941: see above, note 24. Sylvia Pankhurst, who followed events in Eritrea with keen interest and visited the territory in 1944, also makes a connection between the preparation for the celebration of the Liberation Day of Ethiopia and the founding of the Mahbär Feqri Hagär. See Sylvia and Richard Pankhurst, *Eritrea and Ethiopia: The Last Phase of the Reunion Struggle, 1941-1952*. (Essex: Lalibela House, 1953), 61; see also Mamo Wudeneh, *Ye Eritrea Tarik*, p. 123, for similar information on the date of establishment. One other source claims that the initiative to organize came out of the effort to collect contributions to be sent to the Emperor for the reconstruction of Ethiopia, "Yä Qeññ Gezat Astädadär Bä Eretra," 41. Brigadier Longrigg, the Chief Administrator, also mentions a drive by "unofficial representatives" to collect money for "Ethiopian-relief," Longrigg, "Ethiopian Irredentism in Eritrea," 25 March 1943, in FO371/35631.

⁴⁴ A report in the mid-1940's refers to Gäbrämäsqäl Wäldu as "the idol of the youth in Eritrea," Liaison Office Papers. Abdulkadir Kebire, a Muslim merchant, was elected vice president.

⁴⁵ Mohammed Omar Qadi in his memorandum to the United Nations Commission for Eritrea wrote that on the basis of economic, ethnic and historical considerations, the organization's objective was the incorporation of Eritrea into Ethiopia. Wäldä'ab Wäldämaryam, then a leading member of the Mahbär Feqri Hagär, who later became an opponent of union with Ethiopia, also confirms this view: Wäldä'ab Wäldämaryam, letter to Emperor Haile Selassie, 29 April 1947, in Liaison Office Papers.

⁴⁶ Fessehaye Tesfamikael, "Ala Adehenene Emkulu Ekuy Atsene' Walteha Tehetel Selameha," in Liaison Office Papers.

⁴⁷ Quoted in Trevaskis, *Eritrea*, 61.

⁴⁸ Cited in, Giacomo Magri, *La Politica Estera EtiopicaE Le Quesioni Eritrea E Somalia, 1941-1960* (Milano: A. Giuffrc, 1980), 57; see also Sylvia Pankhurst and R. Pankhurst, *Eritrea and Ethiopia*, pp.66-67. A 1946 petition by the Unionist Association said: "We know there exists a generally believed and trite opinion among Europeans, that coloured people (particularly African) are not capable of fully realizing what they wish for, when they want freedom in an economically stable home-country." Mahbär Feqri Hagär, "British Administration Police Action Against Unionist Association - Protest to the Chief Secretary, BMA," in Liaison Office Papers.

⁴⁹ Magri, *La Politica Estera Etiopica*, p. 57. A Tegrä elder in Kärän reportedly told the members of the Four Powers Commission of Investigation when asked about the future of Eritrea: "We all belong to the Habäsha race. We would like to be ruled by Haile Selassie who is black like us. We do not want any from among the white hyena," reported by Fessehayé Täsfamikaél, "Report on the Investigation of the People of the Lowlands, Kärän, Aqordät, and Baräntu, by the Representatives of the Four Powers" [Tegreñña], in Liaison Office Papers.

⁵⁰ Lt. Col. Crawford, the officer in charge of the British Ministry of Information in Eritrea, in a letter on 4 December 1944, FO 371/41510. Trevaskis also wrote that the Advisory Council had a "pronouncedly pro-Ethiopian outlook" by the end of 1942:

Trevaskis, *Eritrea*, 61. Sylvia Pankhurst, who met this group during her visit to Eritrea in 1944, said that they made an earnest appeal to her for support in their struggle for reunion with Ethiopia: Sylvia Pankhurst, *British Policy in Eritrea and Northern Ethiopia*, 24.

[51] Trevaskis, *Eritrea*, 65.

[52] Petition of Abraham Negussu (a former member of the Eritrean Police) to Emperor Haile Selassie, In Liason Office Papers.

[53] U.S. National Archive, (Suitland) Box 3, 800, Intelligence Report by S. Nystrom, Office of Strategic Service (OSS), 8 November 1944; "Yä Qeñň Gezat Astädadär Bä Eretra," 45.

[54] Rhodes Library, MSS British Empire, S 365, Fabian Colonial Bureau, Box 180.

[55] Their demands included an end to placing Eritreans under ex-Fascist officers, and the use of Italian judges to try the cases of Eritreans. They also refused to accept the uniforms which the BMA introduced, claiming that they were the kind used in colonial countries to create a clear distinction between colonized subjects and their white officers: Ibid.; "Yä Qeñň Gezat Astädadär Bä Eretrea," 13-14; see also Trevaskis, *Eritrea*, 65; and *New Times and Ethiopia News*, 8 April 1944.

[56] U.S. National Archive, (Suitland) Box 2, 800.1, "Letter to President Roosevelt by an American Historian of Project 19 at Gura," March 22, 1943.

[57] FO/371/35631, S. H. Longrigg, "Ethiopian Irredentism in Eritrea," 25 March 1943.

[58] Cited in Trevaskis, *Eritrea*, 60.

[59] Longrigg, see note 51.

[60] Emilio De Bono, *Anno, XIII: The Conquest of an Empire* (London: Cressent Press, 1937), 169.

[61] Bereket Habte Selassie, *Conflict and Intervention in the Horn of Africa;* Basil Davidson, Lionel Cliffe and Bereket Habte Selassie (eds.), *Behind the War in Eritrea*; Jordan Gebre-Medhin, *Peasants and Nationalism in Eritrea: A Critique of Ethiopian Studies* (Trenton, N.J.: Red Sea Press, 1989), xiv, who argues that Ethiopia accomplished the annexation of Eritrea "by promising the Church and the nobility a return to their former position of power and privilege." Even the less partisan works like John Markakis's *National and Class Conflict in the Horn of Africa*, repeat this misperception of the structural capabilities of the Ethiopian Church. Markakis claims: "His [Haile Selassie's] main agent was the Abyssinian Church, which had a large and efficient organization on the ground," 63.

[62] For a contemporary account of the dependence of the clergy on the laity, see "The Hamasén - A Social Survey," 35-36, in Trevaskis'Papers, Rhodes Library; see also Tadesse Tamirat, *Church and State in Ethiopia 1270-1527*, (Oxford: Clarendon Press, 1972), 112-114, in which he states that the "clergy lived in, and completely depended on, society, of which they constitute an integral part."

[63] Foreign Office Research Department, "Eritrea and Italian Somaliland," 2 February 1944, 140., in FO 371/35658.

[64] Interview: Qäññazmach Gäbräselassé.

[65] Longrigg, "Some Problems of Administration in Eritrea," March 1944, 9-10.

[66] Petition to His Excellency Brigadier Stephen Longrigg, Chief Administrator of Eritrea, in Liaison Office Papers; see also, Shumet Sishagne, "Yä Eretra He'zboch yä Andenat Tegel," Dialogue, 3rd Series, Vol. 1, No. 2, (Addis Ababa, 1992).

[67] A report from the Chief Administrator's Office stated that the "Committee has been fairly successful in Asmara where many Eritreans - Copts, Catholics, Swedish-Mission Protestants as well as Mohammedans - have signed the petition". S. Nadel for Chief Administrator to C.C.A.O., G.H.Q., Middle East Force, 6 January 1944.

[68] These were the suggestions made by General W. Platt, General Officer commanding the East Africa Forces, FO 371/41525, 24 April 1944.

[69] FO 371/27582, report of G. Mackereth of the Foreign Office, 15 July 1941. A Middle East War Council held in Cairo from the 10th to the 13th of May 1943 broadly agreed along these lines as regards the future of Eritrea, FO/371/35633. See also Henderson, *The Making of the Modern Sudan*, pp. 331-32, for the accounts of Sir Douglas Newbold, one of the participants in the Council; and Haggai Erlich, "Tigrean Nationalism, British Involvement and Haile Selassie's Emerging Absolutism in Northern Ethiopia," in *Asian and African Studies*, XV (1981), pp. 191-227. Another meeting by the Middle East Defence Committee in July 1944 also came out with similar recommendations: FO 371/41451, "Middle East Defence Committee," 7 July 1944.

[70] FO 371/27522, Secretary of State for Foreign Affairs, "Memorandum", 15 October 1941; and FO 371/35608, Howe to G. Mackereth, Addis Ababa, 15 October 1943.

[71] State, Report No. 150, American Consulate General at Nairobi, "Italian Colonies in Africa," 22 June 1946. The Consul claimed to have obtained his information from "a high ranking officer in the East African Command." See also FO 371/41520, 20 April 1944, for the arguments of the British Air Ministry in support of the creation of a new Greater Somalia under British trusteeship.

[72] Quoted in Wilfred Thesiger, *The Life of My Choice* (Glasgow: Collins, 1987), 316.

[73] General Platt, "Memorandum, Head Quarters - East Africa," 24 April 1944, in Fo 371/41525.

[74] Christopher Sykes, *Orde Wingate*, 253-257

[75] "The Ethiopian Problem," 11 August, 1941, p.84, in FO 371/27520. Ato Heywot Hedaru who returned from Khartoum in June 1941 mentions that Ethiopians were not allowed to enter some of the Italian bars and restaurants in Addis Ababa which were frequented by South African and British officers: Heywot Hedaru, *Yachi Qän Täräsach*, 419-430. For further description on the tense relation between British political officers and officials of the Ethiopian government in the provinces, see, Käbädä Täsämma, *Yä Tarik Mastawäsha* (Addis Ababa: Artistic Printing Press, 1962 [E.C.]), 432-442.

[76] Anthony Eden to David Margesson, 10 October, 1941, in FO 371/27514; see also FO /371/27522, October 10, 1941, for a War Office assessment of how Sir Phillip Mitchell's draft treaty would have made Ethiopia virtually a protectorate.

[77] Lord Rennell, British Military Administration, p. 75.

[78] Sir Reginald Wingate to Major Desmond J. Morton, April 28, 1941, in FO 371/27518.

[79] The strategy of building up an East African Empire to make up for the potential loss of Egypt and India was described in detail in the editorials of the influential British colonial journal, *East Africa and Rhodesia*, May 16, 1946. See also Haggai Erlich, "Ras Alula, Ras Seyum, Tigre and Ethiopia's Integrity," a paper presented at the Eighth International Conference on Ethiopian Studies (Addis Ababa, 1984), on how the Sudan was to replace Egypt as the main British stronghold in the region.

[80] In a memorandum of 20 January 1942, the Foreign Office suggested that Britain's policy should focus on carrying the Sudan frontier down into Eritrea in order to unite the Beni Amer, recreate "the old Kingdom of Tigre by attaching Eritrean Tigre to Ethiopian Tigre," and set up minor sheikdoms or sultanates for the Danakil and Somali tribes in Italian Somaliland, FO 371/35606, Forign Office Memorandum of 20.1.1942.

[81] A Foreign Office assessment in 1945 concluded: "For the last three years Ethiopia has devoted her energies... with success... to throwing off what she conceived to be the bonds of attempted British tutelage," FO 371/46053, "Ethiopia," 16 April 1945. For more detailed information on Anglo-Ethiopian relations at this time, see Harold Marcus, *Ethiopia, Great Britain and the United States, 1941-1974: The Politics of Empire* (Berkeley: University of California Press, 1983), 8-78.

[82] Henderson, *The Making of the Modern Sudan*, 232.

[83] Colonel Cheesman, "Memorandum on Internal Situation in Ethiopia," 25 May 1943, in FO 371/35626.

[84] Wäldä'ab Wäldämaryam (one of the leaders of the Separatist Movement in Eritrea) who had been close to the British Military Administration in Eritrea since his employment as editor of the Tegreñña section of the *Eritrean Weekly News* in 1942, wrote to Emperor Haile Selassie that the British appeared to be working to create an Ethio-British condominium as had been done in the Sudan. Wäldä'ab Wäldämaryam, to Emperor Haile Selassie, Asmara, 29 April 1947, in Liaison Office Papers.

[85] FO 371/35633, "Committee on Ethiopia, Report on Future Policy Towards Ethiopia," 18 May 1943; and FO 371/41510, Howe to Foreign Office, 6 November 1944. See also, John H. Spencer, *Ethiopia at Bay: A Personal Account of the Haile Sellassie Years* (Hollywood, Ca.: Tsehai Publishers and Distributors, 2006), 139. Spencer, a former adviser to the Ethiopian Ministry of Foreign Affairs, claimed that British officials had approached the U.S. State Department twice in 1943 to discuss the Greater Somaliland project, and to solicit support for their proposal to establish a trusteeship over all of Ethiopia: see Spencer, "Ethiopia and the Horn of Africa: Hearings before the Subcommittee on African Affairs of the Committee on Foreign Relations," United States Senate, August 4, 5, and 6, 1976.

[86] Brigadier F.G. Drew, FO 371/63175; see also the letter from Major H.F. Kynaston-Snell, Head of the Educational Department, letter to Hinden, 19 April 1946, on expectations of permanent rule over Eritrea, in Rhodes Library, MSS, British Empire, S 365, Box 180. The American Consul in Asmara also reported that British officials told him that Great Britain should not abandon its control in Eritrea, especially in view of the need to find a replacement for British military positions surrendered in Egypt, "Secret Memorandum," 20 September 1946, in State, 711.9.

[87] Colonel Trevaskis, Senior Civil Affairs Officer in Eritrea, wrote: "many British officers found it difficult to conceal their dislike of the bitter and touchy young men in the Mahbär Feqri Hagär," Trevaskis, *Eritrea*, 61.

[88] Four Power Commission of Investigation for the Former Italian Colonies [hereafter FPCI], Report on Eritrea, 1948, Appendix 22.

[89] Longrigg, "Some Problems of Administration in Eritrea," March, 1944, p. 10, in FO 371/46116.

[90] Cited in Sylvia Pankhurst, British Policy in Eritrea and Northern Ethiopia, 10; see also, "Yä Qeñ̃ Gezat Astädadär Bä Eretra," 12.

[91] Negga letter to the Emperor, 19 September 1946 in Liaison Office Papers.

[92] British Military Administration in Eritrea, *The Eritrean Gazettee*, Vol. V, Proclamation No. 23, 23 June 1945.

[93] Among those who lost their positions were Däjazmach Haylämäläkot, son of Ras Wäldämikaél (a chief of great fame in the late nineteenth century), and members of the Barakhi family (influential in the Hamasén throughout Italian times), Däjazmach Hagos Gäbré and several others in Akälä Guzai and Säraé. Those exiled included Azmach Barakhi Habtä'ezgi, Qés Dimétros and Azmach Georgio Habtit. Käntibai Osman Hadad, chief of the Habab, was also put under house arrest in Naqfa to prevent him from spreading irredentism among chiefs of the Western Province: "Dati Sull'atteggiamento parziale dell'Amministrazione Britanica," Liaison Office Papers.

[94] The five members of the Mahbär Feqri Hagär detained were Grazmach Zärré Bakit, Blatta Fasil Oqba'ezgi, Grazmach Täsfamikaél Worqé, Blatta Asfaha Abreha, and Araya Sebhatu. A later Unionist memorandum described this action as an administrative measure designed to convince all the people of Eritrea that the Administration was against the Unionist movement, Liaison Office Papers, Mahbär Feqri Hagär, "All'Amministratore Capo Dell'Eritrea: Protesta," Asmara, 4 January 1946. Thirty prominent residents in Asmara contributed the 1000 Pounds Sterling required to bail out the prisoners, Sylvia Pankhurst, *British Policy in Eritrea and Northern Ethiopia*, 14-16; and Mamo Wudeneh, *Yä Eretra Tarik*, 13; Four police officers, Inspectors Asfaw Agostino, Gäbrämaryam, Gäbräiyäsus, and Sergent Täklägiorgis Tämäleso were imprisoned in Fort Baldissera for taking "an active part in politics," see Rohdes Library, MSS British Empire, S 365, Fabian Colonial Bureau, Box 180.

[95] U.S. National Archive, A Report From the Office of Strategic Service, 8 November, 1944.

[96] FO 371/41520, "Extract from Intelligence Summary - Eritrea," No. 31, February 1944.

[97] Trevaskis, *Eritrea*, 36.

[98] These techniques were openly advocated by Longrigg in his "Some Problems of Administration in Eritrea," March 1944, in FO 371/46116.

[99] FO 371/41531, Overseas Planning Committee - Ministry of Information, "Plan of Propaganda to Eritrea," November 1944. The semi-official French newspaper, *Le Monde*, wrote in its 27 November, 1945, issue that "Great Britain is conducting an active propaganda campaign not only in Eritrea but also in Tigre in view of the formation

of an Eritrean State which would also include the Ethiopian province of Tigre, which State would be placed under British control for a certain length of time."

[100] Letters of S'ägay Iyasu and Bärhé Beieke to Sylvia Pankhurst, Asmara, 15 February 1946, Liaison Office Papers, mentioning the works they had accomplished together with an Englishman, Bert Storey, in gathering evidence of BMA harassment of Unionists.

[101] Mumford, British Ministry of Information, Asmara, 4 December, 1944, in FO 371/41520.

[102] Ibid.

[103] Margery Perham to Scrivener, 12 June 1945, FO 371/46100. A U.S. State Department account also mentions that Perham was using her "formidable social and academic contacts" to expound the cause of a `Greater Somaliland,' State, "The Reserved Areas and Somaliland," 10/7/1945.

[104] His articles appeared in the *Spectator*, 27 July 1945, and 10 August 1945; *International Affairs*, Vol. 21, July 1945; *The Times* (reproduced in New Times and Ethiopia News, 6 October 1945); *East Africa and Rhodesia*, 20 June 1946; and United Empire, September 1946. His book, *A Short History of Eritrea* (Oxford: Clarendon Press), was also published in 1945.

[105] Wäldä'ab Wäldämaryam, testimony (August 1985) to Stefano Poscia, *Eritrea Colonia Tradita*, 33.

[106] See for instance, *Nay Eretra Sämunawi Gazéta*, 3 August 1944. This article asserted that Ethiopia had neither the spiritual nor the material capacity to administer Eritrea. Fitawrari Gäbrämäsqäl Wäldu, replied on 31 August 1944, arguing that the genuine interests of the people of Eritrea were tied up with Ethiopia. He wrote: "If we are going to maintain our identity we have to give our best assistance to Ethiopia."

[107] Longrigg, "Some Problems of Administration in Eritrea," March 1944, p. 6, in FO 371/46116.

[108] Longrigg, "Italy's Colonies", *The Spectator*, July 27 1945.

[109] Idem., "Mischief-making in Eritrea", in Rhodes Library, Mss British Empire S 365 (Fabian Colonial Bureau, Box 180).

[110] A report of the U.S. Office of Strategic Service indicates that the `Greater Tigrai' movement "was born in the office of the British Ministry of Information in Asmara." The report says that *The Eritrean Daily* (the official newspaper published by the British Ministry of Information) favours the idea of the `Greater Tigrai' movement. State, Office of Strategic Service, No. 60687, "Report from Addis Ababa," 8 November, 1944.

[111] S. Nadel for the Chief Administrator, 6 January 1944, in FO 371/41478. The Foreign Office Research Department's assessment at the beginning of 1944 indicated that most of the Eritrean chiefs would oppose the irredentist movement, FO 371/35658, Research Department - Foreign Office, "Eritrea and Italian Somaliland," 2 February 1944, 59.

[112] Täsämma Asbärom (then a Däjazmach) was considered by the Italians as one of the most important chiefs as far back as 1917. See, Governo Dell'Eritrea,

Elenco dei capi e notabili indigeni stipendiati e del personale indigeno in servizio dell'Aministrazione civile dell'Eritrea al 1 Febbraio 1917 (Asmara, 1917).

[113] He reportedly felt so insulted by the Hamasén chiefs who had not consulted him on matters of such grave importance, that he vowed to fight them to the end. Interview: General Nägga Hayläsellasé (London, 1989), and Bitwoded Asfeha Wäldämikaél (Addis Ababa, 1983). Ras Täsämma's son, Däjazmach Abreha Täsämma, complained to Gäbrämäsqäl Habtämaryam, the President of the Addis Ababa branch of the Mahbär Feqri Hagär, that his father was not accorded a position in the Mahbär Feqri Hagär fit to his rank and that the notables of Akälä Guzai in general were excluded from the movement. He reportedly boasted that he would see to it that this organization which had alienated Akälä Guzai did not get anywhere. Gäbrämäsqäl Habtämaryam's report to the Ministry of the Pen, cited in "Eretra Bä Tarik Yä Ityoppya Akal Selämähonuwa" [unpublished manuscript in Amharic compiled from documents in the Archives of the Ethiopian government, Ministry of the Pen].

[114] A 1947 estimate put the urban population in Hamasén to 95,350 compared to 5,370 in Akälä Guzai and 9,000 in Säraé. See, FPCI, *Report On Eritrea*, App. 5.

[115] When asked to lend his support to the irredentist movement, Ras Täsämma Asbärom reportedly said: "it would be highly improper for chiefs, who were paid servants of the Government, to have anything to do with any subversive movement." Quoted in FO 371/41520, "Extract from Intelligence Summary - Eritrea, 1-29 February 1944."

[116] Chief Administrator, Eritrea, "Ethiopian Irredentism in Eritrea," 25 March 1943, in FO 35631.

[117] Longrigg, "Some Problems of Administration in Eritrea," 9.

[118] Hayläsellasé Gugsa, who was entrusted with the command of part of the Tegréan army had defected to the Italian side at the beginning of the invasion in 1935. After the fall of Italian power in Ethiopia he wrote to the Commander of the British troops in Eritrea offering to put himself under the "protection of a civilized European power." Leul Hailc Selassie Gugsa, Mesfin del Tigrai, "A S.E. Il Comandante delle Truppe Inglesi in Eritrea," Mekelle, 10 April 1941, in Liaison Office Papers. The Ethiopian government repeatedly requested the extradiction of Hayläsellasé Gugsa to try him for treason. However, the British refused to comply and removed him to the Seychelles instead. While in exile in the Seychelles, Hayläsellasé Gugsa reportedly agitated through his followers in Tegray that upon his return he would establish an independent Tegray whose boundary in the east would stretch to the river Allawaha: Gebru Tareke, "Rural Protest in Ethiopia, 1941-1970: A Study of Three Rebellions" (Ph.D. Dissertation, Syracuse University, 1977), 122.

[119] "La Situazione Dell'Eritrea," 13, in Ibid.; see also Gianluigi Rossi, *L'Africa Italiana Verso L'Independenza, 1941-1949* (Giuffre, 1980), 73; and Trevaskis, *Eritrea*, 63, for Ras Täsämma's close attachment to Hayläsellasé Gugsa and other great families in Tegray.

[120] Azmach Zäre'om Wäldämikaél's letter to Nägga, Adi Qäyeh, 30 July 1947, "Yä Eretra Guday Bä Amareñña," in Liaison Office Papers.

[121] Trevaskis, *Eritrea*, 63.

CHAPTER THREE

Fission and Fusion in Eritrean Politics: Internal Actors and External Sponsors, 1945-1951

The end of World War II and the beginning of the international discussion on the future of the ex-Italian colonies brought to light the complex interests involved in the Eritrean question. In addition to Great Britain and Ethiopia, who had made their claims known while the war was still in progress, Italy also made a determined effort to recover her lost colonies. Egypt, too, made a brief, but staunch attempt to gain Eritrea.[1]

The major powers who assembled to decide the future of the territory viewed the issue from the perspective of the evolving new international order. The Eritrean question became a cog in the wheel of the intense rivalry which characterized the post-war East-West relationship.

Domestic political forces were also propelled into renewed activity. Different interests and views regarding the future of the territory, which had remained dormant, were reactivated by the prospect of an approaching settlement. New forces were also created as each of the external powers attempted to advance its claims on Eritrea by sponsoring local support groups. The old forces, too, carried out extensive reorganizations to cope with the new challenges.

The first internal interest to respond to this new challenge was the irredentist group which had practically monopolized indigenous Eritrean politics until 1945. It was the only force to come forward with a relatively well articulated view on the future of the territory, and it engaged itself in practical activity to achieve its goal.

The irredentist movement was, however, encumbered by a rather nebulous organizational structure. The new challenges it faced, especially from the emergence of a separatist force in the highlands, as well as the stiff opposition from both the British Military Administration and the Italian interests in Eritrea, underscored the need for change.

The more organizationally conscious element within the irredentist leadership had for some time realized that the rather loose and amorphous structure of the Mahbär Feqri Hagär could not be relied upon for effective mobilization purposes. As early as 1943, some of the militant elements had formed a separate wing of the youth to implement the more radical aims of the movement which could not be achieved directly in the name of the main body of the Mahbär Feqri Hagär. To ward off the suspicion of British officials the group called itself the Sunday Association ("Sänbäté Mahbär"), a name it changed into Association of Eritrea with Ethiopia ("Mahbär Eritrea Mes Ethiopia") when the British officially permitted open political expression in 1946.[2] In turn, this association was affiliated with a radical youth group called Union (Andenät) which in time virtually grew into a vanguard of the Unionist forces.

The new challenge which they faced at the end of 1945, and the task required to surmount it, convinced a number of the irredentist leaders of the need for a major reorganization of the Mahbär Feqri Hagär. Pressure for change was also building up from below. A popular petition submitted to the head office of the Mahbär Feqri Hagär in January, 1946, demanded that the leadership should "wake from its slumber" and give a more active leadership.[3]

A decision was finally reached at the end of January, 1946, to carry out the task of reorganizing and reforming the Mahbär Feqri Hagär. The changes primarily focused on setting up a more compact organizational structure with an effective central committee, a strong executive body, and an efficient staff working fulltime for the organization. A new statute was drawn up, and the branch offices set up in the districts were reorganized along similar lines.

The process of transforming the rather loosely organized Mahbär Feqri Hagär into a relatively centralized and efficient body with a clearly focused political agenda involved a radical departure from the earlier informal approaches to organizational problems. The change brought with it major changes in the apportionment of power and caused shifts in alliance among the contenders for power. There were those who saw the opening of new avenues for themselves in the new change, while others saw it essentially as a threat to their established positions. This created notable dissention in the old Mahbär Feqri Hagär. Factional strife intensified as groups tried to ensure dominance in the evolving organizational hierarchy.

In addition, differences which had been hidden under the carpet began to surface as the projected change involved a much clearer definition of goals and a more concrete plan of action. In place of the rather vague and simplistic aims which had mostly been pronounced orally and variously interpreted by different interest groups, the Mahbär Feqri Hagär was adopting a well defined organizational structure. Groups that had stayed within the organization on the basis of vague promises and ill-defined objectives were now able to see more clearly where they stood in the new arrangement.

Most affected were the few Muslim members who failed to persuade their Christian compatriots to take their special interests into account. They argued that the new statute should contain provisions which would guarantee the rights of Muslims in a union with Ethiopia where Christians monopolized political power. The failure of the organization to pay attention to this plea alienated its minority Muslim adherents. Some constituted themselves into a separate interest group and began to mobilize support for their demands for a union which would provide a special guarantee for Muslim rights. Others withdrew totally from the Mahbär Feqri Hagär and began to organize an exclusively Muslim party.

The cohesion within the dominant Christian group in the leadership of the Mahbär Feqri Hagär was also affected by jockeying for power in the new apparatus. Following the decision to implement the reorganization of the Mahbär Feqri Hagär, the Central Committee was split into two major blocks: those who supported the president, Fitawrari Gäbrämäsqäl Wäldu, and those who stood in opposition to him led by Däjazmach Araya Wassé and Azmach Zäreom Keflä.[4]

The division within the leadership of the Mahbär Feqri Hagär was further complicated by the growing involvement of the Ethiopian government and representatives of the Addis Ababa branch of the Mahbär Feqri Hagär. Delegates coming from Addis Ababa reportedly aggravated the internal conflict by siding with one or the other faction.[5]

Although personality clashes and rivalry for power were apparent, there did not seem to be any major differences among the Christian elements over the fundamental political objective of the Mahbär Feqri Hagär. The manner in which the internal conflict was shelved, and the speed with which differences between the contending parties were ironed out when the threat from outside increased, indicate that the issues which divided them were not deeply rooted.

The threat of Britain's ambitions for Eritrea and the fear of losing ground to the separatist forces were compelling factors which persuaded many of the irredentist leaders to accommodate their differences and to close ranks.

A council of notables led by the Abunä Marqos and Ras Kidanämaryam Gäbrämäsqäl was called upon to arbitrate the conflict. The council first obtained the resignation of all incumbent members of the Central Committee and then undertook a new election in November, 1946.

Almost all the old guard in the Mahbär Feqri Hagär, including those who had withdrawn from leadership owing to disagreements with the president, Gäbrämäsqäl Wäldu, were returned to the Central Committee. But there were significant new additions to the Committee from among the more radical and professional groups in Asmara. Some major reshuffling also occurred. Gäbrämäsqäl Wäldu was dropped from the presidency, although he still retained a seat in the Central Committee.[6] Ras Kidanämaryam Gäbrämäsqäl, one of the only two surviving members of the high aristocracy in Eritrea with the title of Ras, was given the title of Honorary President. Däjazmach Bäyänä Barakhi, a member of a powerful family which had managed to establish a significant influence in Hamasén and in the native quarters of Asmara under the Italians, was elected president. Effective power passed into the hands of the secretary general, Tädla Bairu,[7] a product of Protestant mission education and a school teacher during the Italian rule. As assistant to the senior Civil Affairs Officer in Asmara under the British, he held the highest office given to Eritreans until his resignation in August, 1946, in protest at British policy in Eritrea.

Aided by a dedicated professional staff, Tädla was able to forge an efficient organizational machine whose network soon spread over much of Eritrea. Following the British declaration allowing open political activity to the indigenous population, the Mahbär Feqri Hagär constituted itself into a formal political party under a new name: Nay Eretran Ethiopian Hebrät Mahbär Feqri Hagär-Eretra Mes Ethiopia Hanti Ethiopia (The Eritrea-Ethiopia Union Patriotic Association-Eritrea with Ethiopia-One Ethiopia), which came commonly to be known as the Unionist Party. Its branch offices in the districts were reorganized along new lines. The formal inauguration of branch offices in such places as Kärän, Massawa, Addi Ugri, Addi Quala, Däqämäharäi, Säganäiti, Ghinda, Addi Qäyeh, Sänafé, Aqordat, Baräntu, Tässänei, Om Hajär and Naqfa provided the occasion for organizing massive demonstrations in support of unionism.[8] The party also launched a Tegreñña weekly newspaper called *Ethiopia*, which soon became a highly influential organ of Unionist propaganda.[9]

The Anti-Unionist Movement

Although their influence was not as widespread as that of the Unionists, various groups opposed to Ethiopian annexation were also beginning to make their presence felt. Chief among these were the Separatists, who, while not coming out openly with a concrete plan of their own, still refused to go along with the irredentist call for an unconditional union with Ethiopia.

Although Muslim opposition to irredentism was still incoherent, there were signs of a religious-based agitation in the Western Lowland. Some prominent Muslims, especially in Asmara, who originally belonged to the Mahbär Feqri Hagär were, by 1946 openly expressing reservations about joining Ethiopia unless they were guaranteed special protection.

As becomes evident from a review of the memorandums, petitions, and manifestos in 1946 originating from the various groups who stood opposed to the Unionists, that most of them were not actually against unionism per se, but against an outright annexation of Eritea by Ethiopia as advocated by the Unionist Party. They appeared to be more intent on modifying the Unionist proposal than on providing a radically different alternative. Except for the occasional tendency to repeat the British position, no formula which treated Eritrea as a separate political body with an identity of its own was forwarded at this stage by any of the local forces opposed to the Unionist program. Most of them were unable, or as yet unwilling, to envisage a political alternative which would deny the essential Ethiopian identity of Eritrea. The leaders of these groups claimed that their objective was not to prevent the unification of the two territories, but to set conditions on the type of union which should be formed.[10]

Until the end of 1946 the prevalent wish of those who were not in favor of the Unionist position of direct annexation appear to have been a type of union which included safeguards for their special interests. Each group, of course, interpreted differently what these safeguards should be depending on its relative anticipated fear of union with Ethiopia. Most Muslims feared that they would fare badly in a Christian-dominated Ethiopia unless their rights were officially recognized. Their demands included legal recognition for Islam and its institutions including the Sharia and the use of the Arabic language in schools and for other official purposes.[11]

Most Christian proponents of conditional union expressed the fear that if they were joined to Ethiopia without special provisions to protect them they would be at the mercy of the Amhara oligarchy. They argued that the Shäwan aristocracy which had dominated Ethiopia since the death of Yohannes the IV had practically monopolized political power, uprooted local rulers, and subjected all areas to rigid control from Addis Ababa. They feared a similar fate for Eritrea. Some of the more politically enlightened elements within this group also feared that unconditional union with Ethiopia would expose them to Haile Selassie's archaic and despotic rule. They asked for a form of union that would guarantee local autonomy and basic political rights. They hoped to achieve these by persuading the Unionists to modify their demand for an unconditional union.

The first major attempts to reach a rapprochement with Unionist forces was made towards the end of 1946. A tentative understanding involving a federal type of union with Ethiopia appears to have been reached between a minority group in the Unionist Party, led by Fitawrari Gäbrämäsqäl Wäldu, and Separatist forces at the end of October 1946.[12] The proposal was, however, rejected by a majority of the Unionist leadership, which questioned Gäbrämäsqäl Wäldu's mandate to reach such an understanding on behalf of the Unionist Party.[13]

To gain a wider acceptance for this proposal a much larger conference attended by leading members of both groups was held at Bét Giyorgis in Asmara, in November 1946. The most influential figures in the anti-Unionist camp were Wäldä'ab Wäldämaryam, Däjazmach Abreha Täsämma, Däjazmach Hassen Ali, and Azmach Berhanu Ahmäddin. The last two were emerging as the principal champions of Muslim interests in Asmara. Wäldä'ab and Däjazmach Abreha belonged to the Separatist movement led by Ras Täsämma. The Unionist representatives included Fitawrari Gäbrämäsqäl Wäldu, Azmach Giorgio Habtit, Mesghena Gäbrä'ezghi, Tädla Bairu, Mohammed Omar Qadi, and Fitawrari T'aha Adäm.[14]

The conference failed to produce a satisfactory compromise. The meeting ended in disagreement as each side stuck firmly to its previously stated positions. The Conditional Unionists accused the Unionist Party of slavishly following the wishes of the Ethiopian government.[15] The Unionists countered that those who advocated conditional union had a history of close collaboration with the British administration and the Italian interests in Eritrea and that they were trying to put limitations on the union to safeguard the interests of their foreign patrons.[16] They argued that the demand for a special form of union with Ethiopia amounted to questioning the Ethiopian identity of Eritrea.[17] Their reply to the Conditionalists was summed up by one Unionist leader: "Either get in or go out"[18] — rejecting compromise over the nature of the union with Ethiopia.

The meeting was also marred by mutual recrimination and personal attacks. In the end it dispersed after a heated quarrel between Wäldä'ab Wäldämaryam and Tädla Bairu,[19] two formidable protagonists who were to remain locked in deadly combat for a decade. Efforts to call another meeting were unsuccessful.

The failure of the Bét Giyorgis meeting has often been taken as a landmark in contemporary Eritrean politics. Discontented "Conditionalists" were said to have been driven into adopting extremist positions by Unionist intransigence."[20]

Most of the principal leaders in the anti-Unionist movement attribute the hardening of their position towards association with Ethiopia to this event.²¹ Wäldä'ab Wäldämaryam, a noted figure in the anti-unionist movement, drew a direct link between the failure of the Bét Giyorgis meeting and the formation of anti-Ethiopian parties, including the Muslim League.²²

However, the significance of the Bét Giyorgis meeting in shaping future political trends may have been over-stated. It is true that a few of the leaders of the separatist element in the Christian group may have been kept within the Unionist Party had Unionists been willing to make certain concessions. However, even after the Bét Giyorgis meeting Christian Separatists remained an insignificant minority, limited largely to the Akälä Guzai area. They claimed only seven percent of the highland and .04 percent of the lowland constituencies, even by their own admission.²³ The group's close connection with the British authorities aroused suspicions among the local population that it was a political tool of the Administration.

The Christian following of the Unionist Party does not seem to have been seriously affected by its refusal to accommodate the conditionalists. If at all, the months following the Bét Giyorgis meeting were marked by successful expansion of irredentist political activity in the highland regions, as was witnessed by the opening of new offices, staging pro-union demonstrations, and the signing of petitions in preparation for the arrival of the Four Power Commission of Investigation.

The group whose opposition had the most serious consequences for the irredentist movement was the Muslim community. Muslims represented about half of the population in Eritrea and most of them were totally alienated from the Unionists. A number of influential Eritrean Muslim supporters of unionism were antagonized by the inattentiveness of the Unionist Party to their interests. Most of those who attended the Bét Giyorgis meeting came out convinced that no Christian, not even those who were arguing for conditional union, were willing to consider the Muslims as an important component in the future political life of the territory. They believed that the Christians were basically of one mind in their indifference to Muslim concerns and viewed the differences among Christians at the meeting as personal squabbles among brothers. Ibrahim Sultan, who was soon to emerge as the most important leader of the Muslim faction, said of the Bét Giyorgis meeting: "No one said to us-you are sons of Eritrea. What is your opinion?"²⁴

Unionist effort to win the support of the Muslim community appears to have been very weak. This might partially be explained by the low level of ordinary interaction between the two communities. Geographically the territory was defined largely along Christian-Muslim lines. Christians predominated in most of the highland areas with a small minority of Muslims interspersed among them. The eastern coastal areas and the western lowlands were mostly inhabited by Muslims. Religious and regional differences reinforced ethnic differences. The two communities had remained separate and in most cases no love was lost between them. Even half a century of Italian colonial rule did not seem to have changed the situation appreciably, especially with regard to the rural population.

The absence of a tradition of friendly interaction between the two communities was a serious handicap to the Unionists.[25] They could not follow up their impressive success in the Eritrean highland regions by similar mobilization of the Muslim pastoral population in the lowlands. There appears to have been no effective mechanisms of interaction which the Unionists could have utilized to capture a significant Muslim constituency, especially at the grassroots level. Failing to do this, they opted instead to confine themselves to winning a few adherents in the towns and some notables in the countryside.

While the difficulties of winning over Muslim sympathy were quite evident, Unionist failure was also to a large extent a result of a lack of serious desire to involve Muslims in the political process. Traditionally, Christians had monopolized the politics of northern Ethiopia, and most of the Christians in the Unionist movement were not willing to revise the status quo.

Unionist disregard for the Muslim community was also reinforced by the marked apathy which prevailed among the Muslims. While much of Christian Eritrea was fervently involved in the issues concerning the future of the territory, the Muslim community largely remained indifferent. The pastoral Muslim population was not seriously affected by the kind of desperate rural overcrowding which characterized the Christian peasantry's life in highland Eritrea. Since the nomadic population's integration into the market economy was also marginal, it was not as severely affected by the economic crisis which hit the highland peasants and the urban areas following the Italian defeat. This, in effect, lessened the chances of rapid politicization of the dominantly Muslim pastoral population.

In addition, the pastoral communities were fragmented into small tribal and clan units living in relative isolation, and were affected very little by what was going on in the major towns and on the plateau.[26] They had many fewer schools even by the standards of Eritrea and had produced very few of the modern intelligentsia who were playing crucial roles in other parts of the territory. Also, most of these communities, especially in the Western Province, were too immersed in their own parochial conflicts to pay attention to other, broader issues. For example, after 1942 the Bäni Amer tribes in the Barka area had fought intermittently with the Hadendowa in the Sudan. The disorder spilled over into the Gash and Sätit region where the Baria and Kunama battled against each other as well as against frequent Bäni Amer raids. The

British Military Administration had been able to establish some form of order in the region only toward the end of 1945.[27]

Although they were not as insulated as their rural kin, the urban Muslims also tended to keep aloof from the political issues which greatly agitated the Christian community. For one thing, Muslims in the towns had not done badly following the Italian defeat. Since they had traditionally dominated business they were not greatly threatened by the general economic insecurity which plagued the urban Christian community, which, by contrast, largely depended on wage earnings and other forms of employment associated with the state. Apparently, a large number of Muslims living in the highland towns were doing better under the British owing to the lifting of some of the restrictions imposed by the Italians. The economic crisis which created massive impoverishment among the urban and highland population also played into the hands of the Muslim merchants who prospered by mortgages and exorbitant interest rates. There appeared to be little reason for this relatively contented group to upset the status quo.

As late as 1946, Unionists appeared to have banked very much on the indifference of the Muslim community. Colonel Trevaskis, who was then the British Senior Civil Affairs Officer of the predominantly Muslim region of the Western Province, wrote in January 1947: "The leaders of the Unionist Party have long counted on the political silence of the Muslim areas and any suggestion that the Muslims might not welcome Ethiopian rule have been pooh poohed with great casualness."[28]

Although their participation in the broader political forums was inconspicuous, some basic changes were, nonetheless, occurring at the local level, especially in the Western Province. The most significant development, which was soon to have a profound effect on the political landscape in Eritrea, was the serf movement which started soon after the fall of Italian rule. The uprising by Tegré serfs against the onerous demands of the *shumagellä* (aristocracy), started first in the Sahel region. By the beginning of 1946 it had engulfed much of the Western Province.

The British Administration had its own axe to grind against the ruling caste in the Western Province. Its various privileges and the onerous demands on its subjects hindered the introduction of direct taxation in the region. As part of its plan to eventually annex the region to the Sudan, the Administration was also keen on introducing certain reforms which could bring the area closer to the Sudan. It was partially for this reason that it had merged the former divisions of Kärän and Aqordat into one single unit called the Western Province now consisting of the districts of Kärän, Aqordat, Baräntu, Tässänäy, Om Hajär, and Naqfa. Colonel Trevaskis, one of the ablest officers of the British Military Administration in Eritrea, was placed at the head of this vast province.[29] British officials viewed the existence of archaic feudal obligations and practices not only as an administrative encumbrance but also as an obstacle to the projected union of the Western Province with the Sudan. Hence, the Administration's enthusiasm for the movement for the emancipation of the serfs.[30]

However, as tribes and clans refused to place themselves under the authority of their former aristocratic rulers, the whole area was thrown into a state of confusion and administrative anarchy. Small groups, sometimes consisting of only a few families, tried to set up themselves as autonomous political units. In order to end this state of affairs, the Administration intervened directly and began to chart the direction of the movement, which it sought to organize and unify by bringing in more capable leaders from outside. For this it turned to the towns where it struck a deal with some ambitious and able merchants and former civil servants in Kärän and Aqordat. The most outstanding of these recruits was Ibrahim Sultan Ali, a former interpreter in the Italian administration. He had worked as a civil servant in the initial years of the British Administration and was engaged in trade in the western lowlands when he established liaison with the British over the leadership of the serf movement. He had been among the earliest members of the Mahbär Feqri Hagär.[31]

Ibrahim Sultan and his colleagues helped the Administration in bringing the scattered and disorganized serf communities together and in reorganizing the nomadic population into new and larger political units better suited to administrative purposes. While they were doing this, they also put themselves at the head of the movement. This gave them command of a constituency that was becoming accustomed to being organized in larger groups and to participating in political matters concerning wider issues. In a short time Ibrahim Sultan and his allies changed the direction of the movement from its declared aim of emancipating serfs to advocating Muslim interests and challenging the dominant Christian desire to annex Eritrea to Ethiopia.

The transformation of Ibrahim Sultan's group into a political force seeking Muslim power over the whole of Eritrea was speeded up by the sense of urgency created in the middle of 1946 by the prominence given to the future of the ex-Italian colonies at the Paris Peace Conference. Talk of an impending visit to Eritrea by an International Commission of Investigation created fear among some Muslims that the Christians might carry the day in the absence of an opposing voice.[32] After picking up the support of some Muslims in the towns who were disillusioned by Unionist intransigence and who felt threatened by the increasingly aggressive Ethiopian nationalism of the Christian highlanders,[33] Ibrahim Sultan hurried to set up a counterforce to the irredentist movement.

A few preliminary meetings in Kärän and two general conferences of Muslim notables on 3 December, 1946, and 21 January, 1947, resulted in the foundation of the Muslim League of Eritrea (Rabit'a El Islamia), an organization which supposedly united all Muslims in the territory. Nominal leadership was vested in Said Abubaker El Morghani, the local head of the Khatmiya Brotherhood, who was elected president. Effective power was, however, held by Ibrahim Sultan, the secretary-general of the League.

The Muslim League maintained that its objective was the "conservation and defense of Muslim rights, strengthening of relations between Muslims and organizing the community for the benefit of Muslims as regards their economic, political, social and educational interests."[34] It claimed that Eritrea was predominantly Muslim and that the eastern and western lowlands in particular were "inhabited only by Muslims of Arab origin."[35]

By the time of the arrival in Eritrea of the Four Powers Commission of Investigation, the leaders of the Muslim League had succeeded in portraying their essentially religiously based following as a political party. Their political program rejected union with Ethiopia or any other nation. They demanded independence which could be preceded by a period of trusteeship, for which the League preferred the British, whose past record it admired and from whom it said it was confident of getting "justice and progress."[36]

The Christian separatist group was also galvanized into action by news of the approaching visit of the Four Power Commission of Investigation. Led by Ras Täsämma Asbärom, it opposed the irredentist demand for immediate and total union with Ethiopia and campaigned to break the political monopoly which the Mahbär Feqri Hagär had established over many parts of Eritrea. However, its own position remained vague and highly fluid. Its political objectives underwent several shifts in the short period of its existence. Its position on the question of Eritrea's relation with Ethiopia and the territory's future was vague and vacillating. At times it admitted the strong bond which linked Eritrea with Ethiopia and considered the former as the principal founder of the Ethiopian civilization and directed its opposition only to the Shäwan aristocracy whom it accused of usurping the Ethiopian throne and of selling Eritrea to the Italians. A 1947 memorandum of the Liberal Progressive Party stated: "the millenary Ethiopian Civilization originated from Eritrea and Tigrai (Axum) and not from Shoa...the latter people being at the time nomad and uncivilized."[37]

A number of prominent separatist leaders continued to express their loyalty to Ethiopia and said that they differed with the Unionists only on the methods of bringing about the eventual unification of Eritrea with Ethiopia. Wäldä'ab Wäldämaryam, perhaps the chief spokesman of the separatist group, wrote that when he and his colleagues asked for 15 years of British trusteeship, our main and unique aim was for the benefit of our dear country Ethiopia.... the Ethiopian government would have finished the work of re-organizing and would have been in position to receive Eritrea...and the Eritreans...would have coordinated their political ideas and better prepared for a real union to the mother country....we were and are firmly convinced that Eritrea is Ethiopia and cannot be of somebody else but of Ethiopia, even if it would still have to be separated for a less or more period, we decided to assume the great responsibility of placing Eritrea under a foreign power for a period of 15 years.[38]

Similar reasons were also given by Däjazmach Abreha Täsämma, who together with his father, Ras Täsämma, founded and led the Separatist movement. In his letter to the Emperor he explained that he was forced to expose himself to the "unpopular and humiliating stigma associated with Separatism" to create the right condition for union which would also bring in the Muslims of Eritrea to Ethiopia.[39] Seyum Mä'asho, who later became the secretary general of the Liberal Progressive Party, also wrote to the Emperor along similar lines.[40]

A recurrent theme in the arguments of the Separatist group was the fear of domination by the Shäwan aristocracy. The rigid centralizing drives of the Emperor aroused as much fear in Eritrea as they did in Tegray, where a futile attempt by its traditional rulers to resist Addis Ababa's encroachment on their positions had been suppressed by force in 1943.[41] Some of the highland notables in Eritrea feared similar treatment. The Separatists underscored this fear in a 1947 memorandum:

> the Government of Addis Ababa keeps as Advisers of the Crown, all the Princes aspiring to the Kingdoms of Tigre, Beghemder, Gojjam and the various sultanates, while the true purpose is to deprive them of their hereditary rights and consequently keep them far away from their population over which they have a very great authority: Ras Seium, Ras Hailu, Ras Kassa, the Sultan of Jimma, the Sultan of Aussa.[42]

The appeal of a separate Tegréan state, combining both Tegray and Eritrea, seems to have been partially motivated by the threat of Addis Ababa's hegemony. This, however, had to be reconciled with a host of other views which in the end created in the party a jumble of conflicting opinions and constantly changing political positions.

Part of the confusion in the Separatist movement originated from its close connection with the British Administration. Separatist leaders attempted to reconcile the British plans for Eritrea with the predominantly irredentist desire of the highland population. Brigadier Longrigg's blueprint for Eritrea was evident in the major political objectives of the Separatist group, which asked not only for the establishment of a separate Tegray state, but also for a British trusteeship.

Partly because of their own divided loyalty, and partly because of their fear of antagonizing the majority of the Unionist-influenced highland population, the Separatist leaders initially hesitated to openly express their demands for complete dissociation from Ethiopia. In their first petition to the chief administrator in December 1945, they wrote: "Although we recognize and feel the territorial, cultural and economic unity which binds us with our brothers in Ethiopia, we understand that an immediate union between Eritrea and Ethiopia will harm both territories." They pointed out that the Ethiopian government had not yet recovered from the disorganization caused by five years of Fascist rule and that it would be better for Eritrea if it was placed under British trusteeship for fifteen years.[43]

The limitation of the Separatist influence outside of the family of Ras Täsämma and those around him in Akälä Guzai is evident from the list of the signatories of the petition. In Asmara, they were able to secure the signature of eighteen Muslims and only one Christian, Wäldä'ab Wäldämaryam.[44] Their close collaboration with the Administration and the coincidence of their political objective with Britain's recommendation on the future of Eritrea exposed them to accusations of being stooges of the British authorities.

The leaders of the irredentist movement were quick to accuse the British Administration of sponsoring a mercenary force, the Separatists, to maintain its control over Eritrea. A Unionist petition early in 1946 which contained the signature of several notables (including those of Abdälkader Käbiré and Mohammed Omar Qadi, who later joined the opposition) alleged that the Separatists and their activities were managed by the British officials in Eritrea and that chiefs who refused to sign petitions asking for separation from Ethiopia were deposed and deported. The petition concluded that Separatism was the work of "some chiefs who played the old role of Judas driven by ambition and personal gain."[45] There was a flurry of similar petitions in the first few months of 1946 from Hamasén, Akälä Guzai, Säraé and Kärän condemning the Separatist demand.[46]

Although it failed to win a large following, the Christian Separatist group took heart from the formation of the Muslim League. Theirs was no longer the only voice which whispered doubts about union with Ethiopia. Now challenging the Unionists appeared feasible.[47] As the date of the visit of the Four Power Commission of Investigation approached, the group pulled itself together and began preparations to present itself as a viable political force and to deny the Unionists the undivided voice of the Christian population.

A meeting of the Separatist forces led by Ras Täsämma resulted in the establishment of a formal organization known as the Liberal Progressive Party. Although a few former adherents of conditional union from Asmara joined it, the party's base of support was still limited to Akälä Guzai. Ras Täsämma's family and Däjazmach Mä'ashio Zäwoldi, together with his six children, constituted the core of the new party. The two occupied the position of president and vice-president respectively, while the former's son was the effective power behind the organization and the latter's eldest son became the secretary general.[48]

The Liberal Progressive Party restated the separatist demand for the annexation of the Tegray, including the territory between the Täkäzé River and the Ala River, and the districts of S'älämt, Wolqayet and S'ägädé, which it said were "populated by people of Tegray origins." It asked for a period of British trusteeship to prepare the territory for independence.[49]

The Italian Factor in Eritrean Politics

Although the Paris Peace Treaty required Italy to renounce sovereignty over her former African colonies, she did not abandon the ambition of getting them back in some form or another. The inability of the Four Great Powers to reach an agreement on the disposal of these territories, and the support Italy received especially from France, encouraged her to pursue her demand with vigor. The prime minister, De Gasperi, pleaded that the return of her colonies was absolutely essential for Italy's stability and for the benefit of her African subjects. De Gasperi noted that the return of her colonial assets would assist in speeding up the reconstruction of war-devastated Italy and ensuring political stability by absorbing the multitude of former officials and small shopkeepers who constituted a discontented element in post-war Italy.[50] In an effort to persuade her European allies Rome argued:

> Africa is an economic, political and strategic necessity to Europe and should offer new market and outlets for her surplus population. She might be peopled by white races and "white" countries might be created there as in South America. The removal of Italian influence from her colonies would destroy the work and capital Italy has expended on spreading European influence,....force the Italians to return to live in poverty in over populated Italy, [and]...benefit those who wish to remove European influence from Africa, thus damaging French and British interest.[51]

The Italian government asserted that the Italians who had played an important role in the colonies should no longer be considered as Italian citizens only but as one of the permanent populations of those territories, "just as the Afrikanders are citizens of South Africa."[52]

With regard to Eritrea, the Italian government opposed returning it to Ethiopia "as it is a vital European interest to have a white settlement on the Red Sea."[53] Returning the territory to Ethiopia, the Italians claimed, "will force back Eritrean civilization by 50 years."[54] They argued that with 60 years of experience Italy was the most suitable power to lead the fragmented society of Eritrea towards a modern political life.[55]

Influential Italians with career or financial interests in Eritrea lobbied intensively to arouse internal popular support and to pressure the government to adopt a much more forceful policy to secure the return of Eritrea.[56] Noted ex-colonial officials with broad experience in Eritrea, such as Enrico Cerulli, were attached to the Foreign Ministry to help prepare Italy's strategy for the recovery of her "first born colony."

Rome opened up intensive campaigns to influence international opinion in her favor. It flooded the international forums with propaganda literature lauding the positive achievements of its rule over Eritrea. The Istituto Agricolo Coloniale di Firenze, in collaboration with the Ministero dell' Africa Italiana, was entrusted with the major task of proving to the world that Italy's rule in Eritrea and her later occupation of Ethiopia had been essentially humane and progressive.[57]

The Italian government also attempted to win the support of its Western allies by emphasizing the relevance of the issue to the peace and security of Europe. It stressed that it was beleaguered by popular demands for the return of its colonies, and failure to meet this demand would create a favorable political climate for the extreme right and left. Repeated appeals were made, especially to the United States, alerting it to the fact that the government was being overwhelmed by protests from all sides and that it was having difficulty ensuring political stability.[58]

Italy was also able to mobilize considerable support by utilizing its Latin connection. Most Latin American countries stood on the side of Italy throughout the debate on the future of the former Italian colonies.

With the commitment of France and the sympathy of the United States, as well as the full support of the Latin American bloc, the prospects for Italy's success had improved tremendously in the two years since the discussion on the settlement of the future of the former colonies had started in the summer of 1945. Even Great Britain, which strongly opposed Italy's return because it conflicted with her own plans, appeared to be overwhelmed by the strength of the powers arrayed in support of Italy. The British Ambassador in Rome advised his government in the fall of 1947: "It is difficult to believe that the Italians would not achieve something through this support and I venture to recommend that we should therefore not get ourselves into positions of general opposition to Italian case from which we might be forced subsequently to retreat with lasting harm to Anglo-Italian relations."[59] Foreign Office officials were alive to the possibility that they "might ultimately be obliged to allow the Italians to get back to Eritrea in some form or another" should Italy insist on getting that territory rather than Somalia.[60] The Colonial Office, too, was of the opinion that Eritrea might have to go to the Italians in order to secure French support for Britain's Libyan plan.[61]

The most serious challenge to Italy's claim came from Eritrea itself where the Unionist force, which had built itself around a strong anti-Italian platform from the beginning, fiercely rejected suggestions of any future Italian role in the territory and harassed Italian elements in Eritrea who ventured to express sentiments favorable to the return of Italy. While the chances of the acceptance of Italy's demand for the return of her colonies appeared slim, both the government and the Italian expatriate population in Eritrea were obliged to keep a low profile for fear of triggering a hostile reaction from the indigenous population. However, increasing recognition of her demand in the international forum encouraged Italy to lay the groundwork for the development of a pro-Italian constituency in Eritrea which could be used to lend some form of legitimacy to her claims and to undermine the Unionist assertion that the indigenous population was totally opposed to Italy's return. In view of the large number of Italian residents still living in Eritrea, the task of organizing a force which would advance Italian interests did not prove difficult.

Italian residents in Eritrea numbering some 55,000[62] at the end of the war still played a considerable role in the economic life of the territory. They practically monopolized the urban sector of the economy and held significant interests in agricultural concessions. Their representation in government jobs, even under the British, was high compared to the indigenous population.

Although they had not fared badly under British rule, the Italians resented the loss of their political power and many of them feared the forced repatriation that was contemplated by the British administration which believed that the Italian population was far larger than could be supported by the limited resources of Eritrea.[63] Returning to war devastated Italy held few attractions for many of them.[64]

Of greater concern to the Italians was the irredentist movement which made no secret of its desire to destroy totally their privileged position in the territory. The settlers, therefore, had a strong motive to commit themselves fully to the task of creating a political force which would be used to advance the political interests of their country and to safeguard their own positions in Eritrea.

The work started first by forming an organization which brought the Italians in Eritrea together. The Italian government relied on the Catholic Church for this task. On his return from a visit to Rome in October 1946, Marinoni, the bishop of the Italian Catholic Church in Eritrea, initiated the establishment of an association of Italians, known as the Fondo Italiano di Beneficeuria. The Church's newspaper in Eritrea, *Veritas et Vita,* was actively engaged in promoting the association.[65] Although its declared aim was to provide assistance to needy half-castes, the association soon became a forum for the articulation of the rights of Italians in Eritrea and for advancing Italy's claim over the territory.

A new organization called Il Comitato Rappresentativo Degli Italiani in Eritrea (C.R.I.E.) grew out of the forums provided by the Fondo Italiano di Beneficeuria. It was formed in March 1947 and represented various professional and business associations as well as corporations in Eritrea. C.R.I.E. declared that its primary objective was to work towards the achievement of an Italian trusteeship over Eritrea and to "oppose the unification of Eritrea with Ethiopia, which is contrary to Italian interest, by showing that there is no ethnic or historical justification for such a union."[66] Its president, F. Ostini, opened the campaign by arguing that "the Axumite Empire was not an Ethiopian creation, but a product of Semitic immigration from Arabia. Medri Bahr was autonomous from Ethiopia and the Bahr Negash did not recognize another sovereign."[67]

C.R.I.E. also expressed willingness to cooperate with other forces which did not wish union with Ethiopia. It singled out the Muslim League and the Liberal Progressive Party as candidates for future collaboration.[68]

While doing so, C.R.I.E. underscored the right of Italians to stay in Eritrea. In a memorandum of November 1947, it stated:

> a further stay of Italians in this country is a real and proper right, consecrated by the sweat and blood of many generations....it is at the same time a duty, as [we] are the best qualified among all the people to continue to guide the... population of Eritrea, who in spite of the great misfortune which came upon us, still and will always follow the Italian example.[69]

The leaders of C.R.I.E. argued that "it is only by the work the Italians have shown they can do that the natives in Eritrea will be able to find their way to progress and civilization."[70]

The establishment of C.R.I.E. opened up a vast avenue for Italian ambitions in Eritrea. The government channeled its assistance to the organization through the Ministero dell'Africa Italiana. Various leaflets prepared in Tegreñña and printed in Rome were shipped to C.R.I.E. for distribution in Eritrea. The weekly newspaper, *Bolletino Settimanale della Stampa Coloniale Italiana ed Estera*, was mailed directly from the office of the ministry of the colonies in Rome to Eritrean notables. *Radio Rome* also beamed frequent messages in Tegreñña and Italian to Eritrea carrying news of the widespread support which Italy's claim had received in the international community and heralding the approach of her return.[71]

In spite of its impressive record in advancing the Italian position in Eritrea, C.R.I.E.'s efforts to project itself as a political force which also represented Eritrean interests met only with limited success. As an organization exclusively composed of foreigners and representing Italian interests, C.R.I.E.'s colonial objectives were transparent. Its pretensions to speak on behalf of the local population were successfully ridiculed by its Unionist opponents. In addition, neither the British administration nor the international bodies were prepared to treat it as anything other than an Italian interest group.

The Italians decided to overcome this handicap by broadening C.R.I.E.'s base and by setting up a few bogus organizations which could claim to have better credentials in representing local interests. The first group to which C.R.I.E. turned for the purpose of expanding its constituency were the thousands of Italo-Eritreans. Born mostly of Italian fathers and Eritrean mothers, these people could claim to represent indigenous interests. As a group they had suffered from alienation both from the local population and from the white community. They were eager to grasp the opportunity which C.R.I.E. provided if only to assert their identity and to be accepted into white circles from which Fascist law had officially debarred them.[72]

The more influential elements of the half-caste group were already coopted in C.R.I.E. and worked with it closely to create an organization which they named L'Associazione Italo–Eriterei (the Italo-Eritreans Association). It claimed to represent half-castes, Italians born in Eritrea, and Italian settlers with long residence in Eritrea, as well as Eritrean women who were wives or mothers of Italians and half-castes. Several prominent half castes threw their influence and resources behind the new organization. Chief among its leaders were: Guido De Rossi, a prominent industrialist, who owned two button factories employing some 3,000 workers; Filippo Casciani, owner of a sisal plantation and a rope factory; Michele Pollera, who had built extensive industrial and agricultural assets; Giovanni Casi, a businessman; Luigi Ertola, a prosperous agricultural concessionaire; and Giacomo De Ponti, industrialist and owner of vast plantation farms in the Barka valley and holder of the sole concession for the extraction of incense over the vast territory extending from Kärän to the Sudan borders.[73]

The Italo-Eritreans Association declared that its primary objective was the "protection and defense of rights and interests already existing, as well those which may arise from contingencies occasioned by the juridical status of the country."[74] The association declared that it was totally opposed to the annexation of a part of Eritrea to Ethiopia or any other country and demanded Italy's return to Eritrea as a trustee power.[75]

Further efforts to broaden the pro-Italian group resulted in the mobilization of some former members of the Italian colonial army. This group was initially attracted by a notice issued in the name of the Italian government which appeared in the Eritrean newspapers asking veterans of the former colonial army to send their lists to the Ministero dell'Africa Italiana to collect arrears of pay due to them from the government. The veterans elected representatives and set up branch committees in the various regions of Eritrea to facilitate their registration.

Out of these activities emerged the Associazione Veterani di Guerra (War Veterans Association) whose initial aim was to recover lost wages and pensions from the Italian government. The association operated with Italian funds, and its leaders were maintained on Italian allowances. In time these controls enabled the Italians to transform the association into a political group seeking Italian trusteeship. Some of the leaders who refused to cooperate with the Italians, including its first president, were purged[76] and those who remained were required to swear an oath of allegiance to the Italian flag before officials of the Italo-Eritrean Association. Its name was changed into the New Eritrea Pro-Italy Party. It declared: "We cannot expect any ill from the Italian administration.... A return of the Italian administration thus means for us assured labour for thousands of our fellow men."[77] The party's favorite slogan was: "God is the Creator of the World, and Italy is the Creator of Eritrea."[78]

Besides the ex-soldiers, some former employees of the Italian Government who hoped for more favorable treatment under an Italian administration also joined the New Eritrea Pro-Italy Party. The Italians were also able to add a few followers by intimidating their employees into joining the party. Some dissident groups from the other parties also joined it.[79] However, the Italians were unable to make substantial headway in creating a new image for Italy and in changing the predominantly anti-Italian feeling which prevailed throughout Eritrea. Their followers remained few in number and largely mercenary.

What the party lacked in numbers was more than made up by the enormous resources at the command of the pro-Italian groups. Generous contributions from its wealthy Italian and half-caste patrons as well as the substantial subsidy that flowed from Rome provided them with strong leverage which enabled them to play a much more powerful role than their numbers warranted. In addition to its own newspapers, the *Eritrea Nuova* and *Mäbraheti Eretra* (published in Tegreñña and Arabic), the New Eritrea Pro-Italy Party was also able to use most of the other newspapers in Eritrea which were owned by Italians, including Il Corrocio and Il Lavoro.[80] Its financial resources enabled it to open branch offices all over the territory, according to a contemporary report, "even in places where there are no followers except the hired committee members."[81]

The pro-Italian faction disbursed substantial sums to subvert rival organizations, mostly by buying off their influential followers,[82] and managed to gradually bring several political groups under its influence. This success, however, produced mixed results. While on the one hand it provided Italy with some influence in Eritrea and allowed her to impress international opinion that there was local support for her return, their presumptuous claims and the overtly colonial character which marked Italian political activities in Eritrea enraged the bulk of the population whose anti-Italian disposition had already been apparent as early as 1941.

This notable Italian threat radicalized the Unionist Party which responded with extraordinary measures including violence against Italians and Italian interests in Eritrea. The intensification of Italy's political activity both in Eritrea and in the international forums also triggered a vigorous reaction from Ethiopia. The Ethiopian government attempted to counter the growth of Italian power in Eritrea by increasing its support for the pro-Ethiopian forces in Eritrea and by adopting a much more aggressive strategy in support of its claim on the international scene.

The Ethiopian government on the Eritrea Issue

Haile Selassie's government expected to reclaim Eritrea after the collapse of Italian control. It made its aspirations known while the war of liberation against Italy was still in progress and pressed the British government for a firm promise that control of the territory would not pass into the hands of another power. The Emperor sought such assurances as early as October 1940 during his meeting in Khartoum with Anthony Eden, Secretary of State for Foreign Affairs. He renewed his request in a telegram to Prime Minister Winston Churchill in June 1941 in which he explained the basis of Ethiopia's claims and asked:

> recognizing that the Government of Great Britain has no territorial ambition, His Majesty the Emperor would like to receive the assurance of the Government of the United

Kingdom of its intention not to allow the people of the territory of Eritrea to be handed over again to the Italian state or to any other foreign power.[83]

The Ethiopian government continued to address similar appeals to Great Britain throughout the war years. Britain, which had its own plans for Eritrea, brushed off such requests by telling the Ethiopian government that the matter could only be considered at the peace settlement.[84]

The British government actively discouraged Ethiopian interference in Eritrea and succeeded for a while in limiting contacts between the Ethiopian government and the forces in Eritrea who desired union with Ethiopia. A request for permission for the Ethiopian crown prince, Asfawossen, to visit Asmara (to reciprocate an earlier visit to Gondär by the Area Commander of the British forces) was denied by the Chief Political Officer in Eritrea for fear that "it might give considerable strength to the irredentist movement."[85]

The War Office, which had already reached a conclusion on the need to keep Eritrea within the British fold was particularly determined to deny Ethiopian interest in the territory. It strenuously opposed the appointment of even an Ethiopian trading agent in Asmara despite the fact that Britain had consulates in a number of provincial towns in southern Ethiopia. In response to an Ethiopian request for the establishment of a trading agency, the Commander-in-Chief, Middle East Forces, telegraphed the War Office in 1943 that an Ethiopian representative in Asmara "will form a useful center for Irredentist movement and give stimulus to such aspirations. Once an appointment is made we could only change holders." The Commander-in-Chief further indicated that the Chief Political Officer of the East African Command in Nairobi was also opposed to the idea.[86] That the War Office had to be informed even when an Eritrean resident was appointed as a bus agent for Ethiopia to book seats for passengers between Asmara and Addis Ababa was perhaps an indication of the zeal with which the British military attempted to prevent possible Ethiopian influence in Eritrea.[87] The Foreign Office concurred with the military and successfully blocked Ethiopia's repeated appeals until 1946.

The British Military Administration in Eritrea kept a watchful eye on Ethiopian activities in Eritrea. It controlled travel between the two territories and imposed a rigid censorship on publications entering Eritrea from the Ethiopian side. It even rejected an Ethiopian request to open a school for its nationals in Asmara.[88]

The Ethiopian government, which had been restored in 1941 after five years of devastating Fascist occupation, was not in a position to pursue a forceful policy in Eritrea. Although the growing irredentist movement in Eritrea provided it with strong leverage, it was unable to take immediate advantage of this factor owing to its own internal and external vulnerability. The government had to grapple with the task of imposing central authority over a country that had lapsed into disorder during the war years. The abundant arms and ammunition left behind by the Italians made the effort much harder. The government had to rely increasingly on British military support to consolidate its authority over the country.

Furthermore, the restored government of Emperor Haile Selassie started with a bare treasury. The financial situation in the country was extremely precarious, and credit was non-existent. Emperor Haile Selassie's government had to wrestle with a fluctuating system of paper and silver currencies, including the ones inherited from the Italians and those introduced from East Africa by the Occupied Enemy Territory Administration (O.E.T.A.).[89] As one War Office memo described it, the Emperor was "in an insecure position, without money, without an organized army, without means of establishing an administration and with some...of the notables ready to take advantage of any weakness in his position."[90]

Financial weakness forced the Ethiopian government to depend on a British subsidy for the first few years of the post-liberation period. This provided the British with clout which they did not hesitate to use, especially with regard to the Eritrean question. There was a standing instruction from the Foreign Office that:

> Payment should be contingent upon the Emperor's following His Majesty's Government's advice and guidance on all important matters of policy...the only feasible sanction against the Emperor's misbehavior is, as in the case of Saudi Arabia, that of the purse.[91]

And the purse string was frequently pulled to bring the Emperor into line. British advisers were appointed over all major government departments, and their advice had to be heeded. To be sure, these impositions were deeply resented by the Ethiopian government, and relations with Britain remained very tense. Ethiopians accused the British of imperialist designs, and the British for their part blamed the Ethiopians of "Oriental ingratitude."[92]

It took the Ethiopians some four years to break out of this apparent British tutelage. A slow but steady economic recovery provided the government with some financial autonomy. The subsidy coming from Britain decreased from £1,500,000 in 1942 to £250,000 in 1945.[93] The country's export earnings, which had almost totally broken down in 1941, had risen to U.S. $14,090,215 in 1945 and almost doubled the next year.[94] Of major importance was the introduction of a new Ethiopian currency made possible through a loan under a U.S. Lend-Lease program. This enabled Ethiopia to free itself from the monetary confusion and uncertainties caused by the use of the British East African shillings and several other currencies of various origins.

These were very modest gains, but they were sufficient to allow a government, which had been largely dependent on the British Exchequer, to adopt some measure of independence in its dealings with Great Britain. Its ability to reject a British offer of a loan of £3,000,000 in 1945 on the grounds that the terms of the loan would compromise Ethiopia's sovereignty[95] was proof of the degree to which Haile Selassie's government had succeeded in minimizing British control.

Britain's hold was further undermined by Ethiopia's success in breaking out of international isolation. Beginning in 1943 she established regular diplomatic relations with the United States, the Soviet Union, Belgium, and Egypt. Closer relations with the United States, especially after the Emperor's meeting with President Roosevelt in early 1945, improved Ethiopia's ability to maneuver between the international powers to enhance her relative autonomy.

These improvements in Ethiopia's position both at home and abroad enabled the government to address itself more seriously to the Eritrean issue. Ethiopia made determined efforts to assert its interests regarding Eritrea in the debates over the peace settlement. It also began to involve itself actively in influencing events inside Eritrea.

The irredentist force in Eritrea had been urging the Ethiopian government to intervene more directly on its side. Many of the leaders of the Mahbär Feqri Hagär were disconcerted by the lack of more forceful Ethiopian support for their cause. Frequent appeals were made to the Emperor by Unionist groups and noted individuals in Eritrea asking him to intervene on their behalf.[96] These calls grew more urgent with the beginning of the international debates on the future of the territory and the increasing threat of Italian intervention to influence the decision in its favor. Many believed that, given the great respect he commanded, the Emperor's direct involvement would boost the irredentist cause both at home and abroad. One petition to the Emperor stated: "The people in Ertirea who are Ethiopians address their sufferings to the creator — God and to you.... We entreat you in the name of God to listen this plight and to help us so that we your people can get the justice we deserve."[97] Even his critics in Eritrea were of the opinion that his intervention would help create consensus among the fragmented forces in Eritrea.[98]

Initial Ethiopian contacts with the irredentist movement were channeled through individual Eritreans in the Ethiopian government. These included Blattén Géta Lorénzo Taézaz, the one-time foreign minister and later Ethiopia's Minister in Moscow, and Blata Dawit Oqbazghi, the vice-governor of Addis Ababa. The establishment in 1944 of The Ethiopian Eritrean Unity Association (also known as Näs'a Hamasén Society) in Addis Ababa consisting of Eritreans living in Ethiopia and patronized by high ranking Ethiopian officials, provided the government with a useful vehicle of communication with the Mähbär Feqri Hagär, the parent organization in Eritrea. Funds were openly collected in Ethiopia in support of the unionist cause in Eritrea. Officials of the Addis Ababa branch made frequent trips to Asmara and maintained liaison between the Unionists and the Ethiopian government. Gäbrämäsqäl Habtämaryam, a noted patriot during the Fascist occupation,[99] and the president of the association, became a key figure in managing this relationship and in soliciting both material and moral support in Ethiopia for the unionist movement.[100]

Meanwhile, with the increasing urgency created by the beginning of the international debate on the future of Eritrea, the Ethiopian government pursued with more determination its demand for representation in Eritrea. At the end of 1945, Britain finally gave way to the persistent Ethiopian demand for the establishment of a representative but under very strict conditions. The Ethiopian government was obliged to agree that "the Liaison Officer shall confine his activities to consular functions on behalf of his nationals and their commerce, and will refrain from political activities, and that if the Liaison Officer does not observe the undertaking the Administration may require his removal."[101]

The Ethiopian Liaison Office was opened in Asmara in March 1946. The Emperor appointed a young officer, Colonel Nägga Hayläsellasé to head the mission.[102] The choice was rather strange because, even on his own admission, Nägga did not possess any experience of consular activities or in Eritrean affairs. He started work with only one assistant, and it took him more than three months to set up an office.[103] More surprising still was the absence of a clearly defined description of his responsibilities. The brief and rather vague guideline which he received from the emperor on 20 March 1946 makes the assignment appear as if it were more of a fact finding mission than an agency which would promote Ethiopia's political objectives in Eritrea.[104]

The hesitation and confusion which surrounded the functioning of the Liaison Office in Eritrea indicate the absence of any concrete plan for Eritrea on the part of the Ethiopian government even at this stage. It had long relied on the irredentist force within Eritrea to advance its objectives in the territory, and its new commitment did not appear to have extended beyond playing a supporting role to the Unionist Party.

Fear of antagonizing the British Government may have also forced Haile Selassie's regime to keep a low profile in Eritrea, where the British Military Administration kept a watchful eye over the activities of the Liaison Office and controlled the movements of visitors from Addis Ababa. The liaison officer was prohibited from flying the Ethiopian flag on his car, when the Administration discovered that its display was exciting the Asmara population.[105] Any high powered Ethiopian political activity in Eritrea would have resulted in a head-on clash with the British.

In spite of its tentative and cautious approach, Addis Ababa was inexorably drawn deep into Eritrean politics. The very fact of the establishment of an Ethiopian representation in Eritrea was locally viewed as the beginning of Eritrea's return to Ethiopia. Very soon the Liaison Office became a center of irredentist activities and Colonel Nägga found himself increasingly drawn into the vortex of Eritrean politics. His office was inundated with requests for assistance from various organizations.[106] The Unionist Party frequently sought his assistance and guidance, involved him in many of its deliberations, and asked him to arbitrate internal differences. He was often asked to intervene with the British Administration on behalf of irredentist forces and was invited to preside over many social and political occasions. Villages and churches competed with each other for his attendance, and his presence provided the occasion for massive displays of pro-Ethiopian sentiments.[107]

The Unionist Party, which by 1946 had to wrestle with a hostile administration and the beginning of a serious threat from the Italian interests, as well as a challenge from part of the Muslim community, was more than eager to enlist Nägga's full cooperation. In time strong attachments developed between Nägga and the leaders of the Unionist Party. He later reminisced: "I was just a naive young officer when I arrived in Eritrea. It was from Unionist notables that I received my political education and they were the ones who helped me develop a keen awareness of Ethiopian history."[108] Less than a year after his arrival, Nägga was fully involved in the affairs of the irredentist movement and his office practically became a conduit between the Unionists and the Ethiopian government. Incessant appeals were sent to Addis Ababa for increased support and the guidance of the Emperor.

Addis Ababa did not, however, move as fast or decisively as Nägga and the Unionists desired. The Ethiopian government focused primarily on the diplomatic aspects of the Eritrean issue, leaving much of the internal situation to the Unionist Party.

Spontaneity and disorganization characterized Ethiopia's handling of the Eritrean case. No single body was established by the government to oversee Eritrean issues. There was no systematic plan or coordination of activities. In fact, even the Liaison Office in Eritrea did not belong to any specific ministry. It was occasionally required to report directly to the Emperor through the Ministry of the Pen, sometimes with the Ministry of Foreign Affairs, and sometimes with the Ministry of Interior.[109] Nägga had to write to the Emperor twice to get approval for the purchase of a camera which he needed to publicize unionist activities in Eritrea.[110] It took repeated appeals to procure an annual budget of

25,450 East African Shillings for 1946 to be distributed among 20 monasteries, 10 mosques, and the Unionist Party and its six branches.[111] Nägga's request for funds on behalf of a group of pro-unionist Muslims, who wanted to start their own newspapers to counteract the Muslim League agitation, was rejected by the Emperor who told the liaison officer that he had to economize his expenses in Eritrea.[112]

The weakness of Ethiopia's activity in Eritrea was so obvious that it surprised even the British Military Administration. The administrator observed that Ethiopia was losing a golden opportunity for her lack of a forceful local policy and by her failure to accord immediate and substantial support and guidance to Unionists.[113] Some of the leaders of Unionist branch offices, especially in the peripheral districts, were reportedly so disheartened by the absence of Ethiopian commitment that they were threatening to quit "unless Ethiopians provided immediate support and guidance."[114]

The handful of young Ethiopian officers, who were playing important roles in reconstructing the post-liberation army, were also growing impatient with what they considered to be a timid and lukewarm policy on Eritrea. They were irritated by the government's inability to provide more direct support to irredentist forces. Colonel (later Major General) Mulugétta Buli wrote to Nägga lamenting the "passivity of our rulers in the struggle to liberate our brothers in Eritrea."[115] Assäfa Ayana (later Lt. General and Chief of the Air Force) and Mängestu Neway (Commander of the Imperial Body Guard and leader of the 1960 coup) both deplored the government's casual handling of the Eritrean case.[116]

What finally moved the Ethiopian government to actively support the unionist movement, was the realization of the limits of its diplomatic campaigns. With Britain determined to keep at least a part of the territory and Italy winning the support of some important powers for the return of her former colonies, Ethiopia's claims to Eritrea were meeting with formidable challenges. This apparently persuaded Ethiopian officials to start focusing on the internal front as well. Unionist leaders, and some officials of the Ethiopian government who sensed the uncertainty of international opinion, had already suggested the need to build up the irredentist force so that it could confront its opponents with "force majeure."[117]

The beginning of intimate involvement in internal Eritrean politics not only brought Haile Selassie's government closer to its Unionist supporters but also forced it to come to grips with other forces. Some were openly hostile, and others were willing to extend their support only conditionally. Some within the latter group had sought the Emperor's support for a union which would grant some form of internal autonomy for Eritrea.[118]

Neither the Emperor nor his subordinates were willing to listen to any alternative other than a complete annexation of Eritrea. Colonel Nägga, the one Ethiopian official who was most intimately connected with the Eritrean affair, resolutely opposed any suggestion which placed conditions on the type of union to be achieved. Together with the Unionist leaders, he argued that no large support existed for conditional union and imposing it would result in serious political instability as it was opposed by a great majority of the people. Nägga had convinced himself that "Conditional Union" was a British ploy designed to frustrate Ethiopia's ambitions in Eritrea. He feared that the implementation of this idea, which he called "cancerous," not only would complicate the economic and political situation in Eritrea, but also would set a catastrophic precedent in the rest of Ethiopia.[119] He advised the Emperor that even if no immediate threat of fragmentation in the country existed, "the whites will surely endeavor to create one by exploiting the parochial sensitivities which still exist among a large section of our society."[120]

By this time Nägga had so closely identified himself with the leaders of the Unionist Party that he was unable to maintain any distance in the feud between the Unionists and their opponents. His office was closed to all except the Unionists. Nägga opposed any suggestion of accommodating "Conditionalists" and made strong representations to the Emperor against officials in Addis Ababa whom he thought were favorably disposed to this idea. One of the targets of his attack was Ato Gäbrämäsqäl Habtämaryam, who, as president of the Addis Ababa branch of the Mahbär Feqri Hagär, had handled relations for the government with the main office in Asmara until Nägga's appointment. Gäbrämäsqäl criticized Nägga for adopting such a partisan outlook towards Unionists on the ground that it risked alienating all other forces. He was of the opinion that most of the "Conditionalists" were chiefs and other government functionaries who were dependent on British subventions. By adopting a line which asked both for a conditional union with Ethiopia and some form of British protection as originally enunciated by Brigadier Longrigg, they sought to play it safe both with the British Administration and the Unionists. Gäbrämäsqäl argued that these men were beginning to realize that the British were not here to stay and that they were seeking to reach an accommodation with the Ethiopian government. He advised against alienating them and opened up his own channel with well-known advocates of conditional union.[121] Nägga would have none of it. In fact he telegraphed the Ministry of the Pen demanding the immediate removal of Gäbrämäsqäl from Eritrea.[122]

Although he frequently chastised Nägga for his unwillingness to establish amicable relation with the "Conditionalists" and was irritated by Unionist intransigence towards their rivals, the Emperor was determined to oppose any suggestion which would put limitations on his authority over Eritrea.[123] In response to a petition from the Independent Muslim League of Massawa for conditional union which would guarantee their special interests he stated: "This is a suggestion which would give a negative lesson for the rest of Eritrea.....Even if we were to accept it as politically expedient it will spoil our future plans and would bring serious harm for the people of Eritrea themselves."[124]

The Emperor, while not prepared for any compromise, was in favor of keeping the door open to the opposition to encourage them to submit. He showed more openness in his dealings with forces opposed to unconditional union than to Unionist leaders and the Ethiopian Liaiason Officer in Eritrea. His messages to Nägga carried repeated warnings against antagonizing the opposition and advised a careful handling of the situation.[125] He was particularly eager to win over the Separatist forces to his side. He overruled Nägga's opposition with regard to starting negotiations with the leaders of this movement. In his letter to the latter he said,

> Your argument that the Separatists are small in number and that they would be overwhelmed by the large Unionist force might be true. However, we should not only take satisfaction at their defeat today, but must also consider the future implication of this action. Those who are defeated today will continue to harbor grievances and may pose serious trouble in the future.... The task of persuading Separatists to come to our side is the most important of all and should be given top priority....Däjazmach Abreha and Wäldä'ab appear to be seeking opportunity to come to our side. It is necessary to approach them with great patience and to forget their past terrors in order to accomplish this.[126]

Nägga continued to evade the Emperor's instructions by creating various excuses not to approach "Conditionalists." He used his office to control communications between the Palace and the opposition in Eritrea. He withheld the Emperor's friendly reply to Wäldä'ab Wäldämaryam's letter of April 1947. He sent it back to the Ministry of the Pen suggesting revisions, and, when this was done, he still found various pretexts not to forward it, although the Emperor kept on asking what he had done about it.[127] In the end Wäldä'ab never received it. Nägga insisted that Wäldä'ab was in the pocket of the British and that he had changed his views on relations with Ethiopia so many times in the past that he should not be trusted in the future or honored by receiving Imperial encouragement. Nägga told the Emperor that Wäldä'ab's aim was to establish Tegréan supremacy by restoring the descendants of the Emperor Yohannes to the Ethiopian throne.[128]

The Unionist leaders and Nägga were unable to respond positively to suggestions requiring some changes in their relations with the opposition. In a way, they may have been prisoners of their own past policies. In an attempt to deprive them of followers, Unionist agitation had demonized Separatists and Conditionalists. They were presented as traitors to their country, violators of tradition, and collaborators with the whites. People were told not to associate with them, and some villages were known to have refused burial places in their church grounds for people branded as anti-Unionist.

Coming to terms with Separatists and Conditionalists would have required repainting the enemy, but the Unionists did not appear to have been ready for this. By removing the stigma associated with the Separatists and Conditionalists, Unionists feared, they might help their rivals to create a better image of themselves. This could possibly have helped the opposition to expand its influence, thereby threatening the dominant position which Unionists had enjoyed since the beginning, especially in the highlands and the towns. By blocking access to the royal palace, Nägga and the Unionist leaders sought to deny their rivals an advantage which would have helped to improve their image in the eyes of the local population.

When the Emperor realized Nägga's recalcitrance concerning relations with conditional Unionists, he called him to Addis Ababa to impress on him the need for a new approach. The Emperor appointed a senior ministerial committee consisting of S'ähafi Taezaz Wäldägiyorgis, Ato Yelma Deréssa, Ato Aklilu Habtäwold, Blatta Efrém, and Nägga himself to draw up plans for starting negotiations with forces opposed to Ethiopian annexation of Eritrea. This was the first serious attempt at a higher level to address systematically the internal situation in Eritrea. The committee recommended that work start with the Separatists, to be followed with the pro-Italian group, and finally with the Muslim League. A mission led by Yelma Deréssa and consisting of four Eritrean officials of the government was sent to Eritrea.[129] The effort did not produce the expected results, partly for lack of cooperation both from the Unionist leadership and the Liaison Office.

The Unionist Party and Nägga's office were also able to scuttle another attempt by the Emperor to bring the various hostile forces together. He brought Däjazmach Abreha, Däjazmach Gäbrä'egzi Guangul, Grazmach Seyum Mä'asho and other prominent Separatists to Addis Ababa to get them reconciled with the Unionists. But the scheme failed because the Unionist Party refused to send a delegation to Addis Ababa to negotiate with the Separatists. Repeated calls and threats from the Ministry of the Pen failed to intimidate Unionists who objected that granting an audience in the palace to Separatists would allow them to win a respectability which they had not commanded in the past and would create a false impression in Eritrea that the Ethiopian government was in favor of conditional union.[130]

In the end, the Emperor was forced to withdraw even the small concession he was prepared to offer the Separatists.[131] This resistance by the Unionist forces inhibited the government's action in dealing with opposition. It found itself caught in a dilemma of either offending its Unionist partisans should it seek to attract the so-called Separatists or of alienating the latter by sticking with the former. Given its own lack of preparation for handling the complex internal situation in Eritrea and its opposition to ideas which suggested limitations on full union, the Ethiopian government felt comfortable in limiting its relations to the irredentist force alone, reinforcing the conviction among the groups opposed to union that they would be left at the mercy of their Unionist enemies should Ethiopia succeed in annexing Eritrea.

Notes

[1] In a memorandum submitted at the Paris Peace Conference, Egypt claimed that Eritrea had been taken away from her by Italy. The Egyptians also argued that there were strong economic and ethnological reasons for bringing Eritrea into Egypt. The Egyptian memorandum asserted that "the most progressive community in Eritrea are Arabs [who] give to this region its predominantly Arab character." The Egyptian Delegation in Paris, 30 August 1946, in FO 371/63191; Government of Egypt, Memorandum Submitted by the Egyptian Government to the Paris Peace Conference, August, 1946; see also "Communications from the Egyptian Ambassador in London to the Deputies," 17 November 1947, FO 371/63204.

[2] Mezhiet, "Relazione Approssimativa Dei Partiti Politici - Attuali Affiliati al Partito Centrale (Mahbär Feqri Hagär)," Asmara, March 1947, in Liaison Office Papers. Ato Wäldu Wäldämikaél was the leader of this group. Former members of the association claim that much of their work had to be done in secret until Brigadier Drew announced permission for open political activity in 1946: Interview, S'ägay Abreha (Addis Ababa, January 1990).

[3] "Memorandum," Asmara, 28 May 1946, Liaison Office Papers.

[4] Those on the side of Fitawrari Gäbrämäsqäl included Azmach Giorgio Habtit, Däjazmach Gäbrai, Fitawrari Pét'ros, Däjazmach Täsfai Barakhi, Däjazmach Asräsahäññ Barakhi, Fitawrari Harägot Abbai, Gerazmach Täsfamikaél Wärqé and a large section of the Asmara youth. The rival faction led by Däjazmach Araya Wassé and Azazh Zäreom Kiflä consisted of Däjazmach Hagos Gäbré, Tädla Dairu, Belatta Dämsas Wäldämikaél, Fitawrari Hadgu Gilagaber, Däjazmach Berhané Germas'ion, Azazh Gäbrämikaél Gurmu, Qäññazmach Fessehayé Täsfamikaél and others: Kidanämaryam to Col. Nägga, 14 April 1946, and Nägga to Emperor Haile Selassie, 6 July 1946, *ibid*.

[5] Colonel Nägga, who was appointed the first Liaison Officer of the Ethiopian government in Eritrea in March 1946, claims that Blatta Dawit Oqbazghi, who had earlier been sent from Addis Ababa to work with the leaders of the Mahbär Feqri

Hagär, contributed to the division by playing favorites with some and alienating others. The distribution of the funds sent by the Addis Ababa branch of the Mahbär Feqri Hagär was said to have been an important source of friction: ibid.

[6] Fitawrari Gäbrämäsqäl Wäldu was accused by his opponents of "indolence, indiscretion and drunkenness," which, they said, was exposing the organization to enemy propaganda. He was also blamed for blocking petitions demanding change in the organization and alienating important people who had differences with him: these complaints were contained in a memorandum by the opposition force, Asmara, 29 May 1946; and Col. Nägga, "Yä Hagär Feqer Mahbär Yä Woqetu Hunéta" [report in Amharic on current condition of the Mahbär Feqri Hagär], 3 May 1946, Liaison Office Papers.

[7] According to his own account, Tädla was sent to Florence at the age of twelve after he finished the fifth elementary class at the Swedish Mission's School. He returned to Eritrea after seven years with a regular teacher's diploma (1926-1933). He worked as a teacher and head-master at schools in Kärän, Aqordat, Ad Täkläsan and Adwa from 1934 to 1940. He worked briefly in 1941 for the British Political Officer in Adwa, before coming to Asmara where he served as Assistant to the Senior Civil Affairs Officer from 1942 to 1946: Tädla Bairu to Colonel Nägga, Asmara, 25 September 1946, Liaison Office Papers.

[8] Patriotic Association - Eritrea with Ethiopia - One Ethiopia", Addis Ababa, 18 August 1947, ibid.

[9] The newspaper *Ethiopia* started publication on 4 May 1947. The editor, Azmach Gäbrämikaél Gurmu was formerly an employee of the Italians and an influential member of the Unionist Party. Much of the funding for this paper came from the Society for the Unification of Ethiopia and Eritrea, an affiliate organization in Addis Ababa.

[10] The letters of Däjazmach Abreha Täsämma and Wäldä'ab Wäldämaryam, as well as the memorandums of Mohammed Omar Qadi and Asbärom Abreha: in Liaison Office Papers.

[11] Mohammed Omar Qadi, one of the founders of the Mahbär Feqri Hagär, mentions how hard the Muslim members tried in early 1946 to persuade their Christian compatriots to accede to these demands: Mohammed Omar Qadi, "Promemoria Della Lega Musulmana Indipendente Dell'Eritrea, Con Sede A Massaua," 1947, in ibid.

[12] A British Administration source reported that the compromise reached between the two groups was communicated by a deputation of four representatives on 30 October 1946. The report mentions that the compromise formula recommended an autonomous status for Eritrea within the Ethiopian Empire: BMA, "Monthly Political Report," October 1946, in FO 371/53530.

[13] Fessehayé Täsfamikaél, a member of the Central Committee of the Unionist Party wrote that Gäbrämäsqäl Wäldu's support for Conditional Union cost him his position in the organization: Fessehayé Täsfamikaél, "Alla Adehanänä Emkulu Ekuy As'ene Walteha Tehtäl Sälameha" [Tegreñña], in Liaison Office Papers.

[14] For a list of the leading participants see, Giuseppe Puglisi, *Chi E'? dell' Eritrea* (Agenzia Regina, Asmara, 1952), 291.

[15] Wäldä'ab Wäldämaryam later recorded that the meeting was interrupted by armed bands paid by the Ethiopian government: Wäldä'ab Wäldämaryam, "Do You Remember?" in *Eritrea Information*, IX, 7(1987), 12.

[16] Tädla Bairu, the chief exponent of the Unionist view, said that those who demanded Conditional Union were "quislings" who were doing the bidding of foreign powers, and individuals "who had done much harm to Ethiopia with the Italians and are now afraid of the Ethiopian government:" Tädla Bairu, "The British Military Administration in Eritrea and Some aspects of its Political Activities in this Territory," 1947, in Liaison Office Papers. Tädla prepared this article for publication in Sylvia Pankhurst's *New Times and Ethiopia News*: Tädla Bairu to Sylvia Pankhurst, 12 August 1947, ibid.

[17] One oral informant said that most Christian highlanders including himself viewed the idea of associating with Ethiopia under conditions as "dishonorable, as if we were not full Ethiopians... like we were step-children and not fully born to the Ethiopian nation": Qäññazmach Gäbräsellasé Barakhi, Rome, summer 1990.

[18] Fessehayé Täsfamikaél, "Alla Adehanänä...," in Liaison Office Papers. When a year later Tädla Bairu, the Secretary General, was asked by the Four Power Commission of Investigation about his organization's position on Conditional Union, he categorically stated, "Our Association does not envisage conditional re-union of Eritrea with Ethiopia, and has rejected such an idea": FPCI, Report on Eritrea, "Interview with the `Eritrea with Ethiopia Union Association' Representative, Asmara, 17 November 1947"

[19] Cited in "Yä Qeññ Gezat Astädadär Bä Eretra," 58; see also *Nay Eritrea Sämunawi Gazét'a*, 26.3.1939 E.C., on the major points of disagreement between the two groups.

[20] Trevaskis to Hiden, 24.7.1947, in Rhodes Library, Mss Brit. Empire, S 365, Fabian Colonial Bureau, Box 180.

[21] Mohammed Omar Qadi, wrote that he was forced to form a separate organization of his own because of Unionist objection to the demand for "autonomy under the Ethiopian crown." See for instance his "Promemoria Della Lega Musulmana Indipendente Dell'Eritrea, Con Sede A Massaua." Similar complaints were made by Däjazmach Abreha Täsämma and his son Gerazmach Asbärom Abreha: Liaison Office Papers

[22] Wäldä'ab Wäldämaryam, "The Liquidation of Eritrea?" mimeo., 1947, and also in his letter to Emperor Haile Selassie, 29 April 1947, inwhich he said that the meeting resulted in a more serious division, and drove the Moslems into establishing a separate party of their own: ibid.

[23] FPCI, Report on Eritrea, 101: the estimates were based on claims made to the Four Power Commission of Investigation by the representatives of the Liberal Progressive Party.

[24] Ibrahim Sultan's Interview, Cairo, June 1974, cited in Mesfin Araya, "Eritrea, 1941-52, the Failure of the Emergence of the Nation State: Towards a Clarification of the Eritrean Question in Ethiopia," Ph.D., City University of New York, 1988.

[25] Muslim-Christian interaction was limited even in the towns. For example, the native quarters in Asmara were segregated along confessional lines: see for instance,

Medhane Tadesse, "The History of Geza Abba Shaul (Asmara) up to 1974" (B.A. Thesis, Addis Ababa University, 1988).

[26] On how serious this fragmentation was among one of the dominant communities in the western lowland, and how little it had changed during fifty years of colonial rule, see: S.F. Nadel, "Notes on Beni-Amer Society," in *Sudan Notes and Records*, 26, 1(1945), 51-94.

[27] Trevaskis, Eritrea, 70-72; according to Lord Rennell, British operations in 1945 against one Bäni Amer group, which had led raids against the Hadendowa, resulted in 44 rebels killed, 207 captured, and 692 rifles being brought in: Lord Rennell, British Military Administration in Africa, 464. The leader of this group was Ali Mohammed Idris (nicknamed Ali Muntaz), an ex-askari in the Italian army.

[28] Trevaskis to Hiden, 4.1.47, in Rohdes Library, MSS Brit. Empire, S 365, Fabian Colonial Bureau.

[29] See Ullendorff, The *Two Zions*, 181, for Trevaskis' role in the creation of the Western Province.

[30] An Ethiopian source claims that the serf movement was masterminded from the beginning by Col. Trevaskis in order to facilitate the annexation of the Western Province to the Sudan: "A Note From the Ethiopian Liaison Officer" [Amharic], Asmara, 11 June 1952, in Ethiopian government, documentation and Information Service, "Federation: 1952-1962," [an Amharic compilation of documents from the archives of the former Imperial Ministry of the Pen] (n.d.).

[31] Colonel Nägga Hayläsellasé, the Ethiopian Liaison Officer in Eritrea claimed that Ibrahim Sultan had for long been in the pay of the British. In his letter of 8 June 1947, Nägga informed Emperor Haile Selassie that he had a document in his possession proving that Ibrahim Sultan had been spying for the British while he had been in the Mahbär Feqri Hagär. Nägga did not attach a copy of the document in this letter to the Emperor: Liaison Office Papers. For background information on Ibrahim Sultan see, Markakis, *National and Class Conflict*, 280; and Puglisi, *Chi E'? dell' Eritrea*, 168.

[32] A British Administration report in October 1946 mentioned that "the chiefs of Massawa, Keren and Aqordat Divisions have stressed the necessity of an Eritrean Moslem League to speak with one voice to the International Commission... expected to tour the territory": BMA "Monthly Political Report", October 1946, in FO 371/53530.

[33] For an argument that the Muslim League was formed in reaction to the growing aggressive Ethiopian nationalism of the Christian highlanders, see: Mesfin Araya, "Eritrea, 1941-52...," 174-5.

[34] Cited in, FPCI, Report on Eritrea, Appendix 20, 3.

[35] Moslem League of Eritrea, "To the United Nation Commission for Eritrea", Asmara, n.d., 5.

[36] FPCI, Report on Eritrea, Appendix 18; see also *Eritrea Daily News*, 24 January 1947.

[37] Progressive Liberal Party, "Memorandum," December 1947, FPCI, Report on Eritrea, App. 101. In the same memorandum, the Separatists alleged that the Shäwans

"are waiting to get the Eritreans into their power and then have recourse to cruelty as has happened in Tigrai." Another prominent Separatist leader wrote: "Hamasén is the head of all Ethiopia. It founded Axum, Adewa, Agamé. The ruling families in Harar, Märsa Täklay, Kassala, Guragé, and Wolamo are all from Tegray. The whole of Ethiopia writes in the Geez script. Hamasén will lead the rest of Ethiopia, and not vice-versa, as the Shäwan government wants us to believe": Fitawrari Wäldäsellasé Täsämma, in Liaison Office Papers.

[38] Wäldä'ab Wäldämaryam, "The Liquidation of Eritrea?" [n.d. mimeo. English]. Wäldä'ab also gave the same account of his objectives in a letter to the Emperor on 29 April 1947: in Liaison Office Papers.

[39] Däjazmach Abreha to Emperor Haile Selassie, November 1946, and Emperor to Nägga, 21 November 1946 on Abreha Täsämma's position: in Liaison Office Papers.

[40] Seyum Mä'asho to Emperor Haile Selassie, 23 March 1950, in ibid.

[41] For the 1943 rebellion in Tegray, see, Gebru Tareke, "Rural Protest in Ethiopia, 1941-1970: A Study of Three Rebellions," (Ph.D. Dissertation, Syracuse University, 1977).

[42] Liberal Progressive Party, "Memorandum," December 1947, in FPCI, Report On Eritrea, Appendix 101.

[43] "To the Chief Administrator of Eritrea" [Tegreñña], December, 1945: Liaison Office Papers. The principal organizers of this petition were Däjazmach Abreha Täsämma, Däjazmach Hassan Ali and Wäldä'ab Wäldämaryam.

[44] FO 371/ 63175.

[45] "All' Amministratore Capo Dell' Eritrea: Protesta," Asmara, 4 January 1946: Liaison Office Papers.

[46] Col. Nägga to Emperor Haile Selassie, 27 May 1946, ibid.

[47] Trevaskis wrote in 1947: "It must be appreciated that had the Moslem League not appeared on the scene this 'Liberal' party could never have developed... once Ethiopian union seemed a doubtful bet many timid or discontented Christians took heart and joined this new anti-Ethiopian party": Trevaskis to Hiden, 24.7.1947, in Rhodes Library, MSS Brit. Empire, S 365, Colonial Bureau, Box 180.

[48] Of the 33 notables listed as founders of the party, some two-thirds were closely related to each other either by birth or marriage: "Constitutive Act of the Eritrean Progressive Liberal Party 'Eritrea for Eritreans'," in FPCI, Report on Eritrea, App. 102.

[49] "Liberal Progressive Party Memorandum", December 1947, in *ibid.*

[50] See Spencer, *Ethiopia at Bay*, 182; also De Gasperi to the British Ambassador in Rome, 24 December 1947: FO 371/63208; and De Gasperi to the Council of Ministers, 10 May 1946, in Archivo dello Stato (PCM), Roma.

[51] Italian Memorandum to the British Government submitted in connection with the opening of the Deputies of the Foreign Ministers of the Four Great Powers, 3 October 1947, in FO 371/63197 and 63198.

[52] "Speech of the Italian Ambassador before the Conference of the Deputy Foreign Ministers," 19 November, 1947, in FO 371/63204.

⁵³ British Embassy in Rome to London, mentioning an Italian note submitted to Great Britain, 3 October 1947: FO 371/63197.

⁵⁴ De Gasperi, 14 July 1945, in ASMAE, B 337 (1945).

⁵⁵ Memorandum from the Italian Embassy in London to the Council of Deputies, 5 November 1947, in State, 865D.00/12-1847.

⁵⁶ Conte Stefano Marazzini, a noted Italian half-caste, observed on his return from a visit in Italy that De Gasperi's government, which was desperately seeking to gain the support of influential politicians, was allied with "a great many former colonial officials in Rome who viewed life without black servants and black concubines as incomplete and aspire to return to it": Nägga, "Selä T'alyanoch" [Amharic], 1947, p. 24, in Liaison Office Papers.

⁵⁷ For some of the Firenze publications, see, for instance, *Some Data on Italian Activity in the Colonies* (Firenze: Istituto Agricolo Coloniale, 1945); *L' agricoltura nella colonia Eritrea, e l' opera dell' Italia* (1946); *Eritrea: Some Photographic Representations of Italy's Action* (1946); *Main Features of Italy's Actions in Ethiopia 1936-1941*; *Note aggiutive al Memorandum su i territori Italiani in Africa* (1946); *Memorandum sulla situazione economica e finanzieria dei territori in Africa* (1946); Universita Degli Studi di Firenze, Centro di Studi Coloniali, *Amministrazione fiduciaria all' Italia in Africa* (Firenze, 1947); Vedovato - Moreno Mangano, *The Question of the Administration of Italian colonies in Africa under Trusteeship* (Firenze, 1947). For additional information on the works of Italian colonial propagandists see also the papers contained: in FO 371/63198 and 371/63200.

⁵⁸ Appeals from the Italian Government to the U.S. Secretary of State are found in: State, 865d.01/4/4-849.

⁵⁹ British Embassy in Rome to Foreign Office, 7 October 1947, in FO 371/63198.

⁶⁰ R.D.J. Scott Fox to Jebb, 6 December 1946, FO 371/53521.

⁶¹ Galsworthy (Colonial Office) to Scott Fox (Foreign Office), 23 January 1948, FO 371/69290B. The Colonial Office suggested that they "should agree to support Italy's claim to a large part of Eritrea on condition that some degree of satisfaction is given to the Ethiopian claims (e.g. by giving Ethiopia Assab and the Danakil coast as an outlet to sea)."

⁶² Lord Rennell, *British Military Administration*, p. 60.

⁶³ Some 3,000 Italians in Eritrea were maintained on British relief. By the beginning of 1947 the Middle East Command proposed that some eleven thousand Italians should be repatriated to their country: Middle East to Foreign Office, 27 February 1947, FO 371/63212.

⁶⁴ It is worth noting that the number of Italian residents in Eritrea had not exceeded 4,000 until the beginning of the 1935 invasion of Ethiopia. Concerning the character of the Italian settlers in Eritrea, a BMA publication wrote that they were composed of "large numbers of government officials for whom nominal jobs had been ingeniously created, unwanted men who had left Italy for the good of their political health, and Fascists who had left Italy to line their pockets:" British Military Administration, *The First To Be Freed*, 11.

⁶⁵ Nägga "Yä T'alyanoch Polätika Bä Eretra" [an Amharic report on the Italian politics in Eritrea submitted to Emperor Haile Selassie], 16 March 1947, in Liaison Office Papers.

[66] Quotidiano Eritreo, 3.4.1947; also F. Ostini [the first President of C.R.I.E.], "Il 'Comitato' e la sua azione politica," June 1947, in Liaison Office Papers.

[67] Ibid. This argument was taken up by the secessionist forces in the 1960s.

[68] Ibid.

[69] Comitato Representativo Degli Italiani in Eritrea, "Memorandum on the General Situation in Eritrea," 15 November 1947, in FPCI, Report on Eritrea, App. 108.

[70] Adi Ugri Representative of C.R.I.E. to the Four Power Commission of Inquiry, 2 December 1947, cited in FO/371/63207.

[71] Nägga, "Yä It'alyanoch Polätika Bä Eretra," 32, in Liaison Office Papers.

[72] The Fascist Law (no. 822), which denied Italian citizenship to half-castes, was issued on 13 May, 1940.

[73] Liaison Office Papers; see also State, 884. 00 (W) 19-949; and Giuseppe Puglisi, Chi E'? dell'Eritrea, for detailed information on these and other prominent figures behind the Italo-Eritreans Association.

[74] "Italo-Eritreans Association", November 16, 1947, in FPCI, Report on Eritrea, App. 110, Annex B.

[75] L'Associazione Italo-Eritrei, "Situazione Degli Italo-Eritrei Nel Futuro Della Eritrea," 2.2.1947, in Liaison Office Papers.

[76] Those removed included Azmach Asfeha Himbir (president), Fitawrari Haylä Semrit (treasurer), Fitawrari Anwar Abderkassim (vice president), and Fitawrari Ibrahim Mohammed (controller). These men complained to British officials that the organization was taken over by the Italians. The person who was instrumental in facilitating Italian control over the organization was Comm. Kaffel Hassebenabi, the Honorary President. He was an old veteran who was said to have held the highest military rank among the askaris. He served in Libya from 1924 to 1943, and then moved to Italy where he stayed until 1947: "War Veterans Association," November 18, 1947, in FPCI, Report on Eritrea; FO 371/63206; Nägga, "Yä It'alyanoch Polätika Bä Eretra" [Amharic], 1948, pp. 22-30; Eritrea Ethiopian Union (Keren Branch) to S.C.A.O. Western Province, "Formale protesta contro l'influenza italiana," 5/8/1947; and Azmach Asfeha Himbir to Nägga, 12 October 1947, in Liaison Office Papers. See, also *Eritrea Weekly News*, 4 December 1947: for an open letter by 48 ex-askaris in which they announced their withdrawal from the Veterans Association, protesting the Italian demand to use them against the irredentist movement.

[77] "War Veterans Association", November 18, 1947, in FPCI, Report on Eritrea; see also, *Quotidiano Eritreo*, Asmara, 31.7.1947.

[78] *Mäbruheit Eritrea* [organ of the New Eritrea Pro-Italy Party], May 14, 1948.

[79] J.C. Gray, L. Silberman, and an Observer from Eritrea, *The Fate of Italy's Colonies: A Report to the Fabian Colonial Bureau* (London: Fabian Colonial Bureau, 1948), p. 39; see also, Oscar Rampone, *Avvenne in Eritrea* (Nuovi Autori: Milano, 1985), p. 13.

[80] For the Italian newspapers published in Eritrea at this time, see: ibid, 12.

[81] Nägga to Emperor Haile Selassie, February 16, 1950, in Liaison Office Papers.

⁸² The Unionists frequently complained of the corrosive effect of Italian money. The Muslim League too complained initially that its members were being bought off by the pro-Italian group: "Memorandum of the Moslem League", in FPCI, Report on Eritrea, App. 107.

⁸³ FO 371/31608.

⁸⁴ Aden to Howe, June 27, 1942, in ibid.

⁸⁵ Brigadier H.R. Hone, Chief Political Officer (Eritrea), to Maj. General Commanding Troops in the Sudan, 14 August 1942. Hone wrote, "This movement is already giving my Administration some cause for anxiety:" FO 371/31608.

⁸⁶ C- in- C, Middle East, to War Office, 1 March 1943 and 2 March 1943, FO 371/35631; see also, FO 371/35031.

⁸⁷ Civil Affairs Branch, Asmara, to Directorate of Civil Affairs, War Office, 27 July 1945.

⁸⁸ The BMA's response to the Ethiopian request to open a school was, "the existing facilities in Asmara are fully adequate for the needs of the whole population - Ethiopian subjects included:" BMA to British Legation, Addis Ababa, 17 November 1947, in FO 371/63216.

⁸⁹ For a revealing account of the grave monetary situation in the country from 1941-45: see, State Bank of Ethiopia, *Report on Economic Conditions and Market Trends*, no. 59, December 1963, 6-8

⁹⁰ FO 371/27562.

⁹¹ Foreign Office Minute, 26 August 1941, FO 371/27514; see also, *New Times and Ethiopian News* (London), 24 October 1943; and FO 371/35626: for information on the extent of Britain's financial control over the country.

⁹² Howe [the British Minister in Addis Ababa] to Foreign Office, 15 January, 1945, FO 371/46078.

⁹³ FO 371/35626.

⁹⁴ U.S. Department of Commerce, International Reference Service, U.S. Department of Commerce, no.12, May 1947, p. 2; see also, Margery Perham, *The Government of Ethiopia* (London: Faber and Faber Limited, 1947), 185-216, for the steady improvement of the revenue of the Ethiopian government.

⁹⁵ Marcus, *Ethiopia, Great Britain, and the United States*, pp. 40-41.

⁹⁶ Mohammed Omar Qadi, a later opponent of the Ethiopian government and one of the early founders of the Mahbär Feqri Hagär, noted that the irredentist movement was severely hampered by the lack of support from the Ethiopian government. He mentions that a group of Muslim and Christian notables mainly from Asmara were forced to address a memorandum to the Emperor in 1944 asking his government to interest itself in the future of Eritrea: Mohammed Omar Qadi, "Promemoria Della Lega Musulmana Indipendente Dell'Eritrea, Con Sede A Massaua." See also FO 371/41478 for reports of similar appeals made to the Emperor in late 1943; and Liaison Office Papers for petitions from individual notables including Ras Kidanämaryam Gäbrämäsqäl, Digläl Jällani (Chief of the Bäni Amer), Däjazmach Haylämäläkot Wäldämikaél (son of Ras Wäldämikaél) and from a number of monasteries and villages.

[97] "From the Ethiopian people of Eritrea to His Imperial Majesty Emperor Haile Selassie," September, 1946, Documents Department, Institute of Ethiopian Studies, Addis Ababa University.

[98] Wäldä'ab Wäldämaryam wrote to the Emperor that "no one but you [the Emperor] could unite the fragmented forces in Eritrea:" Wäldä'ab Wäldämaryam to Emperor Haile Selassie, Asmara, 29 April, 1947: Liaison Office Papers.

[99] On the exploits of Gäbrämäsqäl Habtämaryam during the five years of Fascist occupation, see, Mockler, *Haile Selassie's War.*

[100] For information on this association and the role of its leaders, see, Yä Hamasén Dems'e [the organ of the association], 14 October 1944; The Ethiopian Herald, 16 December 1944, 26 August 1946, 2 September 1946; State, 884.01/9-2645; and FO 371/63222.

[101] British Legation, to the Ministry of Foreign Affairs, Addis Ababa, 19 October 1945, in Liaison Office Papers.

[102] Nägga Hayläsellasé was educated at the Täfäri Mäkonnen School and the Holeta Cadet School before the Italian invasion. He went into exile during the occupation and was one of the small group of officers who helped organize the Emperor's army in the Sudan in 1940. After liberation he was appointed Secretary General of the Ministry of War, and later Director of Public Security. He spent the last two years before his appointment without any official assignment. Nägga claims that he was appointed to the post in Eritrea to break the circle of young officers which the Emperor feared would grow into a threat to his power: Personal interview, London, October 1989; see also FO 371/46117: British Embassy to Foreign Office, 26 October 1945, for a brief biographical sketch of Nägga.

[103] Nägga said that considering the vagueness of his assignment and the restrictions imposed on him by the British authorities, he did not at first know whether to take his appointment as an exile or as a serious job: Interview.

[104] The instructions which Nägga received from the Emperor said that he should make efforts to: 1) strive to understand the causes which separated Ethiopia and Eritrea; 2) receive people of Eritrea with an open heart, and seek all possible ways to win over those who oppose union through love and understanding; 3) investigate and report the conditions which exist in Eritrean towns and in the countryside; the nature of the administration, and the schools; the differences between the Muslims and Christians; the educational condition during the Italian time and under the present administration; 4) understand the division of power between the whites and the indigenous notables and to assess the types of taxation; 5) find out if the local elders and notables are included in counseling; and 6) report his findings regularly: Imperial Ethiopian government, Ministry of the Pen, to Colonel Nägga, 20 March 1946, in Liaison Office Papers.

[105] The official reason given was that only flags which should be saluted by the British troops were allowed to fly from vehicles, the Ethiopian flag not being one of them: B.A.E. Headquarters, Asmara, Cook to Nägga, 24 January 1950, in Liaison Office Papers.

[106] One petition from the Hamasén Branch of the Mahbär Feqri Hagär said, "We believe that you would not fail to appreciate the genuinely Ethiopian patriotic sentiment of the people of Hamasén. However, we are deeply concerned by your

failure to extend your support at a time when so much work is awaiting us:" Afäwärq Nämaryam, President of Hamasén Branch, to Col. Nägga, 19 November 1947: Liaison Office Papers.

[107] Nägga wrote to the Emperor that his office was flooded with so many invitations from schools, monasteries, churches and villages, that, unless some additional staff was assigned, he would be unable to meet even a fraction of the requests: Liaison Office Papers. The elders of the district of Sewuaté Ansäba wrote a letter to Nägga expressing their disappointment at his absence during their annual festival to which they had invited him. They reminded the Liaison Officer that their district was "among the first in Eritrea which started the custom of ostracizing those who do not love and honor their country, refusing to establish relations with them or even to attend funerals with them:" Mamher Mäbraté to Nägga, 20 May 1950, in Liaison Office Papers.

[108] Nägga: Interview.

[109] The confusion was such that at the end of his term, the Liaison Officer did not know to which department he should submit all the files and office equipment. He finally decided to keep it at his house in Addis Ababa, where it stayed until the Revolution in 1974: Interview, Nägga.

[110] Nega to Emperor Haile Selassie, 13 May 1947, Laison Office Papers.

[111] Nägga to Emperor Haile Selassie, [? 1946], in ibid. The sums allocated for such purposes increased substantially, especially after 1949, in preparation for the visit of the United Nations Commission of Inquiry.

[112] Emperor to Nägga, 29 June 1950, Liaison Office Papers.

[113] Paddock [American Consul in Eritrea] to Department of State, Asmara, 25 August 1949, State, 865D.01/8-2549: Paddock reported that both he and the British Administrator, Brigadier Drew, were of the opinion that Ethiopia relied too much on the international sympathy she had generated in the 1935 invasion.

[114] U.S. Embassy (Military Attache), Addis Ababa, 19 August 1949, in State, 884.00 (W) 18-1949.

[115] Mulugétta Buli to Nägga, 13 August 1946, in Liaison Office Papers.

[116] Assäfa Ayänä to Nägga, 8 December, 1946, ibid.

[117] This was particularly emphasized by Däjazmach Bäyänä Barakhi, the President of the Unionist Party, and by Nägga Haile Selassie.

[118] Among the Conditionalist leaders, who wrote to the Emperor asking him to consider their proposal, were Wäldä'ab Wäldämaryam, Däjazmach Abreha Täsämma, Seyum Mä'asho, and leaders of the Independent Moslem League of Massawa: Emperor Haile Selassie to Nägga, 2 July 1947; Moslem League of Massawa, "Questions addressed to the Imperial Ethiopian government," 28 June 1947, in Liaison Office Papers.

[119] Nägga to Emperor, Asmara, 7 August 1947, Liaison Office Papers.

[120] Nägga to Emperor, 19 June 1950, ibid.

[121] Minutes of a meeting between Ato Gäbrämäsqäl Habtämaryam and Colonel Nägga, 13 January 1947, ibid.

[122] Nägga to Ministry of the Pen, 5 February 1947, ibid; "Eretra Bä Tarik Yä Ityoppya Akal Selämähonuwa," 65.

[123] Asked in 1947 about his attitude to giving local autonomy for Eritrea the Emperor said that it was an unpopular idea even in Eritrea: Daily Telegraph, May 10, 1947.

[124] Emperor to Nägga, 2 July 1947, Liaison Office Papers.

[125] Ibid., 23 January 1947.

[126] Ibid., 15 January 1947.

[127] S'ähafi Taezaz Wäldägiyorgis Wäldäyohannes to Ato Wäldä'ab Wäldämaryam, June 1947, and Emperor to Nägga, 3 and 5 May, and 1 July 1947, ibid.

[128] Nägga to Emperor, 8 June 1947, ibid.

[129] The other members of the committee were Blatta Efrém, Blatta Kidanämaryam, Ato Keflä'egzi, Fitawrari Abreha Wäldäéwost'at'iwos, and Salih Kekia: "Minute of the meeting in the Ministry of the Pen," July 16 and 18, 1949; also S'ähafi Taezaz Wäldägiyorgis to Nägga, 25 July 1949, Liaison Office Papers.

[130] Ministry of Pen to Nägga, 24 February 1950, and Emperor to Nägga, 15 and 28 February 1950, ibid.

[131] The concession which the Unionists aborted involved a public statement by the Emperor promising to accept some of the demands of the Separatists: Emperor to Nägga, 28 February, 3 March and 26 April 1950, ibid.

CHAPTER FOUR

FEDERATION, 1952-1962

Enmeshed in a web of complex issues and interests, the question of the disposal of Eritrea proved to be the most difficult problem to resolve as far as the ex-Italian colonies were concerned.[1] International opinion on the possible solution for the future of the territory was fragmented as was opinion inside Eritrea.

Although the Fourth Session of the General Assembly of the United Nations established a number of committees to examine the Eritrean issue in detail and invited the major interested parties in Eritrea to once again represent their opinions, all of the proposals forwarded foundered for lack of consensus among the different protagonists.[2] Unable to break the stalemate, the General Assembly voted on 21 November 1949 to once again send a commission to Eritrea "to ascertain more fully the wishes and the best means of promoting the welfare of the inhabitants of Eritrea, to examine the question of the disposal of Eritrea and to prepare a report for the General Assembly" with suggestions for a possible solution. The resolution stressed that the commission should take into account: a) the wishes and interests of all political, religious, ethnic, and social groups, as well as their capacity for self-government; b) the interests of peace and security in East Africa; and c) the rights and claims of Ethiopia based on geographical, historical, ethnic or economic reasons, including her "legitimate need for adequate access to the sea."[3]

The United Nations Commission for Eritrea consisted of the representatives of Burma, Guatemala, Norway, Pakistan, and the Union of South Africa and carried out its work in Eritrea from 14 February to 9 April, 1950. There was wide-spread skepticism as to whether or not this commission could produce any tangible results in seven weeks since its predecessor, the Four Power Commission of Inquiry, had failed to do so in three months. Given the extremely disturbed political atmosphere in Eritrea under which it had to function, and the sharply conflicting differences among the Commission members themselves, the skepticism proved justified.

The arrival of the Commission exacerbated the political tension in Eritrea as each of the contending parties tried to prove its viability by resorting to extremist positions. The *shifta* (banditry) problem, which had seriously undermined law and order in the countryside over the last year, reached a new peak of ferocity as partisans of the various groups embarked on campaigns of terror to intimidate opponents to stay away from the sites visited by the commission and to mobilize supporters who could be displayed in front of the Commission. The haphazard manner in which the Commission conducted its investigation encouraged such practices. Pressed for time, its members usually assessed the strength of the various parties by the size of the crowds which they assembled during meetings in the districts it visited.

The futility of the whole exercise was increased by the divergent views held by members of the Commission and the lack of cooperation among them. Each of them stuck firmly with the previously stated position of their respective governments. They were more interested in gathering facts which could be used to strengthen their preconceived ideas than in seeking information which could help to throw light on the complex situation in Eritrea. Describing the transparently slanted manner in which some members of the Commission conducted their investigation, Trevaskis wrote:

> The Guatemalan and Pakistani delegates, who were both professional lawyers, made it their practice to question Eritreans appearing before the Commission as though they were witnesses in a court of law. Representatives supporting the Independence Bloc were guided along with adroit inquiries and leading questions to make the very best of their case; those who opposed it were tripped up and trapped into admissions and contradictions in a most questionable form of cross-examination. The brusque, hectoring, and at times positively discourteous treatment which some of those appearing before the Commission received was widely commented on.[4]

The Guatemalan and Pakistani delegations, although for different reasons, came from the start determined to champion the cause of independence. As a member of the Latin bloc, Guatemala had consistently supported the Italian position and had been appointed to the Commission to ensure that Italian interests in Eritrea would not be adversely affected. And Pakistan had been at the forefront of the group in the United Nations which championed Muslim interests in Eritrea. In addition, the Pakistani government had established liaison with the Muslim League of Eritrea since its creation in 1947. On the election of Pakistan to the commission, the Chilean delegate to the General Assembly stated that Pakistan's inclusion was an important safeguard for the Muslims.[5]

Of the remaining three delegates on the UN Commission for Eritrea, the Burmese delegate initially sided with the pro-independence group since, by his own admission, his government had instructed him "to go along with Pakistan as far as possible." After realizing that the Pakistani position was untainable, the Burmese delegate requested his government to allow him a "fairly free hand" to consider other options. The South African delegate, whose country had repeatedly voted against Ethiopia's claim to Eritrea, had by this time adopted the British proposal of partitioning Eritrea between the Sudan and Ethiopia.[6] The Norwegian delegate reflected his country's pro-Ethiopian position by strongly favoring a complete union between Ethiopia and Eritrea.

Such divergent views ruled out a joint proposal to the General Assembly. Actually, the Commission was unable to agree even on essential factual matters and had to present two separate reports, one by Pakistan and Guatemala, which was referred to as the "minority report," and the other, commonly known as the "majority report," by the delegates of Burma, the Union of South Africa, and Norway.

The Pakistani and Guatemalan report claimed that no significant affinity existed between Ethiopia and Eritrea, and that the Unionist upsurge in Eritrea was a result of intimidation by terrorism and the propaganda of the Orthodox Church. The report pointed out that the continuing participation of Italians and half-castes was essential to the territory's economy and that independence was the best possible solution "from the point of view of this important minority." The Pakistani and Guatemalan delegation admitted that the territory was not ready for immediate independence and suggested a ten-year period of United Nations trusteeship, which would be assisted by a council composed of representatives from Ethiopia, Italy, the United States, one Muslim country, a Latin American state, as well as two Eritreans, a Muslim, and a Christian. They also proposed the establishment of free zones in Massawa and Assab for Ethiopia and the eventual economic unification of the two countries.[7]

The majority report emphasized the existence of strong unionist sympathy in Eritrea, the territory's essential economic interdependence with Ethiopia, and the absence of a self-sustaining economic and political foundation which precluded a viable independent state. In opposition to the views of the Pakistani and Guatemalan delegations, which considered the irredentist movement as the creation of clerical influence and shifta intimidation, the majority report observed:

> The Unionist movement in the highlands has many of the characteristics of an expanding popular movement. Operating with simple and easily understandable slogans, it reflects the fact that the Tigrinya-speaking Copts undoubtedly consider themselves as Ethiopians. The salute "Ethiopia!" not only resounded at their meetings but met the Commission all along the highways in southern Eritrea, whether from a few tiny children on a hill-top, casual passers-by or village communities massed along the roadside.[8]

> The report cautioned that in view of the marked pro-unionist sentiment in the Eritrean highlands "outright frustration of these wishes would make the position of internal security in Eritrea untenable" and that Ethiopia might readily come to the aid of the Unionists should they require it.[9]

On the question of the economic viability of the territory, the majority report emphasized that Eritrea was "a poor country, without any prospect of progressing as a separate economic entity, and dependent in most vital respects on Ethiopia's rich farming resources and transit trade." The representatives of the three countries were of the opinion that this reality ruled out the prospect of the establishment of a viable separate Eritrean state, "whether in the immediate future or after an interval of international trusteeship."[10] The majority report concluded:

> In such circumstances [of economic impoverishment] and in view of the acute internal political division and state of tension in Eritrea, the conclusion is ineluctable that the creation of a separate Eritrean State entirely on its own would contain all the elements necessary seriously to prejudice the interests of peace and security in East Africa, now and in the future.[11]

Although there was no disagreement on their evaluation of the situation in Eritrea and the essential links which existed between that territory and Ethiopia, the representatives of the three countries differed in their recommendations on the type of association which should be established between the two countries. The Burmese and South African delegates supported a close political and economic association with important guarantees for the Muslim population "who on the whole are afraid to join Ethiopia, and to safeguard the position of the Italian settlers and Italo-Eritrean half-castes who have a permanent stake in the country."[12] Accordingly, they recommended a federal arrangement which they argued would satisfy both the aspirations of the Unionists and Ethiopia, while at the same time providing local autonomy to the groups who opposed annexation by Ethiopia.

In a separate recommendation submitted to the General Assembly the Norwegian delegation proposed the total incorporation of Eritrea into Ethiopia. It argued that the majority of the highland population had always considered itself Ethiopian, as was manifested by the surge of an irredentist movement starting in 1941, and that subsequent opposition to union with Ethiopia was "born out of the political possibilities presented by the discord between the powers about the future of Eritrea, and were created by a handful of ambitious Eritreans."[13] The recommendation noted that in case the predominantly Muslim area of the Western Province did not wish to be incorporated into Ethiopia a decision on its future could be deferred until such time as the population was in a position to choose to join either Ethiopia or the Sudan.[14]

In opposing the federal solution suggested by the Burmese and South African delegations, the Norwegian representative said,

> To impose obligations on Ethiopia to organize its relation with Eritrea on the basis of a federative status, without any knowledge as to whether this would be the best constitutional solution, could easily lead to future conflict and unrest, and in the end endanger the peace of East Africa.[15]

The Fifth Session of the General Assembly, which sat to consider the reports of the Commission on Eritrea, found very little help in their mutually conflicting recommendations in bridging existing differences. Member nations regrouped themselves behind one of the Commission's three proposals, i.e., independence, federation, or total incorporation into Ethiopia. The General Assembly found itself once again in the stalemate which had characterized its previous deliberations on Eritrea. It would have remained there had it not been for a change in position by the United States.

The absence of a firm position by the United States on the Eritrean question and its inability to provide leadership in the General Assembly which most countries expected was an important factor in allowing the inconclusive situation to develop. Most of the Latin and Central American countries, who tended to vote with the United States, had sided with Italy and thereby had prevented any solution other than the one which favored Italy because of the absence of American pressure. In the words of a State Department official, the United States "gave a clear field to the Italian government which was successful in exacting firm promises of support for Italian claims."[16]

The United States had remained rather detached throughout much of the discussion on the future of the ex-Italian colonies, intervening actively only to prevent the Soviet Union from getting a foothold in either of them. With regard to Eritrea, the United States chose to follow the objectives developed by Great Britain rather than develop its own policy. U.S. military strategists were of the opinion that their installations in Eritrea would be more secure under an arrangement in which Great Britain maintained a presence in the region.

The United States was also in a dilemma concerning the claims of Italy, a country which it sought to stabilize and boost into becoming a major partner in the newly evolving structure of the North Atlantic Treaty Organization. Incumbent Italian politicians skillfully exploited U.S. fears that Italy would fall into the hands of either the Communists or the extreme rightists should Italian national ambitions be frustrated by the loss of her ex-colonies. Expressing this fear, Dunn, the U.S. Ambassador to Italy, wrote to the Secretary of State:

> I am convinced that we would make a grave mistake if we support a solution for Eritrea and Tripolitania that completely excluded Italy....Both the forces of extreme nationalism and Communism will be permanently aided in their violent attacks against Italy's cooperation with western democracies by the lasting resentment which would be created by a settlement in total disregard of all that Italy has aspired to and accomplished in her former colonies.[17]

On the other hand, the United States could not ignore the claims of Ethiopia, with whom it was beginning to establish friendly relations. Ethiopia's potential as a gateway for the spread of U.S. influence in the rest of black Africa was appreciated. In addition, the Department of State was continually besieged by petitions from its own black population about its lack of support to this African nation.

At first, the United States sought to assuage Ethiopian grievances by advocating a territorial concession in southern Eritrea which would provide her with access to the sea. This, however, was found to be neither practical, nor satisfactory to the Ethiopians. Faced with a set of complex alternatives and divided loyalties, the U.S. chose to maintain a low profile in the General Assembly with regard to the Eritrean question as long as possible.

What finally brought a change in the U.S. attitude was its need to mobilize international support behind it on the Korean question. The United States had to intervene aggressively to free the General Assembly from its deadlock over the Eritrean question and to push it to concentrate on the Korean problem. Accordingly, the U.S. lobbied to secure the votes required to reach an Eritrean settlement. It first concentrated on the Latin American countries.[18] In a telegram to U.S. diplomatic offices in the Latin American countries, Secretary of State Dean Acheson noted: "In view of critical character [of the] present world situation with special reference [to] Korea the U.S. regards definitive recommendation on Eritrea by IC [Interim Committee of the General

Assembly] at current meetings as indispensable."[19] American pressure was also brought to bear on Italy[20] and intensive behind-the-scenes discussions and negotiations were carried out with Ethiopia and other interested parties, before the issue came to a final vote in the General Assembly.

The federation solution proposed by the Burmese and South African members of the United Nations Commission was taken as a formula which offered something to all parties concerned with the future of Eritrea and which appeared the most likely to succeed. The Four Power Commission of Investigation which disagreed within itself on many points was, however, unanimous in its verdict that the economic and political foundation of Eritrea was too weak to sustain an independent state. The majority report of the United Nation's Commission had ruled out an independent Eritrea, and Pakistan and Guatemala had deemed the territory not ready for immediate independence, in need of ten years of UN trusteeship, and some form of economic association with Ethiopia.

Latest developments inside Eritrea appeared to make federation an attractive proposal. The fragmentation of the Independence Bloc in 1950 and the defection of several of its members to form an alliance with the Unionist Party had shown how tenuous the position of the independence parties was. After the Muslim League of the Western Province reached an understanding with the Unionist Party to cooperate in opposing the Bloc,[21] the forces opposed to union with Ethiopia were visibly weakened.[22] A delegation consisting of some 70 Eritrean notables representing all the Eritrean districts attended the Ninth Anniversary of Ethiopian Liberation from Fascist Occupation in Addis Ababa on May 5, 1950. The Liaison Office was inundated with requests from various districts in Eritrea to be included in the delegation.[23]

The Italians in Eritrea, who had been in the forefront of the independence movement, were no longer vocal in 1950. They had suffered heavily from the shifta attacks and their interests were threatened with liquidation, so they finally decided to dissolve C.R.I.E. and to make their peace with Unionist forces.[24]

The Italian government, too, found out that its anti-unionist position had imperiled the interests of its nationals not only in Eritrea but also in Ethiopia. In retaliation to Italian hostility the Ethiopian government dumped hundreds of Italians living in Ethiopia across the border into Eritrea and threatened to curb Italian interests in Ethiopia. On the suggestion of Unionist leaders and the Ethiopian Liaison Officer, the Ethiopian government began to introduce various restrictions on Italian business originating from Eritrea.[25]

An association of indigenous Eritrean businessmen, established with the help of the Unionist Party, was trying hard to take away some of the key trade with Ethiopia from Italian hands. The Ethiopian liaison officer in Eritrea was fully behind the association and instrumental in soliciting his government's support for the scheme.[26] These efforts underscored the fact that an Italian victory in Eritrea would be fruitless as long as Ethiopia closed herself to Italian interests. In light of such developments, the Italian government appeared to be more amenable to some form of face-saving in 1950.

Another important factor in enhancing the prospect of a federal solution was a change in the British position. Unionist intransigence and the widespread shifta activity which ensued from it had made the territory practically ungovernable. Britain's proposal to annex the Western Province of Eritrea to the Sudan was rejected even by the Muslim League of the Western Province, an openly pro-British party which demanded British trusteeship. The Liberal Progressive Party, which the British had sponsored in its early days, was now splintered. An important section of its leadership had constituted itself into the Liberal Unionist Party and was reporting enthusiastically to the Emperor about its success in garnering a growing number of adherents.[27]

Faced with dwindling internal support and a deteriorating security situation in the territory, the British government was looking for an honorable exit from Eritrea. Therefore, it readily rallied behind the United States, hoping to bring about a speedy solution to the Eritrean problem.

The federal formula also appeared to stand a good chance of winning acceptance because it promised to satisfy Ethiopia's claims. Although they opposed a total annexation of Eritrea, the principal opponents of the Ethiopian claim, the Soviet bloc, the Latin countries, and the Islamic group, were all in favor of concessions to Ethiopia, especially with regard to granting her some portion of the territory to give her access to the sea.

The vigor with which Ethiopia pursued her claims in the international forums and the commitment and strength of her Unionist partisans in Eritrea had demonstrated to the international body that no solution which ignored this reality would ever stand a chance in Eritrea. Ethiopia's determination to get her own ports was such that she had already bought three ships in 1947 and had them sailing in the Red Sea. Significantly, these ships were named Adulis, Bahr Nägash, and Wälwal – the first two associated with ancient Ethiopian maritime prominence and the last symbol of Ethiopian resistance against external aggression.[28]

Observing the popular enthusiasm for the Ethio-Eritrean unification, the American Minister in Ethiopia wrote in 1948: "There is certainly very strong feeling... on the part of Ethiopians of all classes and it is unlikely, I believe, that the Ethiopian government and people will peacefully accept the return of Eritrea to Italy."[29] The "majority report" of the United Nations Commission had cautioned that Unionists would cause serious trouble if their aspirations were frustrated and that Ethiopia would most likely come to their aid.[30]

The Ethiopian Emperor had openly declared that the Eritrean question was "a matter of life and death for Ethiopia's security,"[31] and her representatives to the United Nations had repeatedly expressed Ethiopia's determination to prevent an unfavorable resolution by all means available. At one of the sessions of the General Assembly in 1949, Blatén-Géta Efrém Täwäldä-Mädhen, head of the Ethiopian delegation, and himself an Eritrean, reminded the member nations of Ethiopia's experience of betrayal at the hands of the League of Nations and declared:

> After all the sufferings Ethiopia had gone through [the 1935-41 Italian invasion], she will not allow herself to be sacrificed on the altar of the United Nations to appease Italy as was done at the League of Nations. She will abandon all hope in justice from the United Nations and will take all measures for legitimate self-defence as provided in the Charter of the United Nations.[32]

Those who observed Ethiopia's determination and the resolute position of the Unionists in Eritrea, understood that this was no idle threat. Few could fail to see the potential danger to the security of the region should the international body fail to reach a formula acceptable to Ethiopia and to the irredentist forces in Eritrea.

Its proponents also believed the federal idea to be the best practical concession to those forces which opposed the Ethiopian annexation of Eritrea. The wide range of internal autonomy proposed in the federal formula was expected to comfort those who feared coming under Ethiopian control.

The formula also contained various provisions which were intended to safeguard the continued interests of the foreign, specifically Italian, community in the territory. This helped to placate the pro-Italian group in the United Nations, which had so far viewed the Eritrean issue entirely from the perspective of Italian interests.

The draft resolution for a federation was discussed first in the Interim Committee and later in the Ad Hoc Political Committee. When it was finally presented in the General Assembly on 2 December 1950 it was adopted by a vote of 46 against 10 and 4 abstentions. Only the Soviet bloc, which saw the arrangement as another imperialist ploy to extend American hegemony in Africa, put up stiff resistance.[33]

The General Assembly's resolution stated that its decision was based on considerations of the wishes and welfare of the inhabitants of Eritrea and their capacity for self-government, the interests of peace and security in East Africa, the rights and claims of Ethiopia, and the need for the continued collaboration of the foreign communities in the economic development of Eritrea.[34]

The resolution reiterated that the disposal of Eritrea should be based on its close political and economic association with Ethiopia. This association was to be established on the principle of "the widest possible measure of self-government, while at the same time respecting the Constitution, institutions, traditions and the international status and identity of the Empire of Ethiopia."[35]

The resolution also determined that "Eritrea shall constitute an autonomous unit federated with Ethiopia under the sovereignty of the Ethiopian crown." The Eritrean government was to take charge of domestic affairs. Defense; foreign affairs; currency and finance; foreign and inter-state commerce; and external and interstate communications, including ports, were placed under the jurisdiction of the Federal government. The resolution provided for the establishment of an Imperial Federal Council composed of equal numbers of Eritrean and Ethiopian representatives to advise on the common affairs of the federation. There was to be a single Ethiopian nationality for the federation.[36]

The resolution provided for the appointment of a United Nations Commissioner who was to prepare a constitution in consultation with the local population, the British administration, and the Ethiopian government, and to oversee the organization of an Eritrean administration. All this was to be accomplished before 15 September 1952. The Bolivian, Eduardo Anze Matienzo, was chosen for this task on 14 December 1950.

The Eritrean Constitution and the Establishment of an Autonomous Administration

Although the United Nations Commissioner to Eritrea, called the federal idea "a middle-of-the-road plan...which should give satisfaction not only to those who want to be united with Ethiopia, but to those who want Eritrea to be independent,"[37] he soon found that selling the compromise formula to the major protagonists in Eritrea was a daunting task.

To be sure, the idea of union with Ethiopia under some form of Eritrean internal autonomy was not an innovation of the General Assembly. A group known as the Conditional Unionists had been asking for similar arrangements since the mid-1940s. Subsequently, the forces which sought a federal solution for Eritrea had rallied behind the Liberal Unionist Party, the Independent Eritrea United with Ethiopia Party, and the Independent Muslim League. Since the end of 1949, they were in contact with the Ethiopian government, and had, to some degree, succeeded in winning tacit acceptance from it.[38]

The partisans of a federal formula were, however, a minority. The major political forces in Eritrea remained firmly polarized. The anti-Unionist group led by the Muslim League considered itself a loser under any arrangement which introduced an Ethiopian presence into Eritrea. The leaders of the other major political force, the Muslim League of the Western Province, were opposed to any type of association with the rest of Eritrea, let alone with Ethiopia.

Unionists saw any formula short of the total integration of Eritrea with Ethiopia as a defeat. When the idea of federation was first raised in a subcommittee of the General Assembly in 1949, it created quite a stir among Unionists. In a telegram to the United Nations, they condemned the suggestion as a plan drawn to "satisfy the pretension of an Italian foreign minority."[39]

Ethiopia acquiesced in the federal resolution only because of American pressure and the realization that her chances of gaining a better settlement within the United Nations framework were slender. The creation of an autonomous Eritrean administration had risen more from the desire to appease foreign interests than to solve local problems. John H. Spencer, an American advisor in the Ethiopian Ministry of Foreign Affairs and a principal participant in the U.N. discussions, later wrote:

> ...for Ethiopia, the federation represented a triumph of European - Latin American colonialism. After losing outright union under the Bevin-Sforza proposals to the opposition of Italy and its Latin American agents at the General Assembly, federation appeared to most Ethiopians to have been a concession to the dictates of pre-war Fascism.[40]

The Ethiopian government also felt uncomfortable about an arrangement which limited its power in Eritrea and required it to operate within a certain constitutional framework, a task which it did not confront in the rest of Ethiopia.

Ethiopian reluctance to accept the federal solution also originated from fear of disappointing its unionist partisans in Eritrea. When Ethiopia's delegation in the United Nations requested the Emperor to instruct them to accept the federal proposal, he reportedly withheld his approval for some time for fear that the Unionists might consider it a betrayal of their cause.[41] Two days after its adoption in the General Assembly, the Emperor stated that the federal formula "does not entirely satisfy the wishes of the vast majority of the Eritreans who seek union without condition, nor does it satisfy all the legitimate claims of Ethiopia," and added that he accepted it because it was the only formula "that could obtain the necessary two-third majority for approval by the United Nations."[42]

The United Nations Commissioner found himself in the unenviable position of getting these reluctant partners, negatively disposed towards federation from the beginning, to cooperate in drafting a constitution acceptable to all.[43] Each group was determined to interpret the General Assembly's resolution according to its own views rather than adjust its position to fit the spirit of federation. The Commissioner observed that during his consultations on the Constitution the various parties were attempting "to steer the Federation towards a pattern differing as little as possible from their previous ideas."[44]

Opinions on the nature of the Eritrean constitution were sharply divided between the two main political factions, the Unionists and their opponents. Since these two factions tended to draw their support along linguistic, religious, and regional lines, the differences also appeared to reflect the Tegreñña- and non-Tegreñña-speaking, the highland and lowland, as well as the Christian-Muslim cleavage in Eritrean society.

Among the main issues of contention were the questions of the Emperor's representation in Eritrea, the type of legislature to be set up, the Eritrean flag, and the official language. The Unionists favored the appointment of an imperial representative with certain prerogatives in Eritrea. Some among the Unionists wished that the Emperor be allowed to appoint the members of the Eritrean Executive, while others wanted to limit his power to approving the executive officials elected by the Assembly.[45]

The Independence Bloc, consisting of remnants of the Muslim League of Eritrea, the Liberal Progressive Party, the New Eritrea Party, the Independent Party, the Italo-Eritrean Association and the War Veterans Association, reconstituted itself under the name of the Eritrean Democratic Front and vigorously countered any attempt to give Ethiopia a strong hand in Eritrea. It was opposed to having a representative of the Emperor in Eritrea. The Muslim League of the Western Province also opposed the interference of the Emperor's representative in Eritrean internal affairs.[46]

With regard to the legislature, the Unionists and their allies wanted a single elected assembly. The Democratic Front demanded a bicameral legislature, which would consist of a senate composed on a regional basis and an elected assembly. The leaders of the Democratic Front calculated that a senate established on a regional basis would serve as a safeguard against unionist domination should they succeed in winning a majority in the assembly.[47]

The Muslim League of the Western Province asked for two regional assemblies one for the Muslims and one for the Christians. This was a disguised method of implementing its former plans of creating two separate states, Christian and Muslim, each of which could then be federated individually with Ethiopia.[48]

On the language question, the predominantly Muslim parties asked that Arabic and Tegreñña be recognized as the official languages. The Christians, led by the Unionists and allied parties, maintained that since Arabic was a foreign language and used mainly for religious purposes, only Tegreñña should be adopted as the official language. This, in turn, led Muslim groups to reject Tegreñña and to insist that they would recognize only Arabic as the official language for Eritrea.[49]

Opinions on the subject of the flag were also marked by sharp division along religious lines. The leaders of the Muslim parties were generally opposed to the adoption of the Ethiopian flag. They demanded not only a distinct flag for Eritrea but also insisted that, since the Ethiopian flag has Christian symbols on it, a separate flag should be created for the Federation. The Christian group opposed the creation of a new flag and demanded that only the Ethiopian flag be used in Eritrea.

Nowhere was the polarization of views between Christians and Muslims more evident than it was in Asmara, the region's capital and major urban center. In two successive meetings, held in October 1951, the commissioner found out that the Muslim and Christian views had hardened much more here than they had in the rural areas.

The city was divided between a "Christian Ward" and a "Muslim Ward," and opinions on the constitution were expressed strictly on the basis of "Ward" affiliation.[50] The Muslims were determined to limit the association with Ethiopia to a mere formality, while Unionists struggled to fight off suggestions which undermined that association. After observing the division in Asmara, the commissioner again remarked that each group was determined "to interpret the United Nations resolution to its own advantage, as implying either independence or union with Ethiopia."[51] The commissioner had to remind the political parties in Eritrea repeatedly that his mission was not to ascertain the wishes of the population as earlier commissions had done, but to solicit views which would help him in drafting a constitution based on U.N. Resolution 390 (V).[52]

The commissioner also had to wrangle with the Ethiopian authorities who opposed the major articles in the constitution which limited the Emperor's power. Making a clear delineation between what was to fall under domestic affairs and what was to be the responsibility of the federal authority proved to be a complicated affair. The ambiguities and incongruities contained in the U.N. resolution gave rise to wide divergence in the interpretations of the degree of autonomy to be granted to Eritrea. Invoking Resolution 390 (V), which stipulated that the federation would be effected without prejudice to "the Constitution, institutions, traditions, and the international status and identity of the Empire of Ethiopia,"[53] Ethiopian officials insisted that the Ethiopian government should be recognized as the Federal government. Aklilu Habtä-Wäld, the Foreign Minister, had earlier argued during the debates in the U.N. that "Ethiopia, a sovereign and independent state for hundreds of years, was not about to surrender her sovereignty and disappear from the world scene in order to join in a federation with a territory and population one-twentieth her size which had never known independence."[54] It was in view of this strong objection that the U.N. resolution provided that Eritrea was to be federated with Ethiopia under the sovereignty of the Ethiopian crown.[55]

The Ethiopian government demanded that, since the federation was to be established under the sovereignty of the Ethiopian crown, and if organs of the Ethiopian government dealing with federal affairs were to constitute the Federal government, the latter should exercise some form of control over the Eritrean government to ensure that federal laws and rights were observed in Eritrea and to safeguard the integrity of the federation.[56] Ethiopian officials also asked that in addition to Tegreñña and Arabic, Amharic, the official language in the rest of the country, should be introduced as an official language in Eritrea. On the question of the federal flag, the foreign minister maintained that the issue should not even be raised since one-twentieth of the population of the federation could not "claim to impose its flag on nineteen million inhabitants."[57]

The provisional draft constitution which the commissioner and his Panel of Legal Consultants prepared tried to reconcile the widely different views expressed during its ten months of consultation with the Eritrean public and their various political parties as well as with the Ethiopian government.[58] In an apparent concession to the Ethiopian government and to the Unionists, it recognized that the Ethiopian government was to be the Federal government, and that the Emperor should be represented in Eritrea. Not to antagonize the anti-unionist faction, the Emperor's representative was limited to an advisory role, to promulgating Eritrean legislation (over which he had power only to apply a suspension veto), and to reading the speech from the throne. The provisional draft constitution provided for a strong executive under a chief executive who would be elected by the Assembly. Eritrea was allowed a separate flag, while the Ethiopian flag was maintained as the Federal flag.

After a new round of haggling with the Ethiopian government over the provisional draft constitution in which further amendments were required, the commissioner finally called for the election of a representative assembly to consider it.

In accordance with the mandate it received from the General Assembly, the British Administration set out the procedure for the election of the Assembly.[59] It adopted an indirect system in most places in the territory, except in the towns of Asmara and Massawa where direct elections were conducted. Taking their experience from the Sudan, British officials believed that an indirect system of election was more suited to the largely dispersed pastoral community.[60] Villages and family groups were to elect their delegates in accordance with local customs to regional electoral colleges. The colleges, in turn, would elect representatives to the Assembly by secret ballot.

Deciding the size of the constituencies was a thorny issue. Given the Muslim-Christian cleavage on most issues, there was fear that any imbalance in representation would provide the occasion for a new round of disagreements. The British avoided this possibility by creating, through a complex mathematical balance, 68 constituencies, neatly divided between Muslims and Christians. Each constituency represented 15,000 people. Although the Unionists accused the British administration of underestimating the size of the Christian population,[61] this was a minor problem compared to the trouble that would have ensued if one group appeared to have gained the upper hand.

The results of the elections confirmed the basic socio-political reality in Eritrea. The 68 seats were equally divided between Christians and Muslims. Of these, the Unionists won 32 seats; the Democratic Front, 18; and the Muslim League of the Western Province, 15. The Independent Muslim League and the National Party of Massawa won one seat each. One independent candidate also won a seat.[62]

The results also in some ways debunked the claims of certain self-styled leaders of the independence movement. The Democratic Front led by Ibrahim Sultan, which had consistently claimed a majority support in Eritrea, won only 18 of the 68 seats. Since this was also the only group that advocated the creation of a single independent Eritrean state, the rather dismal results reflected the narrow support the idea commanded. The success of the Muslim League of the Western Province, which was created to advance the secession of the Western Province from the rest of Eritrea, in capturing 15 of the 21 Muslim seats in the region was an ominous sign for the future.[63]

Wäldäab Wäldämaryam, who was considered a popular and leading figure in Eritrean politics, failed to obtain even 10 percent of the votes cast.[64] His failure was particularly significant because he ran in Asmara where direct elections were conducted. Mohammed Omar Qadi, the head of the Independent Muslim League, also lost in Harqiqo, near Massawa.[65]

Ras Täsämma of the Democratic Front was elected by a substantial majority, but he resigned from the Assembly soon after returning from a visit to the Emperor in May 1952, thereby freeing four of his immediate relatives in the Assembly to join the Unionists.[66] His son Grazmach Gärakidan Täsämma was elected in his place.

The fear that the equal distribution of seats between Christians and Muslims might prevent the creation of a working majority in the Assembly was dispelled by the formation of a coalition between the Unionists and the Muslim League of the Western Province. Fortunately for the Unionists, the antagonism between the leaders of this group and those of the Eritrean Democratic Front was such as to preclude these co-religionists from working together. The Unionists seized the occasion and made concessions necessary to keep the Muslim League of the Western Province on their side.

On the second day of its inauguration on 28 April, 1952, the Assembly elected Ato (later Däjazmach) Tädla Bairu, secretary of the Unionist Party, as president, by 49 votes for to 11 against, with two abstentions.[67] Sheikh Ali Mohammed Mussa Redai, the head of the Muslim League of the Western Province, was elected vice-president by 48 votes to 17 with one abstention.[68] On 10 July, 1952, it adopted the Eritrean Constitution unanimously. The Emperor approved it on 11 August, 1952. The Federal Act was ratified in Addis Ababa on 11 September, 1952. On 15 September, 1952, the British Administration relinquished its power to the Emperor's representative and to Ato Tädla Bairu, the newly elected chief executive of the government of Eritrea. Tadla declared on the occasion of the ratification of the Federal Act that "the federation of Eritrea and Ethiopia marked the end of sixty-seven years of struggle."[69]

The Vicissitudes of the Federation

The Ethio-Eritrean federal formula originated primarily out of a desire to end the impasse created both in Eritrea and in the General Assembly about the future of Eritrea. Federalism was neither desired, nor even understood properly, by a great majority of the political forces in the region.[70] Viewed by many as an external imposition, the federal arrangement had few supporters either in Eritrea or in Ethiopia.

The chief executive, Däjazmach Tädla Bairu, was an ardent Unionist, as were most of his Christian colleagues both in the executive and legislative branches. Given their staunch irredentist records, many of them were bound to view federation as but a partial victory and to attempt to use it only as a transition towards full integration with Ethiopia.

The Ethiopian government, for its part, accepted the federation reluctantly and subsequently did everything possible to dilute Eritrean autonomy. The Emperor was speaking of the need to plan for the full integration of Eritrea with Ethiopia even before the federation was formally declared.[71] In May, 1953, he reportedly told the British Ambassador that "union" and "federation" were words which most people did not understand and that to him both meant the same.[72] The rather awkward structure of the federation, in which the Imperial

Ethiopian government also doubled as a federal government,[73] opened up wide avenues for the Emperor to absorb the territory fully.

Neither were the forces opposed to union with Ethiopia prepared to give the federation any better chance. They searched for every pretext to discredit the Ethiopian government and embarked on an incessant campaign to disrupt the operations of the federation. Some of them acted on the premise that their continuous outcry against Ethiopia and the newly established Eritrean government might induce the United Nations to reopen the entire case of the territory's disposal and come out with another formula more to their liking.

Tolerance and the will to forget past animosities to strike new and workable balances, the basic prerequisites for the smooth operation of a federal system, were practically absent in Eritrea. The various political forces in the country had a much longer tradition of fighting each other than working out a mutually satisfactory solution to their complex problems.

Eritrea's fragile institutions were unable to cope with the pressures emanating from the demands of a federal system. The Constitution drafted by the U.N. sponsored panel of legal experts, supposedly to inaugurate a democratic system in Eritrea, remained a dead letter when confronted by a hostile environment in which people found it expedient to fall back on their traditional mechanisms rather than surrender themselves to unfamiliar dictates.

The experiment with Eritrean autonomy was also encumbered with inadequate resources. Imports had surpassed exports throughout the colonial period, and the revenue raised inside Eritrea fell far short of covering expenses even for the highly simplified administrative structures of the Eritrean government. The Italians, and later the British, maintained the territory through a continued flow of subsidies from the metropolitan treasuries.

The new Eritrean government inherited a tattered economy from the British. As an occupying power, the British made few investments and tried to limit their expenses to the bare minimum. The Eritrean economy was unable to recover from the severe slump it had entered into after the Italian defeat. The high rate of unemployment, precipitated by the demobilization of thousands of the colonial army, continued to rise unabated throughout the decade of British rule. The general political instability in the country, especially in the last years of the British administration, further aggravated the already desperate situation.

Still worse, on the eve of their departure, the British had stripped the territory of the few valuable assets built by the Italians. Several buildings (75 in Massawa alone),[74] bunkers, barracks, oil reservoirs, and the airfield at Gura were destroyed and the scrap metals sold to neighboring countries. The rails and railway cars which had been brought to extend the line from Aqordat to

Gondär were sold to the Sudan. Many of the port installations at Massawa and Assäb were dismantled. Several harbor boats and the floating dry-dock at Massawa, together with the harbor's cranes, were sold to foreign bidders. The cement factory in Massawa was dismantled and the machinery transferred to the Sudan.[75] Some important Italian assets, which, according to the U.N. Resolution, should have passed to the Eritrean or the Federal government, were transferred to British holdings. Such was the case with the AGIP installations in Eritrea which were transferred to the Shell Oil Company.[76]

On top of this, the British demanded and received 950,000 pounds sterling from the Ethiopian government to reimburse expenses which they had incurred in Eritrea during their occupation from 1941-1952.[77] No such demands had been made on the Italian government which took charge of Somaliland from the British two years earlier.

Having received an empty treasury at its inception, the new Eritrean government found it difficult to maintain its rudimentary administrative machinery let alone alleviate the dismal economic situation in the country. At the beginning of the Federation, it was feared that the new Eritrean government would not last for more than two or three months.[78] In fact, it was kept going on a month-to-month basis depending for the most part on quarterly payments by the Ethiopian government from the Eritrean share of customs duties collected at the ports. Although the Eritrean government had added only a few hundred new employees over that of the British, some 58 percent of its total expenditures went for personnel salaries. A large portion of this amount represented pay for the largely British and Italian expatriate staff.[79]

The transfer of power also brought with it a change in the currency, the second in a decade. The replacement of the East African Shilling by the Ethiopian currency required a period of painful adjustment. The East African Shilling, which was valued at Eth.$ 0.35, was treated by traders as equal to a half Ethiopian birr (Eth.$ 0.50). This caused an immediate rise in the price of most items.[80]

This inflationary trend was further confounded by the high customs duties imposed by the Ethiopian government on a number of imported products which it defined as luxury items but which included gasoline and textile products. The increase in the price of gasoline, in particular, caused a rise in the cost of several other basic commodities.

Disillusionment with the Eritrean government was instant. Unionist propaganda had made a great deal out of the high cost of living and growing unemployment under the British. In their eagerness to mobilize massive support, Unionists had led the public to expect bountiful rewards from the association with Ethiopia.[81]

Many expected to see the return of the "good old days," the brief period of artificial prosperity created by the Fascists in the 1930s. A great many functionaries of the various parties aspired to secure jobs in the new government. Unionists hoped to be rewarded for their service to the cause of Ethio-Eritrean unity, while the opposition expected to be adequately compensated for dropping its separatist demands.

Too much was expected from a government which possessed so few resources. When most of these expectations failed to materialize in the months following federation, the Eritrean government was held to account and harassed from several directions. A petition by a group of people claiming to represent the unemployed in Massawa warned the president of the Assembly, "the eyes of a goat gaze at the grass and those of the leopard at the goat...Men under the impulse of hunger will turn into beasts forgetting their being human."[82] Another protest addressed to the Assembly by a group of youth from Asmara which called itself the "Revolutionary Party" said,

> We youth rejoiced at the coming of freedom, but happen to be facing problems, as what happened in the past was better than the present....As you are getting a lot of money for yourselves, you do not look at the Eritrean people and do not realize that it got worse....Foreigners are bringing poverty to Eritrea. Now that we have our freedom the salary which is now going to a European is one received by ten persons. We do recommend you not to do this now. You are eating whilst we are starving. They give us a small salary and when we arrive at the market we find the price high. The people who have been elected are completely useless....They do not know that the people hate them.[83]

The new Eritrean government attempted to stay financially afloat by increasing the tax on the countryside, from Eth. $455,600 for the 1952/53 fiscal year to Eth. $782,342 for the 1953/54 fiscal year, an increase of 71.7 percent. Not surprisingly, this heavy burden on an already impoverished peasantry led to massive protest. Rural community leaders appealed directly to the Emperor, describing the imposition as "unbearable."[84] The monarch ruled that Eritrea's share of the tax for 1954 should be paid by the Imperial Treasury, and that in the future it should be reduced to half of the amount set by the Eritrean government.[85] Further deferments were made by the Emperor in subsequent years, especially in the Western Province that had been gravely affected by drought and frequent locust infestations.[86]

The Emperor's gesture was not, however, appreciated by all. Supporters of Eritrean autonomy perceived it as a prelude to annexation. They feared that the assistance might reinforce the widely held view that Eritrea could not stand on its own feet without help from Ethiopia. Ibrahim Sultan and his associates made an unsuccessful attempt to convene a special session of the Assembly to debate the issue of the Emperor's interference in what they considered was a purely Eritrean affair.[87]

Opponents of the federal arrangement used every adverse development to further discredit the system and to embarrass the new Eritrean government. Foremost in this campaign were the leaders of the Muslim League of Eritrea who resented the monopolization of power by their two worst enemies, the Unionists and the Muslim League of the Western Province. They sought to get even with them by waging a relentless attack against every aspect of the administration's policy. Ibrahim Sultan, the consummate agitator, used all his energy in exposing every conceivable weakness of the administration and in sowing the seeds of doubt against the association with Ethiopia. He and his colleagues bombarded the Eritrean chief executive and the federal government with endless petitions and accusations. They made frequent calls to the foreign consulates in Asmara and wrote appeals to various governments and international organizations asking for intervention against the Ethiopian government. They sensationalized Eritrea's political and economic difficulties to discredit the ruling authorities and to erode public confidence in the federal system. They accused the Eritrean executive body of numerous failures before it had fully constituted itself and decried the violation of the federation even before the federal structures were fully set up.

In a petition signed four days before the federation came into effect, Ibrahim Sultan and 15 of his followers objected to the presence of Ethiopian troops in Eritrea and to the assignment of Italian buildings for use by the federal government.[88] In the succeeding few weeks the Muslim League of Eritrea organized the signing of petitions in the name of various Muslim groups including the Asmara Muslims, Muslim members of the Assembly, and notables and chiefs of the tribes of the Division of Kärän and Sahel, accusing the federal government of taking over among other things, the administration of customs tariffs, post offices, telephones and telegraphs, railways, interstate highways and ports. Although the United Nations federal resolution had clearly stated that these facilities were to be placed under the jurisdiction of the federal government, the opposition continued to play with the issue.[89]

Religion was still the most potent weapon which Ibrahim Sultan and his followers employed to undermine the federal arrangement and the Eritrean government. Although the Muslim representation in the Assembly and at the higher level of the executive was about equal to that of the Christians, their overall participation in the government was rather slender. Owing largely to the relative advantages Christians had in education and experience in government employment, they tended to dominate the Eritrean civil service. Five of the six

Senior Division officers in 1953 were Christians. Opponents of the federation viewed the Eritrean administration as essentially Christian in its content and symbolism and worked hard to arouse Muslim fear and suspicion against the government. Twenty-one Muslim members of the Assembly led by Ibrahim Sultan accused the government of gross discrimination against Muslims and declared to the Eritrean Assembly at the end of 1952 that "all the Eritrean Muslims without exception are frightened and doubtful in [sic] the good faith of the Government."[90] A Congress of the Muslim League of Eritrea held in Kärän from 17 to 19 September, 1954, passed a decision that "Muslims of Eritrea should unite politically within the Muslim League to the exclusion of all other parties."[91] The American consul in Asmara mentioned in 1953 that some of the Muslim, leaders including Mohammed Omar Qadi and Ibrahim Sultan, approached him and the Italian consul to express their desire to form a separate state composed of the Western Province with close ties with the Sudan.[92]

The Eritrean government faced no lesser challenge from Christian Unionists who saw its existence as a defeat to their objective of complete union with Ethiopia. Even those who held senior posts in the administration were not averse to its demise. Tädla Bairu, the chief executive, publicly declared on the second anniversary of the federation: "the day when the population of Mareb Mellash, having examined the situation, in lieu of a federative union, should choose complete union, my joy shall be great."[93]

It is worth noting that Tädla deliberately avoided using the name Eritrea in most of his public addresses, choosing the term 'Märäb Melash' to refer to the territory he ruled.[94] A number of Tädla's lieutenants also were not favorably disposed towards the federation. The British consul in Eritrea, who toured the country in March 1954, reported that most of the Senior Division officers and the District officers, as well as officers of the Eritrean Police, were unsympathetic to the Federation.[95]

Former militants of the Unionist Party, who refused to give up their dream of unconditional union with Ethiopia, continued to mobilize significant numbers of followers, especially among the Christian community, under their old slogan of "Union or Death!" The leaders of these groups included such prominent officials in the Eritrean Executive as Embayé Habté, the Senior Division Officer of Kärän; Gäräsellasé Garza, officer of the Labor Directorate of the Eritrean government and former president of the Andenät group; Berhanä Keflämaryam, the Senior Division Officer of Säraé Division; Gäbräyohannes Täsfamaryam, Director of Public Relations; and Azmach Zäreom Keflä, Director of Economic Affairs.[96] The Emperor's visits to Eritrea were invariably used as the occasion for massive Unionist manifestations.[97]

Most of the veterans of the irredentist movement in the highland districts had nothing but contempt for the federal arrangement and the Eritrean administration. They viewed every manifestation of separate Eritrean identity with grave hostility and made repeated calls for the end of the federation. The representatives from the seven branch offices of the Unionist Party in Hamasén Division petitioned the Emperor that, "they desire nothing but total union," and they accused officials of the Eritrean Executive of sinister plans to draw Eritrea away from Ethiopia.[98]

The federation did not command the loyalty of even the members of the Eritrean Assembly. In a petition submitted to the Emperor's representative, members of the Assembly from Hamasén and Asmara complained that the United Nations provision which created a special administration for Eritrea was an affront to Eritrea's Ethiopian identity. They demanded that the territory be placed under the direct rule of the Emperor like any of the provinces in the rest of Ethiopia. They also opposed the creation of a separate flag for Eritrea and the use of the term *mängest* (government) for the Eritrean administration, a word which they said should only be used in reference to the Ethiopian government.[99]

The Eritrean government, which was internally fragmented from the beginning, was not in a position to withstand these multi-pronged pressures. It was mainly composed of individuals who generally lacked experience and were poorly suited for their jobs. Some of them saw themselves first and foremost as Muslims or Christians, Unionists or Separatists, and so forth. Divided by old traditions of antagonism as well as by the more recent bloody feud of the previous decade, Eritrea's new rulers had very little in common to hold them together but plenty of bad memories to set them against one another.

Most of those in government positions worked at cross purposes. Some attempted to draw Eritrea as far away from Ethiopia as possible while others were intent on destroying any vestige of Eritrean autonomy. The net result of these conflicting positions was to reduce the viability of the Eritrean government and to undermine the federal arrangement.

The problem of an autonomous Eritrea was further compounded by the grave weakness of its first chief executive. Tädla Bairu, the dynamic leader of the irredentist movement, proved to be a disappointment as head of an Eritrean government. Perhaps owing to his lack of faith in Eritrean autonomy, Tädla did very little to improve the image of his government. He was accused of dictatorial attitudes toward his colleagues and of gross neglect and mismanagement of the administration. Both the consular reports coming from Eritrea in the first half of the 1950s and oral informants who were closely associated with Tädla's administration widely comment on his authoritarian tendencies. Someone who knew him intimately said that Däjazmach Tädla was transformed from a "diligent leader of the Unionist Party into an arrogant, autocratic and idle Chief Executive."[100] The British consul general in Asmara wrote in March 1953, that Tädla "has become [a] vain and conceited man" during the first six months in office.[101] A similar verdict was expressed by the American consul in Asmara, who reported in July 1954:

> The Eritrean government Administration under the Chief Executive has from the first been quite obviously weak and incompetent. The Chief Executive himself...has developed into a vain and corrupt leader who has largely neglected his duties for enjoyment of the material comforts now in his grasp.... He has shown himself to be vindictive and petty in mind and action....[and] he has been a very real disappointment to all in his high position and has failed miserably to measure up to his own possibilities, for there is no doubt as to his admitted ability and intelligence.[102]

Tädla was particularly vindictive toward his former personal rivals. He harassed a number of them and had them arrested on various pretexts. It was widely believed that the attempt on the life of Wäldäab Wäldämaryam, Tädla's archenemy, on 13 January, 1953 (the seventh attempt since 1947), was ordered by Tädla.[103] The latter had annulled the election of Wäldäab to the Eritrean Assembly in a by-election in April 1953 on the ground that some of the votes were secured through fraudulent means.[104] The chief executive was said repeatedly to have ignored the request of the Emperor's representative for a post for Wäldäab in the Eritrean administration.[105] Wäldäab was finally hounded out of Eritrea in the fall of 1953.[106]

At the end of October 1953 the chief executive arrested Däjazmach Abreha, former leader of the Liberal Progressive Party and the son of Ras Täsämma Asbärom. Abreha and a number of his relatives, including his brothers, were charged with having conspired to assassinate Tädla. It was widely rumored at the time that the chief executive had fabricated the attempt on his life in order to put his main rivals out of commission. Däjazmach Abreha had run against Tädla over a year before for the office of chief executive. Although Abreha was considered one of the most able people in the territory, Tedla refused to offer him a post in his government. This, however, did not prevent Abreha from establishing close links with the Ethiopian authorities, including the Emperor's representative in Eritrea.[107] Tädla appears to have feared that Abreha's flirtation with Ethiopian officials might enhance his chances of winning the next contest for chief executive. He was said to have "cooked" the assassination plot to remove this possible threat.[108] Although the case was eventually dismissed, Tädla was able to reduce the political influence of the Täsämma family by removing them from their positions as chiefs and district officers.[109]

To further weaken his opponents, Tädla passed The Eritrean Public Security Proclamation No. 1 of 1955 by which power was given to the chief executive to order the detention of any person at any place for a period of up to six months if "the public safety or the maintenance of public order so requires."[110] This move further fueled the conflict between the chief executive and the Eritrean Assembly, the majority of whose members were united in condemning Tädla's shabby treatment of the Eritrean Legislature. A statement to the press by a group in the Assembly, which claimed to represent the Majority opinion in the Assembly, said,

> ...the public opinion of Eritrea knows how to consider, value and judge the deeds of the Administration of the Government of Dejazmach Tedla Bairu based on nepotism, personal and family interests...[He] keeps in force such order to use them against all those who would oppose his plans for the increment of personal and family interests, and also in the consolidation of his dictatorial power also with the future in view, particularly, of the next election.[111]

Dissatisfaction with Tädla's irregular activities were building up in several quarters, and his numerous foes were only too eager to cooperate against him. Unionists felt that he had abandoned them after taking office.[112] Members of the Muslim League of Eritrea not only knew him as the old enemy who had led the Unionist struggle against them but also harbored fresh resentment against him for favoring their archrivals, the members of the Muslim League of the Western Province. Orthodox Christians complained that too many positions were given to Protestants. The elite group from Särae and Akälä Guzai felt excluded from power by the chief executive, who, they said, favored his fellow men from Hamasén.[113]

Although harboring different grievances and aspirations, several groups coalesced to overthrow Tädla. Most ironical was a pact in the Assembly between Unionists and members of the Muslim League of Eritrea to oust the Chief Executive. The ardent Unionist leader Qés (Priest) Demét'ros Gäbrämaryam and the staunch separatist Ibrahim Sultan joined forces against Tädla. They planned to undermine his position by first removing his loyal supporter, Sheik Ali Mohammed Mussa Radai, the president of the Assembly.

Tädla attempted to forestall the action by suspending the Assembly for 20 days, an action which the Constitution permitted only in the event of an extreme disturbance. When the members returned to their seats after 20 days, Tädla again suspended the Assembly for another 20 days.

Members of the Assembly petitioned the Emperor to intervene directly to reverse Tädla's arbitrary measure.[114] Ten representatives were sent to Addis

Ababa to make the appeal. Included in the delegation were Ibrahim Sultan and Idris Mohammed Adum of the Muslim League of Eritrea. The Emperor ruled that the suspension be lifted. On reconvening, the Assembly voted Ali Radai out of the presidency and elected Idris Mohammed Adum. Tädla resigned three months later.[115]

Tädla's resignation helped little to build confidence in the government and to stabilize the political situation in Eritrea. A number of influential men from among the Unionists aspired to succeed him.[116] They were distressed when the office passed to Däjazmach (later Bitwädäd) Asfeha Wäldämikaél.[117]

Differences among the major political groups also revived once the immediate task of removing Tädla was achieved. The Unionists and the Muslim League of the Western Province banded together in the Assembly once again against the Muslim League of Eritrea. Idris Mohammed Adum (later one of the founders and the first chairman of the Eritrean Liberation Front) was removed from the presidency of the Assembly and replaced by one of his bitter rivals, Hamid Faraj of the Muslim League of the Western Province.

In subsequent elections most of the members of the Muslim League of Eritrea lost their seats in the Assembly to rivals of the Muslim League of the Western Province. Their leaders, including Ibrahim Sultan and Mohammed Adum, complained of severe restriction and harassment by their rivals.[118] They fled to Egypt at the beginning of 1959 and started to rally other disgruntled elements.

The dismal performance of the Eritrean government and the marked political infighting in the territory opened enormous opportunities for the Ethiopian government to manipulate Eritrean politics. Having lost faith in their own officials in the executive and legislative bodies, many Eritreans turned towards the Emperor for justice and arbitration. The Emperor's representative in Eritrea used the divisions among Eritrea's political groups to advance his own position from a mere titular figure to a formidable powerbroker. Several provisions of the Constitution which were supposed to guarantee Eritrea's autonomy were gradually neglected, and the laws and institutions of the Ethiopian government were introduced at ease.

The Eritrean Assembly, whose Unionist composition had substantially increased in the 1956 election,[119] was easily manipulated into passing laws which undermined the territory's internal autonomy. A British diplomat who visited Eritrea in the summer of 1957 returned with the impression that, "the Federal Government could get a majority at any time to dissolve the Federation."[120]

In 1958, the Eritrean Assembly passed The Eritrean Flag, Seal and Arms (Amendment) Act, which replaced the Eritrean Flag with that of Ethiopia and changed the name of the Eritrean government to the Eritrean Administration, and Chief Executive to Chief Administrator. It was significant that the vote passed unanimously in the presence of 63 of the 68 members, an unprecedented attendance in the history of the Assembly.[121] The enthusiasm with which the Assembly passed the Act was an indication of how little loyalty Eritrean autonomy commanded in the Assembly. According to the acting clerk of the Assembly, "pandemonium broke loose as the members stood, cheered, shouted, clapped and embraced one another" after voting for the motion.[122]

The next year the Assembly approved, with only one dissenting vote, the extension of the Ethiopian Penal Code to Eritrea. After this it only remained formally to declare the end of the federal experiment.[123]

As things stood at the beginning of the 1960s, there existed no viable force in support of the federation. The few opponents of annexation were either effectively silenced or driven into exile. The agitation for Eritrean independence by these émigrés had had, as yet, very little impact inside Eritrea. The great majority of the population was either unsympathetic or entirely indifferent to Eritrean autonomy.

The confidence of the Ethiopian government in the stability of the Eritrean situation could be seen from the prolonged absence of the Emperor's representative from Eritrea. He was said to have been absent from Eritrea no less than 75 percent of the time from 1956 to 1959. The Ethiopian government did not even bother to fill the position of the vice-representative, which it left vacant when Däjazmach Asfeha left it to take the office of the chief executive in 1955. Other important officials of the Federal government in Asmara were transferred to Addis Ababa without being replaced.[124]

To be sure, the Ethiopian government had few supporters in Eritrea at this time. The glorification of Ethiopia and the high hopes of the 1940s had been replaced by frustration at the failure of the regime to meet expectations and resentment against what was generally termed as "Amhara domination." Most of the former partisans of the Ethiopian government had become political bystanders. However, many seem to have been of the opinion that one bad government was preferable to two. This, certainly, was the preference of the business class in particular, which was subjected to double taxation and to two forms of restrictive regulations.

Notes

[1] The Fourth Session of the General Assembly of the United Nations which opened in September 1949 was able to arrive at a compromise formula with regard to Libya and Italian Somaliland. This was made possible by the agreement reached between the two most important blocks in the United Nations, the Arab and Islamic countries on the one hand which championed the cause of an independent and united Libya, and the Latin countries on the other hand, which ardently advocated Italian interests. The compromise solution called for an independent Libya and an Italian trusteeship over Somaliland.

[2] Those who appeared before the hearings of the First Committee of the General Assembly were the Unionist Party represented by Tädla Bairu, the Independence Bloc represented by Ibrahim Sultan, the Independent Muslim League represented by Mohammed Omar Qadi, and the representative of C.R.I.E.

[3] Resolution 289 A (IV), in United Nations, Official Records of the Fourth Session of the General Assembly: Plenary Meetings, 302.

[4] Trevaskis, *Eritrea*, 99. The Ethiopian Liaison Officer also observed, "Since members of the Commission are partisans to certain views, all their questions were designed to support their respective biases rather than to try to understand the issue," Nägga to Emperor, "Political Report Regarding the Work of the United Nations Commission," [Amharic] Asmara, 22 May 1950, in Liaison Office Papers. Commenting on the constant and acrimonious wrangling which characterized the work of the Commission, the American Consul in Eritrea remarked: "It is believed that few Commissions have sunk to lower levels of mutual obstruction, prejudice, and bad manners as did this," American Consulate (Asmara), "A Brief Review of the Eritrean Political Situation," 1950, in State, Suitland, Box 1, 310. For similar comments on the work of the Commission, see also, *The London Times*, 14 July 1950; and Amare Tekle, "The Creation of the Ethio-Eritrean Federation: A Case Study in Post-War International Relations (1945-1950)," Ph.D. dissertation, University of Denver, 1964, 289.

[5] United Nations, *Official Records of the General Assembly*, Fourth Session, First Committee, 246.

[6] The Burmese delegate made this admission to Brigadier Frank Stafford, the British Liaison Officer to the United Nations Commission. See, United States, *Foreign Relations*, 1950, Vol. V, p. 1648.

[7] United Nations, *Report of the United Nations Commission for Eritrea, General Assembly Official Records*: Fifth Session, Supplement No. 8 (A/1285), New York, 1950 [hereafter U.N., A/1285], pp. 30-36.

[8] Ibid., 20.

[9] Ibid., 23.

[10] Ibid.

[11] Ibid.

[12] Ibid.

[13] Ibid. 26. Judge Qvale, the head of the Norwegian delegation told the First Secretary of the U.S. Embassy in Cairo that many of the Eritrean Muslims were rallied

to independence by the Italian Committee, and that he had the impression that their leaders were paid by the Italians: State, Suitland, Box 1, 312.1, U.S. Embassy in Cairo to Department of State, 15 April, 1950.

[14] U.N., A/1285, 27.

[15] Cited in Spencer, *Ethiopia at Bay,* p. 231.

[16] Memorandum by the Assistant Chief of the Division of African Affairs, 27 May 1949, in State, 865.014/5-2749.

[17] Ambassador Dunn to Secretary of State, 29 June 1949, in State, 865.014/6-2949.

[18] Both the United States and Great Britain had come to an agreement on the importance of breaking up the Latin American bloc in order to get the federal formula accepted in the General Assembly: Memorandum of Unites States - United Kingdom Discussions, London, 9 September, 1950.

[19] The Secretary of State to Diplomatic Offices in the American Republics, Washington, 11 July 1050, in United States, *Foreign Relations*, Vol. V, 1950, 1663.

[20] In a discussion with the U.S. Assistant Secretary of State, G. Brusasca, Under Secretary of State for Foreign Affairs of Italy and L. Vitetti, Minister in the Ministry of Foreign Affairs, stated that, "Italy no longer stood for the independence of Eritrea," and was prepared to agree to a settlement based on a federation between Ethiopia and Eritrea, provided that the position of Italians in Eritrea was safeguarded. They also demanded that the final implementation of the federation be delayed in order to allow them time to prepare Italian public opinion: Memorandum of Conversation by the Assistant Secretary of State for European Affairs, 18 July 1950, in ibid., 1658.

[21] See, *Quotidiano Eritreo*, No. 2687, 4 April 1950.

[22] Concerning the condition of the Independence Bloc at the beginning of 1950 Trevaskis noted:

> Behind the brave façade of the Independence Bloc, which was by this time claiming to be a federation of about a dozen parties and associations, there was now nothing but the old Pro-Italy Party and a rump of the Muslim League representing the Muslims of Asmara and Massawa,the Saho, Samhar, and Danakil, and the few Tigray who owed a personal loyalty to Ibrahim Sultan: *Trevaskis,* Eritrea, 98.

[23] Nägga to Emperor, 5 May 1950, 11 May 1950, 19 July 1950, and Emperor to Nägga, 10 May 1950. The representatives of Mai S'ä'ada in Adi Quala to the Unionist Party complaining against being excluded from the visit, 23 May 1950, and the inhabitants of Ad Zämat in Kärän to the Liaison Officer, 13 May 1950, Liaison Office Papers.

[24] Lloyd Ellingson, "Eritrea: Separatism and Irredentism, 1941-1985," Ph.D Dissertation, Michigan State University, 1986, 78.

[25] On the proposals of Colonel Nägga, the Ethiopian government demanded early in 1948 that all Italian truckers should employ Eritrean assistants if they want to enter

Ethiopia. Over 1000 trucks operated between Eritrea and Ethiopia. Specially affected by this regulation was the powerful Italian corporation, Imperial Motor Transport. C.R.I.E. led a campaign against this plan but the Ethiopian government refused to reconsider: Liaison Office Papers, Nägga to Emperor, 17 January 1948. Partly as a result of this policy, Eritreans were able to replace many of the Italian drivers in a few years time.

[26] The "Societa Anonima Commerciale Per L'Economi Eritrea" founded on 22 May 1946 was composed of twelve Christian and twelve Muslim businessmen. Some of its members were in the forefront of the Unionist movement: Liaison Office Papers, Däjazmach Araya Wassé to Colonel Nägga, 9 January 1947.

[27] Seyum Mä'asho, the Secretary General of the Liberal Unionist Party, wrote to the Emperor in March 1950 that they had recruited 67,600 members, of which 19,500 were Muslims from the Saho group: Seyum Mä'asho to Emperor Haile Selassie, 23 March 1950, in Liaison Office Papers.

[28] "The Emperor Speech on the Occasion of the Seventeenth Year of His Coronation," Addis Ababa, 2 November 1947. Some fifty Eritreans from the Massawa area worked in these ships: Nägga to Emperor, 3 January 1948.

[29] George Merrill to Secretary of State, Addis Ababa, 24 September 1948, State, 865.014/9-2448.

[30] U.N., A/1285, 23.

[31] *Feré Känafer*, Part I (Addis Ababa: Berhanena Salam, 1944 E.C.), 388-90.

[32] United Nations Document, A/C. 1/SR 286, 56; for a detailed account of the energetic activities of the Ethiopian delegation at the United Nations, see Zewde Retta, *Yä Eretra Guday* (1941-1963), Addis Ababa, 1999.

[33] See, United Nations, Official Records of the General Assembly, Fifth Session, 316th meeting, 537.

[34] United Nations, *Resolution 390* (V).

[35] Ibid.

[36] Ibid.

[37] Statement made on his arrival in Eritrea on 9 February 1951: United Nations Document A/1959, 16.

[38] See above, 185-187

[39] Unionist Party telegram to the Secretary General of the United Nations, 22 October 1949, in FO 371/73788.

[40] Spencer, *Ethiopia at Bay*, 240.

[41] Ibid., 233-34.

[42] Quoted in David A. Talbot, *Haile Selassie I: Silver Jubilee*, (W.P. Van Stockum & Zoon Publishers, The Hague - Rotterdam, 1955), 382. Aklilu Habtewold, the Foreign Minister, said that "the formula of federation is not at all based on the real desire of the two peoples." See Aklilu's 24 May 1951 interview in *La Settimana,* Rome, 9 June 1951.

[43] A reconciliation meeting was held in Asmara on 31 December 1950 in which all the Eritrean parties promised to forget past animosities, to respect the U.N. resolution and to cooperate with the U.N. Commissioner in its implementations. See, Angelo Del Boca, *Gli Italiani in Africa Orientale, Nostalgia delle Colonie* (Roma-Bari: Laterza, 1984), 9; and Liaison Office Papers, Nägga to Emperor,31 December, 1951. Subsequent developments showed, however, that this meeting had very little impact on the way the various parties perceived one another.

[44] United Nations, Final Report of the United Nations Commissioner in Eritrea, General Assembly Official Records: Seventh Session, Supplement No. 15 (A/2188) [hereafter U.N., A/2188], 36.

[45] Ibid. p. 16; State, Suitland, Box 1, 312.1, U.S. Consul in Eritrea to Secretary of State, 23 August 1951. In a meeting of the Central Committee of the Unionist Party on 18 July 1951, the majority of the members agreed that the head of the Executive should be elected by the Assembly and approved by the Emperor, and that there should be Imperial authority over the Eritrean Executive. Some, including Däjazmach Araya Wassé and Azmach Zäreom Keflä wanted the Emperor to appoint the head of the Executive: "Minutes of the Meeting of the Central Committee of the Mahbär Feqri Hagär" [Tegreñña], 18 July 1951, Liaison Office Papers.

[46] Ibid. 15.

[47] Interview: Bitwädäd Asfeha Wäldä-Mikaél, Addis Ababa, 1983. Bitwädäd Asfeha was an active Unionist and was elected Chief Executive in 1956.

[48] Trevaskis, *Eritrea*, 117. In an earlier memorandum, the Muslim League of the Western Province had proposed the establishment of two independent administrations — for Muslims and Christians, each of which should have their own legislative assembly and executive council. See, United Nations Document A/AC.44/R.24.

[49] The difference on the question of official languages was a delicate issue even in the Unionist Party. In the meetings of its Central Committee, Muslim members insisted that Arabic be adopted as an official language. The Party was able to avoid a serious split by proposing that the issue be decided in an elected Assembly: "Minutes of the Central Committee of the Mahbär Feqri Hagär" [Tegreñña], 18 July, 5-6 October, 8 October, 13 October, 29 October, 5-6 November, 21 November, and 16 December 1951, Liaison Office Papers. The debate on the language issue continued to divide the newly elected Eritrean Assembly. A report of the Ethiopian Liaison Officer mentions that Muslim members of the Assembly were threatening to disavow the federal arrangement altogether if their demand to make Arabic an official language failed. The Christians reportedly responded that Federation was imposed on them and that they would only be happy to get rid of it and to return to their old objective of total integration with Ethiopia: "The Ethiopian Liaison Officer's Notebook," 15 June 1952, Liaison Office Papers.

[50] U.N., A/2188, 17.

[51] Ibid.

[52] Ibid

[53] General Assembly Resolution 390 (V).

[54] Spencer, *Ethiopia at Bay*, p. 233. Matienzo himself said he was aware that "a state with stable institutions and traditions was to be associated with a unit as yet

unformed:" United Nations, *Progress Report of the United Nations Commissioner in Eritrea During the Year 1951*, 16 November 1951, (A/1959) [hereafter U.N., A/1959].

[55] An earlier proposal submitted by the Burmese delegation, which the Ethiopians opposed strongly, called for the establishment of a separate federal government, distinct from the Ethiopian and Eritrean governments.

[56] Aklilu presented these demands to the Commissioner during their meeting in Asmara on July 1951: U.N., A/1959, p. 39. The initial position of the Ethiopian negotiators was for the creation of a strong Executive responsible to and appointed by the Emperor: American Embassy in Addis Ababa to Department of State, 18 October 1951, in State, 775.00/10-1851.

[57] U.N., A/1959, 123.

[58] The Panel was appointed by the Secretary-General of the United Nations, and met in Geneva from November 1951 to February 1952, to discuss the Constitution: Ibid., 19-28.

[59] Resolution 390 (V), Paragraph 11.

[60] Trevaskis, *Eritrea*, p. 118.

[61] Ibid.

[62] The regional distribution of the seats was: Akälä Guzai (12), Säraé (12), Hamasén (7), Red Sea (5), Western Province (23), Asmara (7), and Massawa (2).

[63] See, United Nations, *Report of the Government of the United Kingdom of Great Britain and Northern Ireland to the General Assembly Concerning the Administration of Eritrea (for the period December 1950 to September 1952)*, 8 November 1952, (A/2233) [hereafter U.N., A/2233], 29.

[64] U.S. Consul in Asmara to Department of State, 28 March 1953, State, 320.1-350.

[65] In an apparent reference to Wäldä'ab Wäldämaryam, a British Administration report to the United Nations observed that the election exposed "the hollowness of the claims of the many so-called political partics ... At least one self-styled leader was ignominiously defeated at the polls:" U.N., A/2233, 29.

[66] "Ethiopian Liaison Officer's Notebook" [Amharic], Asmara, 15 June 1952.

[67] There were four spoiled papers: U.N., A/2188, p. 37.

[68] Ibid.

[69] Ibid., 47.

[70] General Duncan C. Cumming, the last British Administrator in Eritrea, wrote: "No Eritrean leader had advocated federation... the federal conception was so foreign to them that none of the vernacular languages of the country contained a word which accurately conveyed its meaning," D.C. Cumming, "The Disposal of Eritrea," *The Middle East Journal*, Vol. VII, 1953, 18.

[71] Emperor to Nägga, 9 January 1951, Liaison Office Papers.

[72] Ambassador Busk to Foreign Office, 24 June 1953, FO 371/102635.

[73] A contemporary diplomat defined Matienzo's arrangement as "a Bolivian's idea of a Swiss federation superimposed on an African absolute monarchy:" quoted in Giorgulli, "Origini E Vicende Della Federazione," 134.

[74] S. Pankhurst, *Eritrea on the Eve: The Past and Future of Italy's "first-born" Colony, Ethiopia's Ancient Sea Province* (Essex: New Times and Ethiopia News Books, 1952), 13. These buildings included customs offices, warehouses, and dwellings of personnel.

[75] Ibid., pp. 13-23. See also Spencer, *Ethiopia at Bay*, 247. Spencer claims that he himself witnessed much of the destruction done by the British, especially in the port area and in Gura.

[76] Ibid.

[77] United Kingdom, House of Commons, *Sessional Papers* (1952-3), Vol. 30, Cmd. 8690.

[78] State, 775a.21/7-2753, American Consulate in Asmara, 27 July 1953.

[79] FO 371/- 96761, 20 October 1952.

[80] A Government report mentions that as a result of this manipulation in the currency, the price of a quintal of t'éf (the staple crop in Asmara and the highlands) had gone up from about Eth.$ 20.00 to Eth.$ 33: "A Report of the Activities of the Federal Offices for 1947 E.C.," in Federation 1952-1962 [Amharic]. Although the cost of grain subsequently declined as a result of the free flow of trade with Ethiopia, the price of most imported items remained very high: State, 775a. 21/4-3053, American Consul in Asmara to Department of State, 30 April 1953.

[81] Unionists in Massawa were telling the unemployed in the fall of 1947 that if they were united with Ethiopia "all the people in Massawa will get job opportunities ... we will no longer be subjected to humiliating alien control. We do not have to take orders from foreigners and we will be able to manage our own affairs like the white-men:" The Massawa Unionist Branch Office, "British Politics in Massawa" [Tegreñña], September 1947, Liaison Office Papers.

[82] A petition to Sheik Ali Redai, President of the Eritrean Assembly, from "the 1450 Office of Unemployed Natives," 23 September 1952, Federation 1952-1962.

[83] "The Revolutionary Party," to the Honorable 68, 18 October 1952, in ibid. Similar sentiments were expressed during a large demonstration in Asmara held on the second month of the formation of the Eritrean administration. The demonstrators protested against the rising cost of living and lower wages and expressed grave doubts about the competence of the members of the Legislative and Executive branches of the Eritrean administration: "Wäya'ati Hezbi Sälamawi Sälfi Asmara" [Tegreñña], 26 October 1952.

[84] American Consul to Department of State, 12 March 1954, State, 775.11/3-1254.

[85] The Emperor reminded the Eritrean government on this occasion that "the Administration has to be proportioned. If the shoes are not of the size of the foot which wears them, it is impossible to walk:" *Quotidiano Eritreo*, 10 February 1954. See also State, 875a. 10/8-754, American Consul to Department of State, 7 August 1954.

[86] State, 775.11/6-2862, American Consul to Department of State, 29 June 1962.

87 FO 371/113515, British Embassy in Ethiopia to the Foreign Office, 8 February 1955.

88 Ibrahim Sultan and fifteen other petitioners, to the Chief Administrator of Eritrea, Eritrean Representative Assembly, and the United Nations Commissioner in Eritrea, Asmara, 7 September 1952, in Federation: 1952-1962.

89 Many of the petitions are included in ibid: see for instance, Notables of the Muslim Population of Asmara, to the Eritrean Representative Assembly, 28 September 1952; Notables, Chiefs, Sheiks etc., of all tribes of the Division of Kärän and Sahel, to the Chief Executive, 18 November 1952; Muslim Members of the Eritrean Assembly, to the President of the Eritrean Assembly, 23 December 1952. See also FO 371/108196 for a series of petitions against the Federal Government and the Eritrean Executive submitted by Ibrahim Sultan in 1954 in the name of the Muslim community.

90 Muslim Members of the Eritrean Assembly to the President, 23 December 1952, in Federation, 1952-62.

91 FO 371/108197, British Consulate in Asmara to Foreign Office, 30 September 1954.

92 State, 775a.14/7-2953.

93 "Address by the Chief Executive of Eritrea on September 11, 1954," in State, 775a.00/9-1754. An American intelligence source reported that Tädla was openly calling for complete union with Ethiopia: Office of Intelligence Report, "The Ethiopia - Eritrea Federation: A Progress Report," no. 7130, 8 February 1956.

94 The name "Eritrea," which was coined by the Italians in 1890, was resented by some of the Christian highlanders who referred to it as the "name of our enslavement." In a petition to Brigadier Longrigg in 1943, a group of notables from Hamasén and Asmara said that they were eagerly waiting for the day when the word "Eritrea" would be obliterated from their country: "Petition to His Excellency Brigadier Stephen Longrigg, Chief Administrator" [Tegreñña], Liaison Office Papers.

95 FO 371/108196, J.H. Wardle-Smith to the British Embassy in Addis Ababa, Asmara, 1 April 1954.

96 Ibid., British Consul in Asmara to British Embassy in Addis Ababa, 22 February 1954.

97 State, 775.11/3-1254, U.S. Consul in Asmara to Department of State, 12 March 1954.

98 The Hamasén Hagär Feqer Committee to His Imperial Majesty, Asmara, 19 February 1958, in Federation, 1952-62.

99 Members of the Eritrean Assembly from Hamasén and Asmara to His Excellency Bitwädäd Andargachäw Mässay, n.d., in ibid.

100 Interview: Bitwädäd Asfeha

101 FO 371/102634, J.H. Wardle-Smith to British Embassy in Addis Ababa, 7 March 1953.

102 State, 775.54/7-1454, Edward W. Clark to Department of State, 14 July 1954. A 1956 report of the U.S. Office of Intelligence Research attributed many of the problems

concerning the federation to "the marked tendency of Tedla to favor arbitrary and autocratic government in disregard of constitutional procedures and guarantees." The report added that Tädla earned the antagonism and scorn of his former followers also through excessive drinking and fondness for women, especially white women. It is said that this weakness was exploited by the local Italians to gain special favors and concessions: O.I.R., *The Ethiopia-Eritrea Federation: A Progress Report*, no. 7130, 8 February 1956. In his annual report to the Foreign Office, the British Ambassador to Ethiopia also dwelt on Tädla's increasingly dictatorial attitude toward his colleagues in the government: FO 371/108194, British Embassy in Addis Ababa to Foreign Office, 4 February 1954. Edward Ullendorff, who knew Tädla in the mid-1940s, characterizes him as the most gifted among that generation of Eritreans and regrets that his achievement was "marred by ambition and an autocratic temperament:" Ullendorff, *The Two Zions*, 181.

[103] There are also reports which indicate that this last attempt on Wäldäab's life may have been engineered by Gäräsellasé Garza, the leader of the Andenät youth movement and head of the Labor Office of the Eritrean government, who was said to have resented Wäldäab's attempt to organize a labor movement. See for instance, State, 775a.00/1-1653, American Consul in Asmara to the Department of State, 16 January 1953.

[104] Il *Quotidiano Eritreo*, 23 April 1953.

[105] Interview: Asfeha.

[106] The American Consul in Asmara described Wäldäab's condition in June 1953 as "utterly discouraged and fearful for his life:" State, 775.00/6-253, American Consul in Asmara to Department of State, 2 June 1953.

[107] The Princess Tänañä-Wärq, the Emperor's eldest daughter and the wife of the Emperor's Representative in Eritrea, later became the godmother to Abreha's grandchild.

[108] Eritrea Governorate General, "Political Conditions in Eritrea Since 1941" [Amharic], (a 93 page study made by order of Ras Asratä Kassa, the Governor General of Eritrea), Asmara, n.d., 58; see also Zewde Gebre Sellassie, *Eritrea and Ethiopia in the Context of the Red Sea and Africa* (Washington D.C: Woodrow Wilson International Center for Scholars, 1976), 92; and State, Consulates Despatch No. 53 of 10/14/53, 26 October 1953. Interview: Asfeha. Däjazmach Tädla is said to have used a certain Mikaél Wäläla to talk Iyasu Täsämma, Abreha's younger brother, into a plot to assassinate the Chief Executive: Supreme Court of Eritrea, Court of Appeal (Criminal) Case No. 51/54, The Law V. Iassu Tesema.

[109] State, 775.11/2-454, Clark to Department of State, 4 February, 1954.

[110] *The Eritrean Gazette*, Vol. XVII, No. 8 (Asmara), 4 July 1955.

[111] "Statement to the Press by the Majority Group of the Members of the Eritrean Assembly," Asmara, 7 July 1955, in Eritrea Provincial Administration Archive [hereafter E.P.A.], File 34.

[112] The allegation that Tädla alienated his former Unionist followers was still repeated in the early 1980s. A group of former Unionists whom I talked to in the town of Kärän in 1982 said, "Tädla relied on us to die for Union with Ethiopia, but threw us out after victory and surrounded himself with the Rabitta [Muslim League] members."

¹¹³ Interview: Däjazmach Embayé Habté (Kärän, 1982). See also State, 611.75/1-1953, American Consul to Department of State, 20 July 1953, for grievances of the Orthodox Christians against Protestants.

¹¹⁴ Under the Eritrean Constitution, although the Assembly could elect the Chief Executive from among its members, it could not bring him down merely through a vote of confidence. Removal was only possible through impeachment which required a two-third majority.

¹¹⁵ He was appointed a member of the Ethiopian Senate first, and later Ambassador to Sweden whence he defected into the camp of the secessionist force in 1967.

¹¹⁶ Aspirants to the Office of the Chief Executive included Fitawrari Harägot Abbai(Secretary of Economic Affairs), Ato Fessehas'ion Haylé (Acting Chief Executive), Grazmach Täsfayohannes Bärhé (Director of Social Affairs), Däjazmach Abreha Täsämma, Däjazmach Araya Wassé, and Ras Bäyänä Barakhi (President of the Unionist Party).

¹¹⁷ Asfeha Wäldämikaél, a former interpreter for the Governor General of the Italian East African Empire, and later a noted Unionist, was the Emperor's Vice-Representative in Eritrea. He entered the contest for the office of the Chief Executive after a delegation of Assemblymen petitioned the Emperor by telegram for permission for him to run for election. He was elected on August 8, 1955, by a vote of 48 against 17: see State, 775a.2/8-1255, American Consul to Department of State, 12 August 1955. Asfeha said that his election was pushed forward by Qés Demét'ros Gäbrämaryam, the powerful Unionist in the Assembly and Sheik Ali Rädai, the former head of the Muslim League of the Western Province, and still the most influential figure among the Tegré in the western lowland. Asfeha rewarded Ali Rädai with a cabinet position. On the other hand, Fitawurari Harägot Abbai, whose relation with the Emperor's representative had visibly soured after he lost the election to Asfeha, was removed from his cabinet position: interview, Bitwädäd Asfeha Wäldämikaél (Addis Ababa, June 1983).

¹¹⁸ E.P.A. File U2/168, Vol.1, Ibrahim Sultan to Ras Andargachäw Mässay and Däjazmach Asfeha Wäldämikaél. Idris Mohammed Adum was said to have been particularly incensed when the Ethiopian government took away the Mercedes car he received while he was President of the Assembly: See Eritrea Governorate General, "Political Conditions in Eritrea Since 1941," 59, and E.P.A. File U1/251, for information on the Mercedes car granted to Idris Mohammed Adum on 14 May 1956.

¹¹⁹ 40 of the 68 seats were said to have been occupied by known Unionists: FO 371/118744, British Consul in Asmara to the Foreign Office, 12 September 1956. The Chief Executive, Asfeha Wäldämikaél, campaigned vigorously during the election to turn a Unionist majority: see State, 775a.00/8-1056, American Consul to Department of State, 10 August 1956. Asfeha claims that he was able to increase the number of his supporters among the Tegré in the western lowland by co-opting new and aspiring men into the local administrative structure. He was able to do this by distributing the offices formerly held by single families. For instance, he created eight "meseläné" (sub-district) positions among the Marya tribe which was formerly held by a single chief: interview, Bitwädäd Asfeha (Addis Ababa, June 1983).

¹²⁰ FO 371/125359, Report of the Second Secretary in the British Embassy to the Foreign Office, Addis Ababa, 6 June 1957.

[121] The Assembly was rather notorious for its poor attendance. It had to postpone meetings repeatedly for lack of quorum. The Assembly which was supposed to debate on a draft budget was adjourned over ten times from July 27 to September 13, 1954, due to the absence of a quorum. The American Consul in Asmara reported in 1957 that it was "a common practice for the clerks of the Assembly to make the rounds of the coffee houses and bars in the vicinity of the Assembly building prior to each session in an effort to round-up sufficient members to make a quorum:" State, 775a.2/12-557, American Consul in Asmara to Department of State, 5 December 1957.

[122] State, 775a. 04/1-459, American Consul to the Department of State, 24 December 1958.

[123] John H. Spencer, the American advisor to the Ethiopian government, claims that the Eritrean Assembly had already expressed the desire to vote for total union in 1955 and 1957, which he said he opposed for fear of arousing the hostility of some foreign powers: Spencer, *Ethiopia at Bay*, 303-305.

[124] State, 775a.00/6-2959, American Consul to Department of State, 29 June 1959.

CHAPTER FIVE

THE BEGINNING OF ARMED OPPOSITION

The transformation of the incoherent opposition in Eritrea into organized dissidence owed a great deal to the work of Eritrean émigrés that lived in the Sudan, Egypt, Somalia, and the Middle East. Some 20,000 of these, predominantly Muslims, lived in the Middle East by the end of the 1950s.[1] Although a majority had moved out of Eritrea in search of jobs, they also included a small but highly vocal group of political activists consisting of student elements and former leaders of the Eritrean independence movement, who made efforts to form a political base among the emigrant population.[2] Chief among the exiled leaders was Wäldäab Wäldämaryam, who carried out vigorous agitation against the Ethiopian government through Radio Cairo starting from 1956 and made efforts to form an organization in exile with a view to carrying out underground political activity inside Eritrea.

The first successful attempt at creating an organized force among expatriate Eritreans was made in 1958 when a group of exiles living in Egypt and the Sudan met at Port Sudan and formed the Eritrean Liberation Movement (ELM). The founders were said to have been "all Muslims who had spent the better part of their lives in the Sudan."[3] This organization later admitted a few Christians including Wäldäab Wäldämaryam and gradually introduced itself into Eritrea where it was known as Haräka Tahrir in the lowlands and the Mahbär Shäwatä[4] in the Tegreñña-speaking highlands.

Apparently inspired by the practices of the Sudanese Communist Party, the Eritrean Liberation Movement organized its members in cells of seven people, and built a network of such cells in the western lowlands and in some of the highland towns.[5] The organization was said to have had a hand in the first successful labor strike in Asmara in March 1958 and in subsequent student demonstrations.[6] Much of the organization's effort was geared towards mobilizing the anti-Unionist elements and infiltrating the police and security forces with a view to overthrowing the Ethiopian administration in Eritrea.[7]

Despite its initial success in making its presence felt among the exiled community and to some extent also in Eritrea, the ELM's effort to broaden its support was mostly met with suspicion and resentment. Its leadership came largely from the Kärän and Sahel region, a fact which aroused intense hostility, especially from the dominant Beni Amer group in the western lowland. There was no organizational link between the cells of the Mahbär Shäwaté which operated among the Christian community and the Haräka in the Muslim lowlands.[8]

The old bickering among the various political factions was revived in exile, and several of the old guards in the pro-independence movement of the 1940s, including Ibrahim Sultan and Idris Mohammed Adum, rejected the ELM outright and hastened to outflank their rivals in the summer of 1960 by forming their own organization, which they called the Eritrean Liberation Front (ELF).

Soon after founding the ELF in Cairo, Idris Mohammed Adum and his colleagues began to plan an armed insurrection in Eritrea. They calculated that thereby the attention of the United Nations could be drawn more urgently and sympathetic Arab leaders could be persuaded to take the Eritrean issue more seriously.[9]

By the middle of 1961 the ELF had made preliminary preparations to start an armed insurrection inside Eritrea. Using ex-Eritrean soldiers who had served in the Sudanese army as intermediaries, Idris Mohammed Adum and his colleagues made contact with Hamed Idris Awaté, a known bandit leader in the Barka and Gash areas in the western lowlands.[10]

Awaté was promised support and urged to convert his shifta followers into fighters of the ELF. Subsequently about a dozen ex-Eritrean non-commissioned officers in the Sudanese Army joined Awaté's band.[11] This change from a traditional shifta band into an armed wing of a liberation front did not bring an immediate change in the character of Awaté's followers.

There was little control over these insurgents from the E.L.F. political leadership, which for the most part stayed out of the field. The rebel force knew no other authority except Awaté's. When he died in the summer of 1962, his death was kept secret for quite a while for fear that the army might disintegrate if it knew the truth. The rank and file knew Awaté's successors as his deputies until 1965.[12] Meanwhile the armed band continued to raid and pillage as in the old days, especially targeting settled cultivators.[13]

Operating within a social milieu where endemic banditry was a common feature, the forces of the ELF were able to survive and even increase in numbers despite their obvious shortcomings. Ordinary brigands who infested the highways of Eritrea sought to enhance their position by associating themselves with the guerrilla movement. In September 1962, the Commander of the Second Division of the Ethiopian Army stationed in Eritrea wrote:

> It is well known that until about a year ago bandits in Eritrea resorted to robbery only to overcome their economic deprivation. However, over the last one year they have been contacted by the Jäbeha and Haräkat organizations and encouraged to claim that they have become shifta for Eritrean independence and not for robbing.[14]

Lacking any concrete guidance from the political leadership, the objectives of the rebellion were left open to different interpretations. The confusion which prevailed in the ranks of the rebels was such that while some of those in exile were declaring their intention to establish an independent Eritrea, guerrilla units in Aqordät were reported to have been agitating at the beginning of 1963 for the return of the federal administration.[15]

Attempts to structure the ELF and to establish a formal leadership started only two years after the formation of the organization when Idris Mohammed Adum, Osman Salih Sabby[16] and Idris Osman Qälaydos,[17] met in June 1962 and named themselves "the leadership of the revolution." They set up a "Popular Revolutionary Command" to take charge of the armed struggle and a twelve-man executive committee to activate the movement abroad. This structure, however, remained only on paper, and most of the organs established in 1962 became defunct soon afterwards.

In a further attempt to restructure the ELF, Idris Mohammed Adum convened in Khartoum what was called a "Congress of the Revolution" in 1965. Later critics claim that the meeting was attended only by handpicked representatives who were loyal to Idris Mohammed Adum.[18] The three leaders officially appointed themselves as members of the Supreme Council. Idris Mohammed Adum was named chairman of the Supreme Council; Osman Salih Sabby became secretary for Military Affairs; and Idris Osman Qälaydos was made secretary for "the affairs of the revolution." A Revolutionary Command headquartered in Kassala was also established to liaison between the Supreme Council and the Military Command in the field.[19]

Once again the newly devised structure remained a dead letter, and personal rather than organizational affiliation played an important role in conducting the affairs of the ELF. The commanders in the field owed loyalty to individuals in the political leadership and not to a central authority as such. The rank and file in the army owed allegiance only to their immediate chiefs, who for the most part belonged to the same ethnic and linguistic group. The organization had not even come up with a clearly defined objective for their rebellion by the second half of the 1960s. That the insurgency managed to sustain itself despite these serious shortcomings owes a great deal to the considerable foreign assistance it received and to the gross incompetence with which it was handled by the Ethiopian government.

The Arab Factor in Promoting and Sustaining the Eritrean Insurgency

Foreign influence and support played a decisive role in the creation and consolidation of the secessionist insurgency in Eritrea. The 1950s and early 1960s witnessed heightened political activity among Ethiopia's neighbors. Gamal Abdul Nasser's takeover in Egypt (1952), the independence of the Sudan (1956) and Somalia (1960), the military coup in Iraq (1958), the civil war in Yemen (1962), and the growth of militant Arab nationalism and Islamic solidarity influenced developments in Eritrea.

New strategic considerations combined with traditional suspicion towards what was considered as the predominantly Christian empire of Ethiopia, inspired Muslim and Arab states to take a special interest in the situation in Eritrea. The exclusively Muslim composition of the ELF and its leadership's assertion of the Arab and Islamic character of the Eritrean people did not fail to influence Arab leaders to view the struggle in Eritrea as part of the Arab cause and to hope that an independent Eritrea would be part of the Arab world.[20]

On this basis the ELF leaders presented their struggle as part of the Arab-Israeli conflict. They claimed that their condition was similar to that of the Palestinians and that they were both suffering from Jewish aggression. The following appeal made by Ibrahim Sultan to the Second Arab Summit Conference in 1964 was typical of the kind of propaganda disseminated to attract Arab support:

> ...the cause of the Eritrean people has a strong connection to the cause of wounded Palestine as both people suffer from Jewish aggression and the connection of the people of the Lion of Judah of Ethiopia with Israel .....It is known to the Arab and Muslim nations that Haile-Selassie of Ethiopia has given active help to Israel and opened up before her Ethiopia with its bountiful riches from Allah....If the Arabs really want to weaken Israel and choke her, they must pay attention to the sources of Ethiopia before dealing with Israel itself. We

Eritreans...are Arabs no less than the Palestinians. We Eritreans fight the Jews of Africa as personified by the Emperor and his government, the offspring of Solomon, the Lion of Judah... just as the Palestinians fight the Jews of Palestine.[21]

As the Arab-Israeli conflict dominated the Middle East political landscape, several Arab countries increasingly became convinced that the secessionist movement in Eritrea could become an asset in the struggle against Israel. The Arab League raised the question of Eritrea in a closed session during its meeting in Riyad and urged Arab countries to extend support to the Eritrean rebellion. In addition to broad pan-Arab interests, each country also had its specific interests which motivated it to become involved in the Eritrean issue.

Egypt's long standing ambition over the Nile Valley and the Red Sea region was revived with the coming to power of Gamal Abdul Nasser, and the Egyptian government sponsored subversive groups in Ethiopia. Egyptian officers were actively engaged in supporting Somali opposition against Ethiopia and in inciting the Muslim population in the country.[22] In Egypt itself senior government cadres were assigned to help organize the exiled Eritrean community.[23]

Cairo became a haven for Eritrean dissidents, and their leaders were cordially received by Nasser in anticipation of using them to advance Egyptian interests in the region.[24] Starting from 1956, Wäldäab Wäldämaryam was allowed to use Radio Cairo to beam a special program in Tegreñña through which he castigated the Ethiopian government and propounded the cause of Eritrean independence.[25] Although Nasser's hostility to Ethiopia subsided somewhat after the formation of the Organization of African Unity in 1963, Eritrean rebels continued to enjoy Egyptian support.

Somali assistance for Eritrean secessionism was motivated by its hope that Ethiopian embroilment in an Eritrean rebellion would create a favorable opportunity for Somalia to realize its "Greater Somali" objectives through the incorporation of the Ogaden region. Within months of its independence in 1960, the Somali government established an organization called the Somali-Eritrean Friendship Association to coordinate support for the Eritrean cause. Liaison between Idris Mohammed Adum and the Somali Defense minister and other high ranking Somali officials was already established as early as August 1960.[26] The Somali government was the earliest source of financial and military support for the Eritrean insurgency. It also provided Somali passports to ELF members and its sympathizers living abroad.[27]

Sudan, the closest of these countries to Eritrea, played a crucial role in the development of the guerrilla movement from its inception. The degree of support varied with the character of the regime which held power in Khartoum.

However, Eritrean insurgents freely used the country as a base and refuge at all times. They established offices in several places in the Sudan including Khartoum, and such towns as Kassala, Gadaref and Port Sudan came under the virtual influence, if not control, of the ELF. Stores and training camps were set up in a number of places in the Sudan and military supplies from other Arab countries found their way to Eritrea through the Sudan.[28] Although the Sudanese and Ethiopian governments signed no less than three agreements between 1964 and 1966 to extradite each others criminals and rebels, none of them were implemented.[29]

Syria provided the largest material and diplomatic support to the secessionist movement in Eritrea. Article II of the Constitution of the Syrian Ba'ath Party defined the Arab homeland as consisting of the area "which extends beyond the Taurus Mountains...the Gulf of Basra, the Arabian Sea, the Ethiopian Mountains,...and constitute one (single) complete unit, and no part thereof may be alienated."[30] Maps prepared in Syria included Eritrea as part of the Arab-lands. Jaysh al-Sha'ab, a weekly journal of the Syrian Army, wrote: "The sons of Eritrea are of various Arab origins...Eritrea formed from the year 84 after the Hejira, part of the Ummayid Caliphate and later on of the Abbassid Caliphate."[31] Competition with Egypt for the leadership of Arab nationalism after the disintegration of the United Arab Republic in 1962 provided an impetus for Syrian involvement in the Eritrean rebellion. A secret Ethiopian government document claimed that in 1965 Syria shipped 32 tons of weapons to Eritrea.[32] *Radio Damascus* carried regular ELF broadcasts starting in October 1966.[33]

Eritrea also figured in the rivalry between the Ba'athist parties in Syria and Iraq for influence in the Arab world. In an apparent attempt to outbid the other, both parties continued to subsidize the ELF generously and provided facilities to train its fighters.

Conservative Arab regimes like those in Saudi Arabia, Kuwait and Libya (under King Idris) also provided considerable support. In addition to their general policy of encouraging Islamic movements, these regimes also extended support to minimize the danger of the Eritrean movements falling under the control of radical Arab governments.

Although not as substantial as the support it received from the Arab countries, the secessionist movement also received assistance from a few Socialist states. As early as 1963, China received some 20 guerilla fighters for military training.[34] Cuba also cooperated in training fighters and cadres. Communist-manufactured weapons came into the hands of the guerrillas from the mid-1960s.[35]

Government Mishandling of the Insurgency

Although support for the secessionist rebellion inside Eritrea was limited mainly to the Muslim population, particularly the nomadic Beni Amer, general indifference towards the regime was widespread. The Ethiopian government had not only failed to win over new supporters but also had practically lost its former partisans in Eritrea.

Unwilling to allow even its supporters to organize independently, Haile Selassie's government whittled the once powerful Unionist Party into oblivion.[36] Neglected for over a decade, most Unionist leaders had by 1960 turned into apathetic bystanders. The few who persisted in trying to sound the alarm and to modify the Ethiopian regime's attitude met with a stone wall.[37]

With power concentrated in the hands of an aging Emperor who was unwilling to delegate authority even as its structure grew increasingly complex, the Ethiopian government was virtually in a state of paralysis. The growing rigidity and formality in the imperial court had made the Emperor practically unapproachable to his subjects.[38] At the same time, his subordinates, who were selected on the basis of their sycophantic loyalty, were less concerned with the efficient administration of the country than they were with intriguing against each other to gain the Emperor's favor. An Israeli diplomat who observed the extreme mediocrity in the government reported in 1960 that "Ethiopia was now in the doldrums."[39] The country entered the 1960s unprepared for the new challenges it faced in the form of hostile neighbors and growing internal dissidence.

Nowhere was the regime's gross incompetence as evident as it was in Eritrea. It allowed grievances to accumulate and did very little to counter growing dissidence. Although it received advance warnings from its embassies in the Middle East that secessionist leaders were planning to launch an uprising in Eritrea, the government took no action to forestall the rebellion.[40]

Eventual government action to suppress the rebellion started very late, and the measures it took were inefficient and inconsistent. More experienced in quelling spontaneous peasant uprisings and palace plots, Haile Selassie's government was helpless in handling the relatively organized and protracted guerrilla operations of the Eritrean Liberation Front.

The forces deployed to crush the insurgency were far too small compared to the strength of the guerrillas they had to deal with (especially after the mid-1960s), and the vast areas and difficult terrain that had to be covered.[41] The government kept only one brigade of troops in Eritrea until 1967, and even these were poorly armed, disorganized and badly commanded. Although the army which the government maintained in Eritrea grew to a division in the late

1960s, this force was, in the words of one of the brigade commanders, "a hollow image of a division with no replacements for those who had died, retired or deserted...a ragtag... walking barefoot and looking more like a volunteer army rather than a regular force." The commander complained that the properly trained officers were all stationed in the offices of the Ministry of Defense in Addis Ababa and that the army in the field was largely left with the non-commissioned officers. He also deplored the antiquated weapons with which the army in Eritrea was equipped. He wrote: "while the guerrilla fighters are arming themselves with sophisticated Communist weapons we are forced to use obsolete American junk." He estimated that the firepower of the guerrilla army exceeded the government's side by about 50 percent. The commander also lamented the absence of coordination between the army, the air force, and the navy. He concluded his appeal to the Emperor: "We cannot continue to live reminiscing on past glories. Events are overtaking us."[42]

The Ethiopian army was not able to develop a well planned, properly coordinated and sustained counterinsurgency operation. Most of its operations were carried out haphazardly by small units. Poor logistics often forced troops to return to camp after brief engagements, leaving isolated regions in the hands of the insurgents. This lack of decisive and sustained action resulted in strengthening the will of the rebels to resist while at the same time undermining the government's prestige and legitimacy in the eyes of the population.

The random and poorly organized campaigns contributed to aggravating civilian bitterness against the government. Frustrated by their failure to crush the elusive guerrillas, government forces frequently resorted to terrorizing the civilian population. This, in turn, was exploited by insurgent propaganda to further alienate the population from the government. An informant who had lived in an area of intense guerrilla activity described this process of alienation:

> Only a handful of people started the insurgency. It is the government that helped them to grow. The rebels would throw a grenade in a town and the government soldiers would shoot everyone they found. People started to flee towards the guerrilla zones to save their lives. The ELF would then agitate that the Ethiopians were determined to exterminate the people.[43]

In a futile attempt to curb the guerrilla activity, the government reinstituted the Banditry Act which had been enacted by the British in the 1940s as a measure to counter shifta activity. According to this act, now sanctioned by the Emperor in 1964, all civilians living within a 10 kilometer radius of a site of guerrilla attack were held responsible for the damage it caused.[44] If it had any effect at all, this measure motivated the guerrilla fighters to carryout more acts of sabotage to provoke the government into taking acts of reprisal which would further embitter the population.

By failing to act urgently the government lost the opportunity to deal with the guerrilla movement while it was at its infancy. The situation became more complicated in time and called for more sophisticated political and military measures which the Ethiopian government was not prepared to institute. Meanwhile, the insurgents were able to use the opportunity to expand their operations and to exercise control over larger communities either through persuasion or coercion. Brutal repressions were carried out against individuals and villages in order to demoralize government supporters.[45] In the towns, ELF assassination squads targeted former Unionist leaders.[46]

The insurgents extorted substantial fees from businessmen and plantation owners, mainly Italians. In an interview to the *Christian Science Monitor,* Osman Salih Sabby admitted: "they pay us large sums of money in taxes. The landowners know that if they do not pay, their plantation will be burned."[47] The Italian Ambassador in Ethiopia reportedly advised the Italian community in Täsänäy to pay what the guerrillas demanded first to save their lives and property and then to inform the government afterwards.[48] The government appears to have been helpless in stopping these extortions. The manager of a factory who was asked by the guerrillas to pay Eth. $40,000, told a reporter that the authorities officially tell them to resist "but they make us understand that it is better to pay....I think there is an underground understanding."[49]

Discord in the Secessionist Movement

Although considerable Arab backing and major Ethiopian weakness enabled the armed struggle to persist, no substantial progress was made in terms of creating a cohesive force in Eritrea based on commonly shared political objectives. Those who led the insurgency abroad were mostly the same people who a decade earlier had failed to strike a working alliance at home to advance their separatist demands. Old rivalries and mutual suspicion still persisted among the old guards, and their new followers quickly regrouped themselves behind one or the other factional group.

The first major rift in the ELF occurred as a result of a fall out between the two most important leaders of Eritrean separatism, Ibrahim Sultan and Idris Mohammed Adum. Both men revived their old rivalries of the 1940s[50] and mobilized their personal and clan followers in the struggle to gain the upper hand in the ELF and to control the exiled community in the Middle East. Although Idris Mohammed Adum later managed to deny Ibrahim Sultan any position of influence in the ELF, the consequences of thereby losing the support of the one man who had been at the head of the struggle for Eritrean separatism were serious. Ibrahim Sultan deprived the ELF of some support in the Kärän and Sahel areas over which he had influence. He was also able to detach a substantial number of his followers in exile away from the ELF.[51]

Wäldäab Wäldämaryam, the only Christian of any consequence among the exiled leaders, had been alienated from the ELF from the beginning. Given to emphasizing the Islamic and Arabic character of their struggle, the ELF leaders considered Wäldäab a liability and an embarrassment in their relations with Arab and Islamic countries. He was accordingly kept at a distance. He was even prohibited from entering Arab countries other than Egypt. The Saudi foreign minister reportedly told him in 1962, "we support the Muslims not the Christians in Eritrea" and denied him entry. Libya also turned down his request for entry in 1964 on similar grounds.[52] Wäldäab himself revealed at the beginning of 1970 that he was refused entry into most Arab countries because of his Christian religion and complained that Arab countries support the Eritrean struggle only for religious reasons.[53]

The ELF's emphasis on the Islamic character of Eritrea was diametrically opposed to Wäldäab's long-standing ambition of establishing a Christian-dominated state by uniting Eritrea and Tegray. He thus remained a bitter critic of the ELF. Throughout the 1960s his stand on the future of Eritrea was, as had been the case in the 1940s, marked by inconsistency. At times he advocated the return of the Federation,[54] and occasionally he urged the creation of an independent Eritrea.[55]

Factional strife characterized the relations between the other leading members in the ELF. Especially acute was the rivalry between Idris Mohammed Adum and Osman Salih Sabby. The latter, coming from the Massawa area, formed a block of the eastern lowlanders to challenge the dominance of the western lowland elements who virtually monopolized the leadership in the ELF. Idris Mohammed Adum also resented Sabby's growing popularity and influence, especially among the governments of the various Arab countries. Idris Osman Qälaydos, the other important figure in the ELF hierarchy, exploited the differences between the two to consolidate his own power.[56] As the organization came to command larger resources as a result of generous foreign assistance, the struggle between the various factions for control of the funds became particularly acute.[57]

The differences and rivalries which plagued the top echelon of the ELF's leadership also found their way into the field. The army itself consisted of a conglomeration of recruits who were attracted to the ELF for a variety of reasons. A good number of them were ex-bandits who found safe refuge in the ELF to continue to live off the local population. Former Italian askaris and ex-soldiers in the Sudanese army welcomed the ELF for providing them with an opportunity to continue with their military careers. Jobless and insecure

Eritrean refugees in Arab countries joined the ELF as a way out of their dilemma. Religious fanatics who viewed the ELF as an Islamic movement joined the front to wage a jihad against Christians. There were also those who joined to settle old scores against rival ethnic groups. Lastly, a few student radicals began to join the ELF, especially after the mid-1960s, hoping to use the ELF to advance a socialist revolution.

Creating a unified army command out of a conglomeration of such diverse elements with mutually conflicting interests and allegiance proved impossible. No single purpose overriding loyalty existed to hold it together. Not surprisingly, internal squabbles and skirmishes became a dominant feature of the army of the ELF, also known as the Eritrean Liberation Army (ELA). Individual members in the political leadership abroad competed with each other to form their respective blocs within the army. They tried to outbid each other by recruiting exclusively their own fellow ethnic and regional compatriots and fought over who should get the lion's share of foreign aid. For all practical purposes, the force did not exist as an army which owed loyalty to a single central authority but as armed guerrilla units which vied against each other.

Intolerance between fighters of different ethnic and regional groups was such that, in May 1964, the Beni Amer guerrillas in the Aqordät region were demanding the expulsion of those who belonged to the Marya, Bilän, Assaorta, and other ethnic groups. They suggested that the non-Beni Amer groups should evacuate the region and operate in their respective areas.[58] And intermittent clashes occurred between the two dominant groups in the ELF, the western lowlanders and those who came from the Red Sea plains.[59]

Ethnic and regional conflict in the ELF had, by the middle of the 1960s, reached such a stage that it was no longer possible to keep the army as a homogeneous unit under a single command. The Supreme Council was forced to assign the fighters to their respective districts. Accordingly, four zonal commands were created, and the fighters were distributed along ethnic and regional lines.

The first zone, which was the largest and best equipped, was assigned for the Barka and parts of Gash and Sätit regions. It was led by Mohammed Dinai, a Beni Amer and an ex-soldier in the Sudanese army. The second zone, led by Omar Izaz, a Bilän and also a former non-commissioned officer in the Sudanese army, operated in the Kärän and Sahel region. The third zone, led by Abdulkarim Ahmad, a Saho, was assigned to the Akälä Guzai area. The fourth zone under Mohammed Ali Omaro from the Red Sea Coast moved into the Red Sea and Danakil areas.[60]

A fifth zone was created in late 1966 to accommodate the Christian fighters, whose number was increasing by this time but were unable to co-exist with the

Muslims in the other zones. This group was led by Wälday Kahsay, a former school teacher. It operated in the largely Christian-inhabited highland areas and was also responsible for political work in Asmara.[61]

The zonal division did not end the strife in the ELF. Rather, it increased the competition and aggravated the antagonism between the various groups. The new structure made each zonal command virtually autonomous and gave a free hand to the commanders. Each zone recruited its fighters from its own localities. The Revolutionary Command in Kassala, which was supposed to oversee the zonal commands, was totally ignored, and, instead, each zonal commander created his own direct link with the Supreme Council.[62]

In the absence of a central organ to direct their activities, the commanders became virtual warlords. They exacted money from the people in the form of taxes, fines, and donations. They frequently resorted to looting cattle and other property from the surrounding population. Some of the zone commanders were known to accumulate considerable property in Kassala through these means.[63]

The leaders of the various zones entered into earnest competition with one another for the acquisition of larger territories because larger areas promised more resources. Each zonal command aspired to strengthen itself at the expense of the others and used every opportunity to weaken them. Cooperation between the zones even against enemy attack ceased. It is claimed that far from helping each other, the leaders of the zones "were rejoicing at the defeat of one another."[64] Military activity against the government almost came to a standstill during this period with each commander trying to preserve his own force for the internal power struggle.[65]

The hostility between Muslims and the few Christians in the ELF continued unabated throughout the second half of the 1960s. The ELF was principally the creation of Muslims, and its leaders had used Islam as a substitute for the political program which they were unable to develop. In this way they sought to win the support of the Muslim population of the lowland areas, where the armed struggle had started, and that of the Eritrean emigrés in the Middle East, which was predominantly Muslim, by presenting their organization as a champion of Muslim resistance to Christian domination and persecution.

The ELF leaders made no secret of their ill feelings towards the Christian Eritrean population and openly declared their aim of establishing Islamic hegemony in Eritrea. The public declarations of the initial members of the Supreme Council were unequivocally anti-Christian in content. Osman Salih Sabby wrote about the ill treatment of Muslims "in the hands of the…infidel."[66] Idris Mohammed Adum declared at a press conference in Damascus that "there are no others in Eritrea but Arab citizens."[67] In an interview over *Radio*

Damascus, Idris Osman Qälaydos also spoke of the persecution of Eritrean Muslims at the hands Christian Eritreans. He said that thousands of Muslims who stood behind the ELF were "languishing in jail while their tormentors, the Christian Eritreans were relaxing in comfort."[68] A 1963 booklet entitled *The Eritrean People's Cause*, devoted much of its space to the persecution of Muslims.[69] Increased dependence on Arab material and diplomatic support strengthened the ELF's Islamic orientation.

Muslim insurgents carried out more frequent attacks on Christian villagers in the western lowlands than on government forces. Several Christian villages were destroyed and their inhabitants massacred. A unit of the ELF force killed 47 Christian peasants at Täkunbia, near Barentu, and stole several hundred cattle on July 4, 1965.[70] Another Christian village in the Kärän district was totally burnt on December 8, 1965. A certain Gerazmach Yoséf Mahs'un and his family perished in the fire.[71] Other atrocities against Christian communities were also reported at Kohayin, S'inadäglé, Hididam, and in the Gash and Sätit districts.[72]

The severity of ELF repression led many Christian villagers living in the western lowlands and at the foot of the highlands to organize themselves for counter-resistance. They demanded arms from the government to defend themselves against insurgent attacks.[73] Christians in the highland areas also requested the government to allow them to be armed and were given some 2,000 rifles and 100,000 rounds of ammunition at the end of 1965.[74] The establishment of these local counter-insurgency commando forces which drew their recruits exclusively from Christians, increased the ELF's determination to step up its attacks on Christian civilians.

Clearly, the Christian minority in the ELF was viewed with suspicion and hostility. They complained that they were "ostracized as kafirs and attacked as an enemy."[75] The inter-religious prejudice was such that Muslims and Christians within the front were not willing to eat together.[76] The minority Christian fighters were subjected to periodic repressions. It is said that as many as 50 Christian fighters were killed in the district of Sänbäré,[77] and another Christian contingent of 25 men was wiped out along with its leader, Gilla Germay, in 1967.[78]

The escalation within the ELF of the threat against Christians in 1967 led to large-scale defections to the government side. Wälday Kahsay, the commander of the fifth zone, who was already being hunted by the Muslim faction, gave himself up with 19 of his men to the Ethiopian Consul in Kassala on August 24, 1967. Twenty-seven others had already given themselves up in the Säraye district a few weeks earlier.[79] These defections triggered even harsher reprisals against the remaining Christians in the front with the Christians in the fifth zone being virtually decimated.[80]

According to the account given by the former commander of the fifth zone, Christians and Muslims in the front viewed each other as virtual enemies and there appeared to be no binding factor to hold them together. He said that preparations were secretly underway in 1967 to organize the Christian guerrillas for an attack against the Muslims. He claimed that he and his deputies, Gilla Germay, Haylé Guangul and Abraha, were planning to arm their Christian followers with the best available weapons in order to destroy the Muslims in a surprise attack. He said that the plot failed because most of their Christian followers surrendered to the government prematurely.[81]

In 1968 the ELF was in an extremely weakened state. The defection of the Christian fighters, the intense rivalry between the zonal divisions, the continuing squabble among the various ethnic and regional groups, as well as the lack of direction and supervision from the political leadership in exile, were seriously crippling it. These weaknesses exposed the guerrilla forces to a severe defeat from a government offensive at the end of 1967.[82]

These reverses, and the generalized dissatisfaction which prevailed in the ranks of the guerrilla force, opened up opportunities for some of the radicals in the ELF to agitate for changes in the organization. An underground movement named the "General Rectification Movement" was created. It asked for the convening of a congress to resolve the crises in the ELF, for the abolition of the zonal structure and its replacement by a unified army under a centralized leadership, and for a more humane treatment of the civilian population.[83]

This underground movement was particularly successful in the third, fourth and fifth zones, where the members generally resented the Beni Amer domination of the ELF. The fact that the Supreme Council and the Revolutionary Command in Kassala, which was said to have been monopolized by the Beni Amer,[84] had little influence over these three zones, helped the opposition to proceed with few obstacles. The three zones came together under a provisional leadership headed by Mohammed Ahmad Abdu.[85]

The growing pressure for the unification of the ELF army finally forced the leaders of the first and second zones (known as the Barka bloc) to join the reform movement. Preliminary contacts initiated between the two zones and the provisional leadership of the already unified three zones resulted in an agreement to convene a meeting of all the zones.

Representatives of all the five zones met at Adobha, in the Aqordät district, from August 10 to 24, 1969. The conference was attended by about 160 delegates comprising zonal commanders and their deputies, unit leaders, political commissars, cadres, and representatives of the various auxiliary bodies in the army. These representatives were nominated by the higher authorities of their respective zones.[86]

The conference passed resolutions calling for the abolition of the zonal division and for the reorganization of the fighting force under a single command. It also resolved to suspend the already defunct Revolutionary Command in Kassala and called for the suspension of the zone commanders and their deputies until their case could be decided by an organizational congress. A 38-man Provisional General Command popularly referred to as Kiyyad Al Amma was to assume the leadership of the army until a "National Congress," which was to be called in about a year should take charge of the organization. A preparatory committee for the convening of the Congress was established.

Although these seemingly impressive resolutions were passed as a result of the intense efforts of the reform minded elements, the mutual suspicion and conflicting objectives which had characterized the ELF from the start, nevertheless beset the conference. In an apparent move to maintain their dominant position in the ELF hierarchy, the first and second zones insisted on, and after acrimonious debates succeeded in receiving a much larger representation than the other three zones in the conference.[87] The Barka bloc (zones one and two) also demanded and got 20 of the 38 seats in the Provisional General Command. Each group separately nominated its own representatives to the Provisional General Command.

The question of the future of the Supreme Council of the ELF brought the conflicting allegiances and the fears of the conference participants into the open. Each protégé of the Supreme Council members stood firmly behind their patrons and resisted efforts to expose their weakness. Some groups, who felt insecure at their lack of strong representation in the newly established leadership, also opposed the move to depose the Supreme Council. By a strange twist of events, most of the members of the tripartite unity (zones three, four and five), who had earlier been quite vocal in their opposition to the Supreme Council, now favored maintaining it as a defense against a total takeover of the front by the Barka bloc.[88]

The failure of the Adobha Military Conference to settle the factional strife and organizational crisis which plagued the ELF became clear immediately after the Provisional General Command started to exercise power. The men in the General Command, who represented mutually hostile groups, entered into fierce competition for key posts. Members from the third, fourth and fifth zones regrouped themselves into two major blocs: those from the Red Sea area and the Christians. Although no love was lost between these two groups, they shared mutual resentment and fear regarding the Barka bloc. Whatever these zones were attempting to achieve by these actions, the Beni Amer group, which dominated the Barka bloc, was meanwhile preparing itself to settle the issue of power by force.

Each of the contending groups in the General Command rallied the support of their respective rank and file by impressing upon them the imminent threat they faced from their rivals. The unity of the entire force of the ELF, which the Adobha Conference sought to achieve, evaporated into thin air as old animosities flared up once again.

In an apparent bid to control fully the organization, the Barka bloc revoked the Adobha resolution and suspended the Supreme Council on December 19, 1969. This move was particularly aimed at weakening the Red Sea area faction which had counted on Osman Salih Sabby's support for the confrontation with the western lowlanders.[89] Opposition to this measure was dealt with firmly by the Barka bloc. Six members of the Provisional Command who were said to have opposed the deposition of the Supreme Council were arrested.[90] All six were from the Red Sea area. A series of such purges and intimidations put the Barka faction in control of the General Command. Thereafter this body ceased to consider itself a transitional leadership and concentrated on the permanent consolidation of its power. The committee established to prepare a general congress was allowed to wither away.

Resistance against the hegemony of the "Barka boys," as the members from the western lowland region were known, was strongest among those who came from the Red Sea region. The General Command ruthlessly crushed the opposition, several hundred fighters from the Red Sea area being killed or driven into exile in the Sudan.[91]

The Christians who had survived the 1967 massacre and those who had joined the front since then also came under increasing repression. In March 1970 the two most important leaders of the Christian group, Kidané Keflu and Wälday Gedäy were executed in Kassala by order of the General Command.[92] Over 200 Christian fighters were killed during this period.[93] Many of these were fresh student recruits from the towns. Over two hundred other Christian guerrillas surrendered to the government.[94]

The ELF's leadership in exile was itself too torn by factional strife to rescue the situation in the field. In fact, each member of the leadership fueled the sectarian differences in the field in order to create more loyal followers for their respective factions. Sabby supported his compatriots of the Red Sea against the western lowlanders. When he realized that his followers were losing the struggle for power in the General Command, he repudiated the new leadership in the field and started to rally his own supporters in exile in an apparent attempt to form a new organization. He called a meeting of his followers in Amman, Jordan, in November, 1969. In January, 1970 he created what was called the "General Secretariat" with himself as the secretary general[95] and openly called for a struggle against the General Command.[96]

Idris Mohammed Adum was not unhappy to see his fellow Barka men taking the upper hand in the field. Instead of challenging the General Command for usurping his power, he chose to combat Sabby's renewed efforts to build an alternative power. He declared his support for the General Command. He was later reelected Chairman of the ELF. The fractures both within the army in the field and among the political leadership abroad were too deep to be mended proving once again that even for those who were ardent supporters of an independent Eritrea, sectarian loyalties far outweighed a common national goal.

Notes

[1] Simret Habte, "Background to the Dilemma of the Eritrean Liberation Fronts," [mimeo.] (Stockholm, Feb. 1978), 2.

[2] An Eritrean Students' Club was established in Cairo in the early 1950s: ELF, *Eritrean Revolution*, I, 4(May-July 1976), 13.

[3] John Markakis, *National and Class Conflict in the Horn*, 106. See also, "Eritrean Governorate General, Kä 1941 Amäta Meherät Wodih Yä Eretra Yä Polätika Hunétawoch," n.d., Asmara [a document compiled in Amharic on political conditions in Eritrea since 1941], 53.

[4] Mahbär Shäwatä literally means association of seven. It got this name, because each cell consisted of seven people.

[5] Mohammed Said Nawud, one of the founders of the ELM, was said to have been in close contact with the Sudanese Communist Party. See for instance, *Stefano Poscia, Eritrea Colonia Tradita*, 69.

[6] Wäldäab Wäldämaryam, "The Truth about Eritrea: Lecture Delivered by Mr. Woldeab Woldemariam, Head of the Eritrean Liberation Movement's Delegation Abroad," mimeo. (Khartoum, 20 January 1965).

[7] Markakis claims that the ELM was "inspired by the facile success of the military coup d'état in the Sudan a few months earlier, and the frequency of such intervention throughout the Arab world:" J. Markakis, *National and Class Conflict*, 107.

[8] See for instance Bereket Habte Selassie, *Conflict and Intervention*, 61-2.

[9] ELF, *Eritrean Revolution*, 16; EPLF, *Hafäshawi Polätikawi Temherti Netegadälti* (1975), 37.

[10] Awaté was born from a Beni Amer and Baria family. He served in the Italian army and spent much of the British period as a shifta raiding Kunama villages near Baräntu, and the Hadändäwa across the Sudanese border. He claimed to support the Muslim League of Eritrea, although he also wrote to the Unionist Party in 1948 professing loyalty to the Unionist cause. He continued his shifta activity in the 1950s, and gained notoriety in addition to his cross-border raids, for attacking agricultural

concessions held by highland Eritreans in the Barka and Gash areas: Liaison Office Papers, Haylämikaél Wäldäsellasé to Colonel Nägga, 1 November 1948; FO 371/53530, BMA Monthly Intelligence Summary, 16 November 1946; and Ethiopian government, *Eretra Keflä Hagär Bä Feudo-Bourgeoise Astädadär Wäqt*, 1962-1974 (A collection of documents selected from various government archives compiled by the Documentation and Information Service of the Wokers Party of Ethiopia), pp. 7-9. For a comparison with another bandit figure drawn into Eritrean nationalist activity, see the case of the Mesazghi Brothersa: E. Hobsbawm, *Bandits* (New York, Pantheon Books, 1981).

[11] Eritrean Liberation Front - People's Liberation Forces (ELF/PLF), *Eritrean Review*, no. 35, August 1976.

[12] ELF, *Eritrean Revolution*, 17. Awaté was succeeded by Mohammed Omar Abdallah, also known as Abu Tyara, from the Marya tribe located between the Sahel and Kärän. His deputy was Mohammed Dinai, a Beni Amer.

[13] A report from the U.S. consulate in Asmara characterizes Awaté's group as "a band of malcontents," who pillaged agricultural concessions in the Barka area and attacked non-Muslims: State, 775a.00/1-462, U.S. Consulate to Department of State, 4 January 1962.

[14] Commander of the Second Division to Army Intelligence Headquarter, September 1962: E.P.A., U1/1426.

[15] Headquarters of the Second Army Division to Lt. General Abiy Abäbä, Asmara, 12 February 1963: E.P.A., U1/1462.

[16] Osman Salih Sabby had been a teacher at Hargigo in the school founded by Salih Kékia (a noted Unionist from Massawa with considerable commercial interests in Addis Ababa). He went into exile in 1960 and met Idris Mohammed Adum and Ibrahim Sultan in Jeddah. From there he proceeded to Mogadishu where he was instrumental in the creation of the Eritrea-Somali Friendship Association: cited in E.P.A., U2/168, Vol. 2, Eritrean Province Security and Immigration Office to the Ministry of Interior, Department of Public Security, Asmara, 12 February, 1961. An elder informant in Massawa claimed that Sabby grew bitter against the Ethiopian government after he was denied admission to the Naval College at Massawa by "Hamasén officials who detested Muslim Eritreans." Sabby was said to have appealed to the Emperor during the latter's visit to Massawa through Salih Kékia, but was still kept out in spite of the Emperor's orders to admit him: Qadi Ahmad Mohammed Nur (Interview, Massawa, 1982).

[17] Idris Osman Qälaydos was a student of law at Cairo University. He was imprisoned around 1961 by the Egyptian Government on suspicion of spying for Israel. After his release, a statement from the ELF Executive Committee to its branch offices on April 21, 1963 exonerated him from the charges. A leaflet of August 15, 1963, distributed by the General Union of Eritrean Students also says that Idris Osman Qäladyos was falsely implicated by "an Ethiopian spy called Ali Ahmad Affendi who was later hanged by the Egyptian government." Both documents and another reference to the release of Idris Osman Qälaydos by the Ethiopian Embassy in Cairo in a letter of July 26, 1963, are found in E.P.A., 186.

[18] Däbäsay Bäyänä, "Yä Jäbeha Tarikawi Anäsasena Bäyägizéw Yakahédachäw Tarikawi Kenewunoch," [an unpublished manuscript on the history of the ELF by

a former member of the organization], Asmara, 1982, 7; Täklähaymanot Abära, "Private Note," Massawa, 1981, 1. See also ELF, *Eritrean Revolution*, 14.

[19] Ibid., 17.

[20] In a broadcast on Radio Damascus, Salih Sabby announced:

> The Eritrean people has always been Arab ... Eritrea's independence is very useful for the Arab world. An independent Eritrea will be a part of the Arab nation:" *Radio Damascus*, 6 September 1967, transcript in E.P.A., U2/1195, Vol. 2. See also Taye Geremew, "Rebellion in Eritrea-Who is Behind it, What are its Aims?" *New Middle East*, 31 (April 1971), 24-28. In its August 5, 1970 issue, the Iraqi newspaper, *Al-Thawrah*, carried an article entilted "The Story of the Arab Revolution in Eritrea."

[21] Ibrahim Sultan, "Statement of Eritrean People: an appeal to the Second Arab Summit Conference," 31 August 1964. Salih Sabby also said over Radio Damascus, "The Eritrean revolution has the responsibility of ending Israeli influence on the Red Sea and to make it a completely Arab Sea," *Radio Damascus*, 25 June 1969, transcript in E.P.A., lä 3/1195.

[22] In November 1956, Lt. Colonel Abdul Aziz Hilmy, Egyptian Military Attaché to Ethiopia was expelled from the country for inciting Muslims to rise up against the Ethiopian government. Before taking up his Ethiopian assignment Hilmy had worked in Khartoum, where according to a British source, "he was notorious for his political agitation:" FO 371/113522, British Embassy in Addis Ababa to Foreign Office, 7 December 1955. See also State, 775.00/3-2058, U.S. Embassy in Addis to Department of State, 20 March 1958. John Spencer claims that according to information he received from the U.S. Embassy in Addis Ababa, the Egyptians were spending more than 1 million birr a year in sponsoring anti-Ethiopian agitation among the Somali elements: Spencer, *Ethiopia at Bay*, 311.

[23] The Egyptian Government took the initiative to hold the "Eritrean Youth Conference" which was held in the Cairo Chamber of Commerce on 28 April 1958. The chairman of the conference, Major Tahawi, was a high ranking Egyptian official. The conference participants called on Eritrean workers "to boycott the ships which load meat and food-stuffs at Massawa Port for Israel because Zionism and imperialism are the same:" State, 875a.46/5-1458, U.S. Embassy in Cairo to Department of State, 14 May 1958.

[24] The Italian Embassy in Cairo reported in July 1959 that Nasser was cordially receiving Eritrean dissidents including Ibrahim Sultan and Idris Mohammed Adum, and keeping them "in reserve" for future use: State 775A.00/8-759, "Summary of Extracts from Reports by the Italian Embassy at Cairo," 24 July 1959.

[25] Apparently worried by the barrage of propaganda coming from Cairo, the Emperor confided to the American Ambassador that he wanted the U.S. President to know "of his growing anxiety regarding the effect of Cairo propaganda on the Muslim population in Ethiopia...an insidious form of subversion which begins to assume important proportion:" State, 775.5 MSP/8-858, U.S. Embassy in Addis Ababa to Department of State, 8 August 1958. See also U.S., Office of Naval Intelligence,

Opportunities For Communist Penetration of Ethiopia and the Horn of Africa (1958), for the extent of the turbulence and excitement which Egyptian propaganda was causing in Ethiopia.

[26] Letters from Idris Mohammed Adum on 23 August 1960 to the Somali Defense Minister and other high ranking officials thanking them for earlier support and requesting further assistance. Osman Salih Sabby also wrote on 15 September 1960 to Somali nationals and their leaders in Saudi Arabia, requesting their assistance for the publication of a planned book on "the ill-treatment of Muslims in Ethiopia:" in E.P.A., U1/251.

[27] E.P.A., 186, Ethiopian Embassy in Cairo to the Ministry of Foreign Affairs, 18 August 1965, and Report No. 85, 15 April 1964.

[28] The extent of the ELF's dependence on the Sudan was described by Wälday Kahsay, a regional commander of the ELF, who defected to the Ethiopian government in 1967: statement on 6 October 1967, in E.P.A., File 513. For further information on the Sudanese contribution to the Eritrean rebellion see also, Eritrea Governorate General "Survey of Counter Insurgency Operations in Eritrea and Draft Proposals," (1968) [also known as "Project Adwa," prepared on request by Ras Asratä Kassa, the Governor of Eritrea, by the Ministry of Defence probably in collaboration with Israeli advisors], 30.

[29] "The People of Eritrea and the Underground Organization" [Amharic manuscript possibly prepared by a government intelligence unit], October, 1966, 11.

[30] Quoted in Zewde Gebre Sellassie, *Eritrea and Ethiopia in the Context of the Red Sea and Africa*, 119.

[31] *Jaysh al Sha'ab*, 17 April 1970 [trans. from Arabic made in the office of the Eritrean Provincial Administration], E.P.A.

[32] "The People of Eritrea and the Underground Organization," p. 10. According to this same source about half of this consignment of arms was said to have been temporarily detained by the Sudanese Government.

[33] Ibid., 12.

[34] Issayas Afäwärqi, the current President of Eritrea and Mohammed Nur Ramadan, Issayas's predecessor as Secretary General of the EPLF, were both trained in China.

[35] See John F. Cambell, "Background to the Eritean Conflict: Differed Results of Colonial Map-Making, Geopolitics and Religion," *Africa Report* (May 1971), 20.

[36] Christopher Clapham wrote that the idea of a political party "would be quite foreign to the Emperor's political techniques, since he has been used to dealing with individuals on a very personal basis, playing one off against another, and has destroyed any organisation which might have emerged as a rival to himself:" Clapham, *Haile-Selassie's Government* (New York: Frederick A. Praeger, 1969), 187.

[37] A noted Unionist leader who was himself unable to convey his ideas directly to the Emperor, and even to his representative in Eritrea, wrote to General Nägga: "As one needs to douse the fire before it creates a conflagration, we should seriously address the Eritrean situation before it gets out of hand, and before the people are alienated from the Emperor they love so much. Should you get access to His Imperial Majesty

please update him about the deteriorating condition in the territory:" Däjazmach Araya Wassé to General Nägga, 17 June 1955, in Liaison Office Papers.

[38] On the tendency toward a growing rigidity and formality in the imperial court under Emperor Haile Selassie, see Merid W. Aregay, "The Settlement of the Status of Eritrea, 1941-52," M.A. Thesis, University of Chicago (August 1959), 98. Merid wrote, "up to the beginning of the twentieth century the emperor and his vassal lords were in direct contact with their people. Now, however, even the personal rule of the emperor has to be executed through an intricate, hierarchical bureaucratic administration."

[39] Hanan Bar-on, Israeli Consul General at Addis Ababa, quoted in a U.S. Embassy dispatch from Addis Ababa.

[40] The Ethiopian Embassy in Cairo reported to the Ministry of Foreign Affairs on 17 April, 1959, that Idris Mohammed Adum, Ibrahim Sultan, and Wäldäab Wäldämaryam were preparing in Cairo to launch an armed insurgency in Eritrea: E.P.A., U2/168, Vol. 2.

[41] Interview: Captain Kassahun Abägaz, Massawa (1982). Captain Kassahun had been engaged in counter-insurgency operations in Eritrea since the early 1960s. The major part of the force was stationed in Asmara, Kärän, and on the Asmara-Massawa road. Some garrisons were also posted in various other towns to guard key installations.

[42] Colonel Wärqu Mäkonnen (Commander of the 12th Brigade), Abiy Riport Lä Germawi Negusä Nägäst [An Important Report to His Imperial Majesty], 16 November 1970, in Library of the Institute of Ethiopian Studies, Manuscript No. 1099.

[43] Interview: Khalifa Idris Osman (Kärän, 1982). He was an administrator of the Hagaz district since the early 1960s.

[44] Inhabitants of the villages around Ginda, for instance, paid a compensation of Eth. $ 17,294.84 for damage done on a train by the guerrillas: Ghinda Wäräda Administration Archive, File No. 3/34/1050/569, Colonel Gétachew Nadäw (Chief of the Airborne Force) to the Awraja governors of Massawa and Hamasén, 10 September 1970.

[45] A report from the district of Sahel to the office of the Eritrean Governorate General mentions that the guerrillas had killed 12 villagers at Sakar in Adi Täkles sub-district on 28 July 1966, for alleged collaboration with the government. Also Interview: Goitom, Solomon.

[46] See for instance ELF, "On the heroic acts in Asmara" [trans. from Tegreñña], 14 April 1970, on the death sentence passed on Däjazmach Hadgu Gilagaber and Däjazmach Zäre'om. The leaflet noted that the Unionist camp was in an "extreme state of terror." See also, "The People of Eritrea and Underground Organization," 7, for political assassinations carried out by the ELF.

[47] *Christian Science Monitor*, 28 March 1969; also E.P.A., File 513, for the testimony of Haylé Guangul, an ex-guerrilla leader, to the 2nd Army Division, on how the ELF extorted large sums of money from Italian plantation owners, 6 October 1967.

[48] The Ambassador offered this advice during a visit to the area: E.P.A., U2/286, report by the Täsänäy Security and Immigration chief to the Eritrean Governorate General, 15 January 1971.

⁴⁹ Quoted by Gustavo D'Arpe, "In Eritrea si combatte per la piena indipendenza," *Il Tempo*, 31 July 1965.

⁵⁰ Idris Mohammed Adum, a Beni Amer from the Western Province, was a member of the Muslim League of the Western Province, a rival organization to Ibrahim Sultan's Muslim League of Eritrea. Later Idris Mohammed Adum allied himself with forces which favored federation.

⁵¹ E.P.A., U2/77, Vol.1, 19 January 1966; and E.P.A. kä 1/702, reports from Jeddah, 25 October 1969 and 28 February 1970, which mentions that Ibrahim Sultan was carrying out a campaign against the rest of the ELF leaders. Also E.P.A., U2/1195, Vol.3, for Ibrahim Sultan's broadcast over Radio Damascus on 26 January 1970, in which he made references to the dangers of "unlimited ambition and greed in the ELF."

⁵² Cited in Fred Halliday, "The Fighting in Eritrea," *New Left Review*, 67(May-June 1971), 65.

⁵³ Transcript of Wäldäab's interview over *Radio Damascus*, 28 January 1970, in E.P.A., U2/77, vol 2.

⁵⁴ In an appeal addressed to the Council of African Ministers at Lagos on 24 February 1964, Wäldäab wrote:

> We appeal begging you to ask Ethiopian government to consider its arbitrary action in abolishing Eritrean-Ethiopian Federation and suppressing Eritrean constitution... We assure you and Ethiopian government that we shall remain faithful to our commitments and safeguard Ethiopia's prerogative laid down in the United Nations resolutions.

⁵⁵ Wäldäab Wäldämaryam, "The Truth About Eritrea..."

⁵⁶ A report from Jeddah passed on to the Ethiopian government mentions that Idris Osman Qälaydos was busy strengthening his own faction in the ELF while Idris and Sabby were intriguing against each other: E.P.A., chä 1/702, Ethiopian Embassy in Jeddah, 14 January 1970.

⁵⁷ There were wide-spread accusations of large scale embezzlement of the front's fund. It was reported from Saudi Arabia, for example, that hundreds of Eritrean émigrés there who needed passports got them from the Somali Embassy after pledging to pay ten percent of their monthly earnings to the ELF. Idris Mohammed Adum was said to have used a large amount of this money "to keep three wives in three countries and to spend extravagantly." T'aha Nur Ibrahim, the ELF representative in Saudi Arabia, was also reported to have used the organization's fund to buy a very expensive villa for himself: E.P.A., chä 1/702, reports from Saudi Arabia (15.4.1969 and 13.5.1969), and from Kassala (15.10.1969).

⁵⁸ E.P.A., lä 5/702, Aqordat Awraja Police Headquarters to the Eritrean Province Police Headquarters, 6 May 1964. Mohammed Omar Abdalla Kälbay, a leader of a guerrilla unit, was reportedly prohibited from operating in the Beni Amer area because he was from the Marya tribe.

⁵⁹ E.P.A., U2/168 and chä 4/133. Also, interview: Qadi Ahmad.

⁶⁰ Detailed information on the zones and their leaders is found in "Survey of Counter-Insurgency Operations in Eritrea." Also E.P.A., U2/168, Report of September 15, 1965.

⁶¹ Wälday Kahsay's interview to the 2nd Army Division, 7 November 1967: E.P.A., File 513. See also EPLF, *Hafäshawi Polätikawi Temeherti*, 40.

⁶² ELF, *Eritrean Revolution*, 17.

⁶⁴ Mahmud Mohammed Dinai, commander of the first zone, reportedly bought two trucks in Kassala by such means: Eritrean Province Police Headquarters to Ras Asratä Kassa, 21 February 1969, in E.P.A., U2/168, Vol.1. See also EPLF, *Hafäshawi Polätikawi Temeherti*, p. 41.

⁶⁴ EPLF, *National Democratic Programme* (1977), p. 11.

⁶⁵ EPLF, *Hafäshawi Polätikawi Temeherti*, p. 40.

⁶⁶ Sabby's letter to Somali nationals living in Saudi Arabia, 15 September 1960: E.P.A. U1/251.

⁶⁷ Idris Mohammed Adum, Press Conference, Damascus, 28 February 1967: E.P.A., File 34.

⁶⁸ Transcript of Idris Osman Qälaydos's interview over *Radio Damascus*, 15 September, 1967: E.P.A., U2/1195.

⁶⁹ ELF, *The Eritrean People's Cause* (Arabic), 1963.

⁷⁰ Interview: Qés Solomon Habtäs'eyon. He claims to have witnessed the massacre.

⁷¹ Eritrea Governorate General, "Kä 1956 Amätä Meherät Eskä 1961 Amätä Meherät Deräs Yätäfäs'ämutena Bämät'änat Lay Yaluten Gudayoch Baçeru Yämiyasay Mäs'ehét," (Asmara, September 1969), p. 14; interview: Goitom, Täkié, and Täklé.

⁷² Täsfamikaél Georgio, "Yä Sha'ebya Amäsärarätena Yalächibät Hunéta," mimeo. [an outline of the birth and development of the EPLF by a former district governor in Akälä Guzai and an ex-member of the EPLF], (January 1982).

⁷³ Christian villagers in Shilalo, for instance, demanded one hundred and fifty rifles, in September 1966, in addition to the one hundred rifles they had received earlier from the government. They claimed that they were already in bitter feud with the guerrillas: Gash and Sätit Awraja Office to Eritrea Provincial Office, 27 September 1966, in E.P.A., U3/24.

⁷⁴ "Kä 1956 Amätä Meherät Eskä 1961," 15.

⁷⁵ Eritreans for Liberation in North America (ELNA), *Harenät*, II (March 1973), 11-12.

⁷⁶ See for instance, Haliday, "The Fighting in Eritrea," 64.

⁷⁷ Zewde Gebre Sellassie, *Eritrea and Ethiopia*, 12.

⁷⁸ Wälday Kahsay (commander of the fifth zone), interview to the 2nd Army Division, 7 November, 1967: E.P.A., File 513.

[79] Ibid.; *Ethiopia* (weekly newspaper in Amharic), Asmara, 27 August 1967; and *Hebrät*, 30 May, 1967. See also Graham Taylor, "Ethiopia's Rebellion," *Africa Report* (December 1969); and Säraye Awraja Administrative Office to Eritrea Provincial Administrative Office, 10 September 1967: E.P.A., File 3/24

[82] EPLF, *Hafäshawi Polätikawi Temeherti*, 41.

[83] Wälday Kahsay, interview to the 2nd Army Division, 7 November 1967, in E.P.A., File 513.

[84] EPLF, *Hafäshawi Polätikawi Temeherti*, 41.

[85] Ibid., p. 42; ELF, *Eritrean Revolution*, 18.

[86] Gash and Sätit Awraja Police Chief to the Provincial Police Headquarters, 15 February 1969, mentioning reports of grievances of the non-Beni Amer fighters against the domination of the Revolutionary Command in Kassala by the Beni Amer: E.P.A., U2/33.

[87] This unity was named the "Provisional Unity of the Eritrean Revolution." Their opponents in the first and second zones ridiculed it as the "Unity of the Three:" Däbäsay Bäyänä, "Yä Jäbeha Tarikawi Anäsasina..." 10; Muhammed Ahmad Abdu was a student in Egypt before he joined the ELF and was sent to Syria for a year-long military training in 1966.

[88] Ibid.

[89] The Barka block (zones one and two), sent one hundred and two representatives, while the three other zones had only seventy: EPLF, *Hafäshawi Polätikawi Temeherti*, 45; interview: Däbäsay.

[90] Ibid. See also EPLF, *Hafäshawi Polätikawi Temeherti*, 45-48; and ELF, *Eritrean Revolution*, 19-20, for expressions of the conference's different attitudes towards the Supreme Council.

[91] See ELF, *Eritrean Revolution*, 19-20, for a justification of the deposition of the Supreme Council; and EPLF, *Hafäshawi Polätikawi Temeherti*, 47-49; and Bereket Habte Selassie, *Conflict and Intervention*, 65, for the opposing views of the partisans of the non-Beni Amer groups. A balanced account of the events of those days is given by Mogäs Fasil (a former EPLF member) in an untitled 38 pages study (Asmara, 1981); also interview: Däbäsay.

[92] ELF, *Eritrean Revolution*, 20.

[93] Mogäs Fasil, p. 1; interview: Qadi Ahmad and Täwäldä. EPLF, *Hafäshawi Polätikawi Temeherti*, 48, claims that some four hundred fighters were forced to flee to the Sudan within two months of the coming to power of the General Command.

[94] *Africa Confidential*, II, 24(November 1970); Zewde Gebre Sellassie, *Ethiopia and Eritrea*, 112.

[95] EPLF, *Polätikawi Temeherti*, 45, puts the number of Christian fighters killed during this period at two hundred and fifty. Lloyd Ellingson, "The Origins and Development of the Eritrean Liberation Movement," Proceedings of the Fifth International Conference of Ethiopian Studies (1978), 622, puts the number at about three hundred. See also *La Stampa* (24 August 1970); *Il Messaggero di Roma* (24 August 1970); and *La Specchio* (10 January 1970), for reports of the bloody fighting among the guerrilla forces.

[96] A government report puts the number of guerrillas that had surrendered from September 1969 to August 1970 at two hundred and eighty-one: Eritrea Governorate General, "Bä 1962 Amätä Meherät Yätäfäs'ämutenena Bämät'änat Lay Yaluten Yäsera Gudayoch Baçeru Yämiyasay Mist'irawi Mäs'ehét," [a report by the provincial administration on the major activities accomplished in the province in 1969/1970 and outlining future projects], Asmara, 1970.

[97] Pliny, "Eclectic Notes on the Eritrean Liberation Front, E Pluribus unum?" *Ethiopianist Notes* (Michigan, 1978), 38; E.P.A., chä 1/702, report from Jeddah, 21 January 1970.

[98] Halliday, "The Fighting in Eritrea," 66.

CHAPTER SIX

Split and Civil War

By the first half of 1970 it could be clearly seen that although the insurgency in Eritrea had managed to linger, the ELF had failed to accommodate all the nationalities and various interest groups in the territory in the ongoing struggle, and that it could no longer continue as a single organization. Convinced that they had nothing much in common with each other, the leaders of the various factions embarked upon preparations to break away from the ELF and form their own organizations.

The faction of the Red Sea area led by Osman Salih Sabby was the first to secede from the ELF. Sabby had already created an alternative leadership by establishing his own "General Secretariat" in opposition to the General Command. He gathered most of the Red Sea area fighters who had fled to the Sudan and lured others still in the field to quit the ELF and join his group in the Sudan. He regrouped this force in the Sudan and moved it into the southern Danakil areas via Aden.

At a meeting held at Sudoha-Ella, in the Danakil, at the end of June 1970, Sabby's group announced the formation of a separate organization which was called the Popular Liberation Forces, also known as "Sha'ebia" in Arabic. Sabby's confidant, Mohammed Ali Omaro was made commander of the army, while Sabby took charge of the political leadership.

On the external front, Sabby campaigned vigorously to discredit the General Command and to channel most of the support to his own organization. He succeeded in winning over a majority of the foreign branches of the ELF. His popularity and energetic campaign in several Arab capitals enabled him to divert much of the foreign aid to his group. Sabby also worked on veteran dissident leaders whose relations with the ELF had soured. Leaders and members of the already defunct Eritrean Liberation Movement, including Wäldäab Wäldämaryam and Mohammed Said Nawud declared their support for Sabby's organization.[1] Sabby also employed the service of Ibrahim Sultan to discredit the remaining leaders of the ELF including Idris Mohammed Adum.[2]

The handful of Christians who survived the new wave of Muslim repression in 1969 also broke away from the ELF and fled towards the highland. Issayas Afäwärqi,[3] who had been a member of the General Command in charge of the Akälä Guzai region, and his compatriots refused the General Command's summons to return to headquarters and instead moved into the more inaccessible hills of Alla, in Akälä Guzai.[4] Issayas's group constituted itself as an independent organization under the name "Sälfi Nas'enät Eritrea." It attributed its split to Muslim repression. In a document that appeared in 1971 entitled *Nhenan Elamanan* (We and Our Objectives), and believed to have been authored by Issayas, the group accused the ELF of waging a jihad against Christians.[5]

At Alla, Issayas and his colleagues began to exhort their former schoolmates and other acquaintances in Asmara, Addis Ababa, and other towns, to join their group and to help them save the insurgency from Muslim domination. Christian sympathizers of the rebellion in the towns were urged to cease supporting the ELF and channel their aid to the new group.[6]

The Christian faction focused particularly on winning the support of the Eritrean intelligentsia, something which had not been given much emphasis by the ELF. One of the leaders of the group wrote at the beginning of 1970: "We are now trying our best to win Eritrea's intellectuals to our side, for without the intelligentsia nothing of importance to Eritrea can be done."[7]

In spite of the energetic efforts it made to ensure its survival as a viable political and military force, the position of the Christian faction in 1970 was extremely precarious. The highland population within which they sought shelter from ELF attacks was largely hostile to the insurgency. In addition, since Muslims had practically monopolized the foreign relations of the secessionist movement, the Christian faction found itself virtually blocked from any source of foreign support. The group's initial efforts to secure alternative sources of assistance from the West were unsuccessful. The Christian faction contacted U.S. officials in the Kagnew Station and solicited support. Issayas himself was secretly brought into the Kagnew Station where he held talks with senior American officers. Issayas and his colleagues told the Americans that the ELF was a Communist backed organization, and that they had broken away from it because of their opposition to Communist and Arab hegemony. The group also approached the Italian Consulate in Asmara to solicit Italian assistance.[8]

The uncertainty of external support and the fear of inevitable attack from the General Command even persuaded Issayas and his colleagues to contemplate coming to terms with the Ethiopian government. In a letter of November 24, 1969, Abreham Täwäldä and Solomon Wäldämaryam, two leading members of the Christian faction expressed their desire to Ethiopian authorities to "start discussions at any time and place."[9] Although a reconciliation committee consisting of influential Eritreans managed to meet with the Christian guerrillas on several occasions, no agreement was reached because the government refused to concede the insurgents' demand for the return of a federal arrangement for Eritrea.[10] The guerrilla's demand that the government supply them with arms to fight the Muslim insurgents was also firmly rejected on the grounds that the government was not interested in fanning Muslim-Christian conflict but in securing the surrender of both groups.[11]

The third group to secede from the ELF was a faction called the "Obél Group." Four dissident members of the General Command,- Adam Salih, Osman Ajib, Ahmad Adam Omar, and Mohammed Ahmad Idris, who, it appears, aspired to overthrow the rest of their colleagues - gathered their followers at Obél in the Barka area and openly rose in rebellion. In December 1971, they named themselves the "Eritrean Liberation Forces" and formally broke away from the ELF.

The General Command which presided over the now much weakened ELF attempted to contain further erosion in the organization and whip up some support for itself by calling what was known as the Awaté Camp Military Conference, held from February 26 to March 13, 1971. It was attended by some 300 delegates from the various units of the ELF. The conference resolution, which was apparently orchestrated by the General Command, called the splinter groups "deviant elements who were and are trading with the blood, tear and sweat of our people and fighters."[12] The conference decided to maintain the General Command until the convention of a general congress, which, it said, should be called within four months. It also recommended the formation of a dialogue committee which should contact the splinter groups.

The various breakaway forces viewed the Awaté Military Conference as a General Command subterfuge to rally support to suppress the opposition. The Christian faction in Alla described it as a "new method conceived by the General Command." Issayas and his colleagues declined the ELF's offer to participate in the forthcoming congress, alleging that it was insincere of the General Command to invite them while at the same time characterizing them as counter-revolutionaries.[13]

Sabby's group condemned the Awaté Military Conference outright. It accused the General Command of leading the "Eritrean Revolution to further crisis and division." The Obél faction also adopted a similar stand.[14]

None of the three splinter groups attended the ELF's "First National Congress" held from October 14 to November 12, 1971. Most of the 560 representatives who attended this congress were said to have been loyal to the ELF leadership. It established a 37-man Revolutionary Council and an Executive Committee to lead the ELF. Idris Mohammed Adum was elected chairman, and Heruy Tädla Bairu, son of the former secretary general of the Unionist Party and the first chief executive of the Eritrean government during the federation, was elected vice-chairman.[15] The new leadership in the Revolutionary Council consisted mostly of the members of the General Command and a few of those who had been suspended at the Adobha conference.

The congress mandated the Revolutionary Council to take "all necessary steps to secure national unity." Although Sabby's group and the Obél faction were openly condemned it advised caution towards Issayas's group, "not because it believed that there were democratic elements in it but because of the threat from the armed 10,000 [Christian] peasants in the highland and Gash area and the threat from Ethiopia's divide and rule tactics."[16]

The ELF leadership set out to suppress the dissident groups soon after the end of the congress. It started with the Obél faction which was the closest. As it was based in the Barka area it posed a more urgent threat to the heart of the ELF's base. Several members of the Obél group were killed or forced to disperse to the Sudan. A few retreated to the Sahel area.[17]

Sabby's PLF and Issayas's Sälfi Nas'enät, who obviously were the next in the line of ELF's attack were alarmed by the onslaught against the Obél. Both groups were in an extremely vulnerable situation. Sabby's forces in the Danakil were already weakened by repeated attacks from government forces, which had forced them to retreat to the more inaccessible Sahel mountains. Sälfi Nas'enät, too, had sustained heavy casualties from government attacks after the middle of 1970. In addition, this group had no source of arms or other supplies.

In desperation, the three splinter groups, which had little in common except the desire to survive the ELF's war of liquidation, decided to stand together. Each of these groups had something to offer to the other. Sabby's faction, although depleted in numbers, was well funded by sympathetic Arab countries. Issayas's group, although poorly equipped, could boast of a potential recruiting ground in the highlands and the urban centers. The Obél faction, although few in number, was the only force which could claim support in western Eritrea and as such was potentially important for any future expansion towards this area.

After a few preliminary talks at the end of 1971, the three groups signed an agreement in Beirut in February 1972 to form a united front "against their common enemies."[18] The union thus established was called the Eritrean Popular Liberation Forces (EPLF). Sabby took charge of the external affairs of the organization as secretary of the Foreign Mission (a new name for the former General Secretariat). All military and internal matters were left to a coalition "Field Administration Committee" led by Issayas and a few of Sabby's lieutenants and fellow ethnic men, including Ramadan Mohammed Nur.

In late February 1972, an all-out war started between the ELF and the newly formed EPLF. This war, which was to continue almost unabated for a decade, was led by Abdullah Idris for the ELF[19] and Issayas Afäwärqi for the EPLF, perhaps two of the most ruthless guerrilla leaders which the Eritrean insurgency had produced.

The theater of the war extended from the Sahel region, the principal base of the EPLF since 1972, southwards to western Eritrea as far as the Gash area. Gradually the war zone also expanded into the highland districts as both groups raced to occupy the highlands for strategic purposes.

The EPLF was able to emerge from its position of inferiority in a short time to meet the ELF challenge successfully. At a time when student radicalism dominated the Ethiopian schools, the EPLF portrayed itself as a vanguard of the left wing and attracted the support of a significant number of relatively educated, politically conscious elements, especially from the highlands where Issayas and his colleagues were active.

The EPLF also drew support from the hierarchically structured highland communities with a marked tradition of cultural and political authoritarianism. This and the radical orientation of most of its student recruits enabled the EPLF to assimilate and implement a Leninist type of organization, a crucial tool which eventually decided the winners and losers in the Eritrean field.

By comparison, the ELF largely depended on pastoral communities that had limited exposure to modern education and little experience in broader political affairs. They pursued a mode of life which generally tended to be averse to the kind of rigid discipline and political conformity required by a guerrilla organization. The looseness and disorder which characterized society in the western lowlands adversely affected the organizational character of the ELF, where disorganization and inefficiency abounded.

The EPLF was also gaining ground on the external front. Sabby, the front's enterprising chief of foreign affairs, was in the good books of most Arab leaders. In addition to his previous patrons, he now had the support of a generous Muammar al-Qaddafi.[20] The EPLF's growing army faced no shortage of arms or money. The EPLF also succeeded in winning over most of the insurgent affiliated mass organizations abroad.

The EPLF's growing strength meant, of course, the escalation of the fighting with the ELF. In this internecine war, which was described as "more serious than clashes with the Ethiopian security forces,"[21] the insurgents increasingly deployed larger units of their armies and employed the most sophisticated of the weapons in their hands. Some 55 major battles were said to have been fought and about 2,000 fighters are believed to have died on both sides between 1972 and 1974.[22]

Nor was the civilian population in the guerrilla-affected areas spared the agonies of the civil war. The people were forced to choose sides by the warring factions and subjected to reprisals by one or the other group for alleged sympathy for the opponent. Some 52 Christian peasants in the village of Däbrä Sina were killed, and 200 houses were burnt by the ELF. At another Christian village in Ademdem, a unit of the ELF army was said to have "ordered residents into their homes, set fire to the village and shot everyone who tried to escape."[23] An ELF guerrilla leader who surrendered to the government was quoted by *The Sunday Times* as saying that his unit alone had killed 90 men between January and April 1971. The ex-guerrilla leader reportedly said: "But it is difficult to tell....It is difficult to round them all up, to know what is happening. We kill them with daggers to save ammunition."[24]

The various contending guerrilla forces were so consumed by these internecine wars that the original objectives of the insurgency, i.e., the struggle to set up an independent Eritrean government, was relegated almost to a secondary position throughout much of the first half of the 1970s. More guerrillas died fighting rival rebel forces than they did against the government army. More acrimonious accusations were exchanged between insurgent groups than directed at the government.

The fratricidal wars eroded the morale of the fighters and increased the number of deserters. Dissention within each group was rife. Issayas was able to quell a major rebellion within the core of the EPLF leadership in 1973 by resorting to extreme repression which almost destroyed the first batch of the Christian leadership of the insurgency.[25] The coalitions that were hastily formed to survive the inter-guerrilla wars were also cracking under the strain of the deep-seated hostility and mutual suspicion which characterized relations between Sabby's group and Issayas's Christian army.

Generally speaking, the insurgency in Eritrea had placed itself in virtual deadlock by the mid-1970s. Although the pressure from the Ethiopian government was not such as to threaten the insurgency with total extinction, its prospects did not appear promising. What finally saved it from stagnation, and perhaps from degeneration into conventional banditry, was the eruption of the Ethiopian Revolution in 1974, and its attendant consequences which favored the insurgency.

The Period of Uneasy Truce, 1975-1979

The general political ferment which followed the outbreak of the Ethiopian Revolution and the urban terror which the new military rulers unleashed at the end of 1974, drove thousands of the youth in Eritrea into the arms of the guerrillas. The flow of new recruits was so large that it had a significant impact on the composition of the guerrilla forces in each of the fronts. The ELF alone was said to have absorbed about 7000 new recruits in the last few months of 1974.[26] About 90 percent of the EPLF rank and file fighters at the beginning of 1975 were newcomers.[27]

The majority of the new recruits fled into whichever front they happened to contact first. In this way, the ELF, which had been a predominantly Muslim and lowland based organization, suddenly found its hands full with a predominantly Christian and urban force. The new recruits also fundamentally altered the balance in the EPLF where Sabby's followers in the field, who were in the minority to begin with, were now completely submerged by the newly arriving Christian force.

This massive infusion of fresh recruits had a diluting effect, at least initially, on the ongoing feud among the insurgents. The new members held no bitter memories of the bloody wars between the opposing factions. They were also more urban and better educated than the veteran guerrillas. Given their exposure to radical student politics, they were also less likely to fall prey to ethnic, regional, and religious proclivities. They were reluctant to join the partisan struggles and even exerted some pressure on the leadership to exercise restraint in persecuting the civil war. Since this new force had not yet been subjected to rigid organizational control and to sectarian indoctrination, it was able to constitute itself as a significant pressure group in the respective organizations.[28] There were some instances where the rank and file fighters refused to obey orders to fight rival guerrilla forces.[29]

Some pressure to end the inter-guerrilla wars also came from the civilian population, especially in the highlands. Taking advantage of the ceasefire declared in the fall of 1974 by the new Ethiopian military leaders, the guerrilla forces were rapidly expanding into the highlands. The ELF and the EPLF raced each other to stake out claims to new territories in the highlands which had hitherto remained off limits to guerrilla activity. This competition triggered a new wave of fierce battles. The local elders and clergy intervened in some instances to stop the fighting[30] and applied some pressure on the leaders to come to negotiations.[31]

These pressures, plus the insistence of some of the Arab supporters of the insurgency to end hostilities, finally brought the two guerrilla factions to talk to each other at the beginning of 1975 for the first time since the split in 1969. A tentative accord signed between field military commanders on 16 January 1975 delimited the spheres of operation of the two forces in order to avoid further clashes. The area lying east of the Asmara-Kärän road was placed within the EPLF sphere, while the western side fell under ELF control.[32] They also agreed on a joint military operation and to a division of any spoils of war in the attack on Asmara, which was due to start at the end of January 1975.[33]

Formal negotiation to end the war and to unify the rival forces started in August 1975. A joint statement at the end of a meeting in Beirut on August 13 and 14, 1975, between representatives of the ELF Revolutionary Council and the EPLF's Foreign Mission said that the two sides had agreed on the need for a unified political leadership and a single army.[34] They agreed to discuss the details of achieving these goals at a joint meeting of the leaders in Khartoum, scheduled to start on September 1, 1975.

At the Khartoum meeting the ELF was represented by Ahmad Nasser, its new chairman, elected at the organization's second general congress in May 1975; Ibrahim Totil,[35] vice-chairman and head of the Political and Organizational Bureau; Abdullah Idris, chief of the General Staff of the Executive Committee and head of the Military Bureau; and Azzein Yassin,[36] member of the Revolutionary Council and head of the Foreign Relations Bureau. Osman Salih Sabby and Wäldäab Wäldämaryam, the titular chairman of the EPLF's Foreign Mission, represented the EPLF.[37] The meeting was held under the auspices of President Numeiri of the Sudan. Iraqi Ba'ath Party officials were also present.[38]

The meeting was concluded on 7 September 1975 with the Khartoum Agreement which provided a plan for the step-by-step merger of the two organizations. They agreed to hold a general unity congress in eight months' time which, among other things, would ratify the unification of the two fronts and set up a single leadership. They also decided to hold a joint leadership conference in November 1975 and to form joint coordinating committees for foreign affairs, military operations, and political and social affairs, as well as a separate 12-member central coordinating committee to supervise their work for the interim period. A special four-man delegation representing the two fronts was dispatched to Arab countries to herald the news of their unity to their supporters and to jointly solicit further aid.[39]

The euphoria that followed the Khartoum Unification Agreement, however, came to an abrupt end when the field leaders of the EPLF publicly repudiated the agreement on the ground that they had not been represented at the Khartoum meeting. They declared that Sabby was not entitled to negotiate for the internal forces.[40] Issayas and his colleagues launched an intense campaign against the unity agreement.

A meeting in Khartoum between the Foreign Mission and the field leadership of the EPLF from 18 March to 23 March 1976 was held in an attempt to resolve the differences. However, the talks became deadlocked as each side maintained that it was the sole representative of the EPLF. The meeting finally ended in a complete rupture between the two.

This break marked the climax of the tug-of-war that had been going on between the Foreign Mission and the leaders in the field over the question of who actually had the ultimate authority in EPLF. New developments in the field seem to have encouraged Issayas to question the value of maintaining Sabby and his Foreign Mission as representatives to the front. The forces in the field no longer reflected the loose coalition formed at the Beirut agreement in February 1972. The force formerly belonging to Sabby and Issayas's Sälfi Nas'enät had been completely merged on 8 September 1973. Issayas, Solomon Wäldämaryam, P'ét'ros Solomon, and Sebhat Efrém from the former Sälfi Nas'enät, and Ramadan Mohammed Nur, Ali Se'id Abdella[41] and Salih T'et'ow of the former Sabby group consisting of the fighters from the Red Sea area, became members of the new leadership. Members of the Obél faction who found themselves in increasing disagreement with the Red Sea group, broke away from the united front early in 1973 and proceeded to the Barka area. The splinter group was annihilated by ELF forces on the way. Its few surviving members rejoined the EPLF.[42]

Meanwhile, the flood of new recruits from the Christian highlands starting in 1974 provided Issayas with a powerful lever to establish himself as the undisputed leader of the military and political forces of the EPLF inside Eritrea. His force was also highly enriched in material resources. Sabby's excellent contacts with several Arab sources had brought the EPLF a large quantity of weapons. The supply had increased tremendously in the months following the Ethiopian Revolution. An EPLF spokesman in Beirut announced in February 1975 that Libya alone had supplied weapons to the value of U.S. $5 million during January 1975.[43]

Sabby had done his job too well. By 1975 he had practically outlived his usefulness to Issayas. The EPLF had become a power to be reckoned with and did not require Sabby's service to mediate with Arab leaders. In fact, he was already beginning to be a liability to the EPLF. The new radical recruits were beginning to get uneasy about the alliance with Sabby, whom they perceived as an arch reactionary. His subsequent expulsion from the EPLF was applauded by radical student organizations, a fact which boosted the front's image as a progressive, socialist movement.[44]

Sabby spent most of his time abroad raising funds for the movement. Not surprisingly, he was out of touch with developments in the field and was not able to check the erosion of his influence in the EPLF. When he at last visited the field in April 1975 he discovered that he had few followers left inside the front.[45] This must have prompted him to push vigorously for immediate unity with the ELF, probably anticipating that his position might be more secure in a new leadership that would be formed out of the merger of the two organizations.

After being kicked out of the EPLF, Sabby once again went about reorganizing his own faction. Most members of the foreign offices; the branch associations, particularly in the Middle East; and some commanders and their fighters, mostly from the eastern lowland area, went along with Sabby. He augmented his force by recruiting Eritrean refugees in the Sudan. This new force which named itself the Eritrean Liberation Front/Popular Liberation Forces (ELF/P.L.F) began operating in the Barka area, close to Aqordät.

The split that occurred in the EPLF not only put a brake on the unification talks but also created a serious division inside the ELF over the question of whether to recognize Sabby's ELF/PLF or Issayas's EPLF. The issue reopened up the old Christian-Muslim differences in the ELF. The old guards led by Abdullah Idris favored alliance with Sabby as deterrence to Christian dominance of the movement and also in anticipation of tapping his rich resources. The new force in the ELF, which was largely Christian and sympathetic to Issayas's group, urged alliance with the EPLF.

The third regular meeting of the ELF Revolutionary Council held in August 1976 was so deeply divided over this question that it stayed in session for 41 days to reach an agreement. The compromise agreement that was eventually reached recognized Sabby's and Issayas's groups as two factions of the same organization, both of whom would be approached through their respective representatives in future talks. The Revolutionary Council meeting also agreed to endorse the earlier unity agreement with Sabby and to work for new agreements with Issayas's group.[46]

The ELF and Sabby signed a further agreement on 24 July 1977 stipulating the need for a speedy realization of unity. This agreement was roundly condemned by the rank and file members of the Christian force in the ELF. It led to factional strife within the front and eventually to the emergence of a dissident movement known as the "Fallul,"[47] which plunged the organization into a very serious crisis. The ELF leaders accused the EPLF of sponsoring dissidence inside the ELF by organizing secret cells.[48]

The EPLF and the ELF differed on the methods of bringing about unity. The former proposed that eventual merger between the two should be preceded by a period of loose alliance in which each of the fronts would maintain its organizational autonomy while coordinating some of their military and political activities. They urged that unity should be preceded by political education of the rank and file members and by the creation of the necessary structures which would integrate the forces from below.[49] The ELF, on the other hand, insisted on total and immediate merger of all groups and the establishment of a unified leadership.[50]

This divergence in the approach to unity was a result of the desire of each front to extract the maximum advantage from the projected merger. The EPLF, which was sure of its organizational capability and effectiveness at the grass-roots level, chose the method which would enable it to win over the rank and file fighters in the other groups without having to share power with the leaders of the ELF, who otherwise would demand a 50 percent share in any projected merger. The latter's insistence on a full merger appears to have been dictated by the realization that they were being rapidly overtaken by the EPLF both militarily and politically. They sought to forestall an EPLF predominance through an immediate merger.

Renewed pressure for unity was created by the military situation in 1977 in which the insurgent forces were gaining the upper hand on Ethiopian government forces. Several towns were overrun, and a large part of the countryside, including the highlands, fell under rebel control. Many of the new gains were falling into the hands of the EPLF. This appears to have worried the ELF, which was falling behind, especially in the capture of strategic areas and towns. It revived its call for unity to share the spoils of the new conquest.

The Arab supporters of the insurgency were also disconcerted by the lack of unity, particularly at a time when victory appeared imminent. The Sudanese government, whose relations with the Ethiopian regime were at their worst during this period, redoubled its effort to bring the fronts together. Other Arab countries, too, pressed their respective clients to get together, and some were said to have hinted that further assistance would depend on unification.[51]

These pressures finally induced the two fronts to begin negotiations for unity. A series of meetings were held in Damascus and inside Eritrea in April and May 1977. In October 1977 some Arab countries, including the Sudan, invited all groups for a dialogue in Khartoum. The EPLF refused to negotiate as long as Sabby's ELF/PLF was represented. The deadlock was broken when Sabby declared that he would absent himself from the meeting and that he was willing to dissolve his organization should the EPLF and the ELF agree to create one front in the field.[52]

The Khartoum talks between the EPLF and the ELF, which were held in the presence of the Sudanese first vice-president, resulted in an agreement which was signed on 20 October 1977. The agreement provided for the formation of a Joint Supreme Political Command which would be responsible for the preparation of a unification congress. Joint committees for military affairs, information, the economy, foreign relations and social affairs were also to be formed. The two sides also agreed to exclude Sabby's group from future negotiations and called on Sabby to disband his group.

The Joint Supreme Command was formed on April 20, 1978. It consisted of the three top men from each of the fronts. Ahmad Nasser, Abdullah Idris, and Ibrahim Totil represented the ELF, while on the EPLF's side were Rammadan Mohammed Nur, Issayas Afäwärqi, and Ibrahim Affa (EPLF's Military Commander). Ibrahim Totil told a cheering crowd on the occasion of the formation of the Joint Supreme Political Command that "they were now one nation and one organization."[53]

Such optimism proved, however, premature. Each front was in reality intent on building its own strength separately as ever before with the aim of outbidding its rival. Mutual mistrust and rivalry for greater territorial acquisition and for wider recognition sometimes brought the two forces to blows.[54] The various joint committees created to facilitate cooperation between the two fronts collapsed one after another for lack of mutual trust and commitment to genuine unity.[55]

ELF's continued dealings with Sabby's ELF/PLF, contrary to the October 20, 1977, agreement, and the EPLF's secret negotiations with the Ethiopian government,[56] despite the agreement which entrusted such negotiations to the Joint Supreme Political Command, deepened the mutual mistrust between the two fronts.

The Ethiopian counteroffensive in 1978 which resulted in severe setbacks for the rebel forces exacerbated the strained relations between the fronts. Each group opted to meet the offensive alone. There are also indications that each of them was hoping for the destruction of the other in the government offensive.

The Ethiopian military offensive concentrated first in areas held by ELF forces. The EPLF watched passively while the ELF suffered heavy defeats and lost much ground.[57] Hussien Khalifa, a member of the ELF Revolutionary Council and Military Bureau, accused the EPLF of ignoring the ELF's call for help and of remaining behind the battle lines "with the purpose of saving their human and material capacities and acquiring gains at the expense of the ELF."[58]

When the EPLF in turn came under heavy attack from government forces, it accused the ELF of collaborating with the government and of opening its defense lines to expose the EPLF to annihilation.[59] It even registered complaints with the Sudanese authorities that the ELF was preparing to destroy the EPLF.[60]

The need for strategic areas of retreat to escape the massive assault from the Ethiopian forces in 1978 led to a race between the two fronts to occupy the Sahel region. Its difficult terrain and its easy access to the Sudan made this area a safe haven for guerrilla forces. The EPLF crushed an ELF brigade that had reached Adobha, and blocked further ELF penetration into the Sahel.[61]

The tremendous reverses both fronts had suffered during the government counteroffensive brought about a brief lull in their internecine conflict. Their Arab allies, who attributed the recent defeat to the disunity which prevailed in the insurgent camps, also increased the pressure to bring them to resume negotiations. New round of talks were began in Khartoum on January 12, 1979. A further meeting, this time including Sabby's ELF/PLF, was hosted by Abu Dhabi, in August 1979,[62] at the insistence of President Numeiri. In October 1979, President Siyad Barre of Somalia invited them for another meeting in Mogadishu. He urged them to achieve unity inside Eritrea "in order to confront Ethiopian occupation and aggression."[63]

Although all sides did their best not to appear a spoiler of the peace initiative, none of them believed seriously that unity was possible through negotiations. The lull continued only long enough to allow them to prepare for renewed hostilities. No amount of Arab pressure or the threat of attack from the Ethiopian army could persuade them, particularly the EPLF, from marshalling all its resources to wipe out its rival once the opportune moment arrived.

The War of Liquidation, 1980-1981

The EPLF made a fast recovery from the heavy losses it suffered in 1978. By the beginning of 1980 it had reorganized itself in the Sahel and was able to make up partially for the fighters it had lost with new recruits who had fled the former EPLF-held towns for fear of Ethiopian government reprisals. In addition, the EPLF was also able to make use of recruits from Tegray sent for training by its ally, the Tegray People's Liberation Front.[64]

After achieving initial recovery, the EPLF began to concentrate on the ELF. The ELF's presence in western Eritrea and in the southern fringe of the Sahel, as well as in some parts of central and southern Eritrea, posed an obstacle to future EPLF expansion. Since most of the highland area and the eastern slopes had fallen into government hands, the EPLF had to look towards the vast and semi-arid regions of western Eritrea for future expansion. In addition, most of the EPLF's previous sources of manpower had dried up as a result of its withdrawal from the highland, central, and eastern regions. It was, therefore, motivated to look towards areas held by the ELF for new grounds for recruitment.

The EPLF also felt threatened by its rival's ability to maintain contacts over wide areas, while it was confined to the northern Sahel region, isolated from the main population areas. Heavy reliance on positional warfare, plus the extremely centralized organizational and military structure of the EPLF had reduced its capacity for mobile operations, and dispersal of forces. By contrast, the ELF's forces were widely scattered, and although fewer in number and less efficient, they were able to keep in touch with the population over wider areas.[65] The EPLF feared that, if the trend continued, the ELF might succeed in recouping its previous loses and emerge from its predicament to threaten the EPLF's predominant position.[66]

The competition for foreign aid also played a significant role in increasing the antipathy between the fronts. This became particularly acute after the 1978 government offensive which left each side desperately short of armaments. The ELF and the EPLF entered into frantic competition to replenish the weapons they had lost. The sudden switch of alliance by Libya and the People's Democratic Republic of Yemen to the Ethiopian side also deprived the EPLF of two of its most important external supporters.

Much of the EPLF's income from the towns and the agricultural areas in the highlands and the eastern slopes had virtually dried up after these areas fell into government hands. Largely confined to the sparsely populated and impoverished northern parts of the Sahel, the EPLF was finding it increasingly difficult to feed and maintain its army. This created an acute need for external assistance, whose volume could possibly increase if there were no competitors. The temptation to eliminate rivals to monopolize foreign aid appears to have been fairly strong.

The fronts also used each other as a scapegoat to explain away the 1978 debacle which had greatly disillusioned the rank and file members. Internal contradictions, which had been shelved during the euphoria which rapid success had created in the 1975-1978 period, began to crop up. Certain basic questions regarding the authoritarian character of the organizations were raised. The EPLF in particular saw these developments as a serious threat to its monolithic structure. It, therefore, sought to avert a potentially volatile situation by diverting the attention of its rank and file fighters towards a major engagement with the ELF. It had already prepared its members psychologically for war with the rival force through intense agitation attributing the 1978 defeat to ELF sabotage.[67]

Perhaps the most important factor which prompted the EPLF to start an all out war against the ELF was the gradual but basic change which was brewing inside the ELF. A significant, although poorly coordinated force in the ELF was beginning to question the fundamental secessionist thesis which viewed the Eritrean problem as a colonial issue. Some members, especially among the student elements, were impressed by some of the revolutionary measures taken by the Ethiopian government including its proclamation on land and its nationalization of industries. Ex-ELF members who later surrendered to the government and those who went to exile are unanimous in their statements that the majority of ELF members viewed the Ethiopian regime as basically progressive.[68]

The positive attitude among the rank and file in the ELF toward the Ethiopian government was contrary to what was rigidly maintained in the EPLF. The latter was worried that if those who entertained positive attitudes toward the Ethiopian government gained control of the ELF leadership they might come to a separate agreement with it. The EPLF was also concerned that the prevailing view in the ELF might find its way into its own ranks and the population in general. Some ex-members in both fronts argued that the EPLF was determined to stamp out this development before it took root both in the field and among the Eritrean people.[69]

The EPLF prepared the ground for attack by accusing the ELF of cooperating with the Ethiopian forces to destroy it. It said that the ELF had become one and the same with "the Ethiopian enemy" and declared that it deserved to be equally attacked.[70]

The EPLF started a major offensive against the ELF on 28 August 1980 by attacking scattered military units in the southern fringes of the Sahel. After annihilating two battalions of ELF forces and capturing supplies at Adobha and Ruba Ansäba, the EPLF forces moved farther into the Barka area.

The ELF was not prepared for this onslaught. Its forces were scattered and unable to regroup in time to check the EPLF advance. Still worse, it was caught at a time when it was in political disarray. It had suffered a major crisis in the middle of 1977 when differences between the newly recruited radical Christians and the old, predominantly Muslim adherents erupted into a bloody conflict over relations with Sabby and the general trend in the organization. This led to the death and desertion of over 1500 fighters from its ranks. Differing views on the ideological character of the Ethiopian government further escalated the conflict inside the ELF. The ELF's Revolutionary Council itself was torn by the intermittent power struggle between the various cliques within it. Differences within the front's leadership, and the presence of the "Eritrean Labor Party," the shadowy socialist party which operated inside the ELF, were other sources of instability. Divided within itself and disorganized, the

ELF by 1980 was indeed a poor match for the highly disciplined and seriously regimented EPLF.

Another EPLF asset was the support it received from the Tegray People's Liberation Front (TPLF). The EPLF had played a major role in strengthening the TPLF by providing it with arms and training. In addition to the service it could render to the Eritrean insurgency by diverting government offensives towards Tegray, the EPLF also sought to use the TPLF in the struggle against the ELF. Since most of the ELF positions were located in territories bordering on the Tegray region, the EPLF counted on the TPLF to arrest ELF expansion and consolidation in southern Eritrea.

The participation of the TPLF in the 1980 war on the side of the EPLF was a major factor which enabled the latter to prosecute the war effectively in areas which were far removed from its base in Sahel. The TPLF army played a major role in crushing ELF forces scattered in the southwestern parts of Eritrea, in Säraye, and Danakil.

Arab supporters of the Eritrean insurgency made intense efforts to stop the war. This time the pressure also came from the Arab League, where the issue was raised during the Arab Summit Conference in Amman in November 1980. The League's secretary, Chadli al-Qulaibi, succeeded in pressuring the fronts' leaders into attending a meeting in Tunis in March 1981.

In addition to the ELF, the EPLF, and Sabby's ELF/PLF, a fourth group called the ELF/PLF-Revolutionary Council, which had splintered from Sabby's faction, also attended the Tunis meeting.[71]

Undeterred by the Arab pressure for peace, the EPLF launched an even more massive attack while negotiations were taking place in Tunis to drive the ELF out of its remaining sanctuary in southern Barka. The cornered ELF fighters, who had no place left to retreat inside Eritrea, were said to have put up fierce resistance. Ex-guerrillas who participated in these battles on both sides observed that the anger and hatred between the two groups was so intense that the fighting was marked by extreme brutality which did not spare even the wounded and the captured.[72]

Outnumbered and outgunned, the ELF was finally forced to withdraw from Eritrea in August 1981. A force numbering about 5,000 fighters crossed the Sudanese border and sought shelter around Kassala while a few surrendered to the Ethiopian government.[73]

Unfettered by rivalry, the EPLF leaders continued to forge a highly centralized and effectively disciplined organization which could be relied upon to impose a consensus which had eluded Eritrean Separatists for so long. By a strange twist of events, a force which originated from the predominantly

Unionist Christian highlanders came to assume full charge of a secessionist movement which was started by Muslim lowlanders who viewed the Christian population in Eritrea as essentially Ethiopian, and hence, worthy to be attacked with equal ferocity.

After it lost the upper hand in the insurgency to the dominantly Christian EPLF, Eritrean Muslims, especially in the western lowlands, entered into a period of political inaction, deeply resenting what it considered Christian hegemony through the EPLF. A few, especially among the Bäni Amer, continued to maintain pockets of military resistance against the EPLF.

Other communities like the Kunama, in the Gash and Sätit area, resisted the EPLF until the mid-1980s, when a massive EPLF assault forced them to submit.

Notes

[1] The Eritrean Liberation Movement (ELM) had sent a force from the Sudan to start its own armed struggle in Eritrea in 1965. However, this force which numbered some fifty men was wiped out in the Sahel by the ELF: "Eritrea Keflä Hagär Bä Feudo-Bourgeoisie Wäqt..."; see also Markakis, *National and Class Conflict,* 109, 283.

[2] For transcripts of Ibrahim Sultan's and Wäldäab Wäldämaryam's anti-ELF broadcasts in January 1970, over *Radio Damascus,* see E.P.A., U2/77.

[3] He was a first year student at the Haile Selassie I University before he joined the ELF in 1966. In 1967 he was sent to China for one year of military training. It is said that on his return, he created good relations with Sabby, and that after the formation of the General Command, Abdullah Idris, a strong man in the General Command and a Beni Amer, suspected this collusion between Sabby and Issayas and was waiting for an opportune moment to eliminate Issayas: Interview, Täwäldä.

[4] The leading figures in this group were Wälday Gedäy (later killed in Kassala by orders of the General Command), Abreham Täwäldä, Solomon Wäldämaryam, Abära Mäkonnen, Häbtäselassé Gäbrämädhen, Wäldämikaél Haylé, Barahi Negusé, Mäsfen Hagos, Täwäldä Iyob, and Asmärom Gäbräegziabhér.

[5] "Our Struggle and Its Goals," November 1971, reprinted in Eritreans for Liberation in North America (EFLNA), *Liberation,* II, 3 (March 1973).

[6] A certain Täsfaledät Täklé, who was brought to an Ethiopian court in Asmara in connection with aiding the guerrillas, testified that Christian sympathizers of the movement were told by the leaders of the Christian faction of the need to recruit Christian followers in the towns in order to weaken the Muslim group: E.P.A., U1/697.

[7] Habtäsellasé Gäbrämädhen's letter to American officers working at the Kagnew, in E.P.A., U1/1942.

[8] Täsfamikaél Georgio's testimony to the Eritrean High Court, in E.P.A., wä/mä/557/62; see also Täsfamikaél Georgio, "Yä Sha'ebya Amäsärarätena Yalchebät Hunéta," 7-10; and Habtäsellasé's letter to his American contacts in the Kagnew Station, in E.P.A., U1/1942; Habtäsellasé's letter to the Italian Consul in Asmara, 5 April 1970, and Baron Emanuel Scammaca, the Italian Consul General, to Däjazmach Täsfayohannes Bärhé, 7 April 1970, in E.P.A. U2/866.

[9] Letter of Abreham Täwäldä and Solomon Wäldämaryam, 24 November 1969, in E.P.A., wä/mä/557/62.

[10] This was revealed by Däjazmach Täsfayohannes Bärhé, the Assistant Governor General of Eritrea Province in testimony he gave to the Eritrean High Court on 16 March 1971: E.P.A., U1/697.

[11] Colonel Gäbräegziabhér Mäharänä (a member of the reconciliation committee), testimony to the Eritrean High Court, 12 March 1971, in ibid.

[12] Quoted in ELF, *Eritrean Revolution*, 30.

[13] EPLF, Hafäshawi *Polätikawi Temeherti*, 41-52.

[14] ELF, *Eritrean Revolution*, 23; Däbäsay Bäyänä, "Yä Jäbeha Tarikawi Anäsas...," 14-16.

[15] His father, Tädla Bairu defected to the ELF in 1966, and joined the Supreme Council briefly. However, he was unable to work with his former political enemies, and soon withdrew from the political scene. Heruy graduated from Haile Selassie I University in 1963.

[16] ELF, *Eritrean Revolution*, 23-24.

[17] Täklähaymanot Abära, "Private Note," 3; Mogäs Fassil, 4.

[18] EPLF, *Vanguard*, I, 1(January 1973); *Africa Contemporary Records* (1972-3).

[19] Abdullah Idris was born from a nomadic Beni Amer family in Hagaz. He attended elementary school in Aqordat. He was sent for military training to the Syrian Military Academy. He was an influential member of the Revolutionary Council and the Executive Committee in charge of military affairs.

[20] Qaddafi was said to have pledged $7,200,000 to the insurgency in Eritrea within a year of his coming to power: J. Bowyer Bell, "Bab El Mandab, Strategic Trouble Spot," *Orbis*, Vol. XVI, no 14. Libyan arms destined for the Eritrean rebels valued at 1 million pounds sterling was captured by North Yemeni troops during their invasion of South Yemen in September 1972: J. Bower Bell, "Endemic Insurgency and International Order: The Eritrean Experience," *Orbis*, XVIII, 2(Summer 1974), 437.

[21] Godfrey Morrison, "Eritrea and the Southern Sudan: aspects of some wider African problems," *The Minority Rights Group*, Report no. 5, (London, 1976), 6.

[22] Interview: Re'esom; Marina and David Ottaway, *Ethiopia: Empire in Revolution* (New York, African Publishing Co., 1978), 207. The authors claim that ELF officials had admitted that the number of deaths were more than two thousand. See also Jim Hoagland, "Eritrea: Rebellion Fading?" *The Washington Post*, 4 June 1972, for reports that several hundred guerrillas were killed in the clashes during the first few months of 1972.

²³ *Time*, 1 March 1971; *The Sunday Times* (London, 30 May 1971); see also Taye Geremew, "Rebellion in Eritrea;" and Morrison, "Eritrea and Southern Sudan," 5.

²⁴ *The Sunday Times*, 30 May 1971.

²⁵ This opposition known as the "Mänka movement" consisted mostly of members from the Akälä Guzai district. Issayas and his supporters portrayed the movement as an Akälä Guzai conspiracy against those from Hamasén. The leaders of the Mänka movement opposed Issayas's monopolization of power and his increasing dictatorial tendency: See Mogäs Fassil, 3; Täsfamikaél Georgio, "Yä Sha'ebia Anäsasena Yalächebät Hunéta," 14; see also *Africa Confidential*, Vol. XV, no. 25, 19 December 1974, for reports of division and several assassinations in the EPLF in July and August 1974, as a result of these differences; see also, Shumet Sishagne, "The Genesis of the Differences in the Eritrean Secessionist Movement," *Proceedings of the Eighth International Conference of Ethiopian Studies*, Vol. II, 1988.

²⁶ Däbäsay Bäyänä, "Yä Jäbeha Tarikawi Anäsas...," 26.

²⁷ Mogäs Fassil, 4. This author, who was in the EPLF at this time, wrote that "several thousand of youth from Asmara were flooding into the bush" during this time.

²⁸ This was particularly true in the ELF where the relative laxity in the organization allowed the newcomers a great deal of latitude. The highly regimented EPLF did not take much time to put its new members under firm organizational control.

²⁹ Däbäsay Bäyänä, "Yä Jäbeha Tarikawi Anäsas..." 26. See also Marina and David Ottaway, *Ethiopia Empire in Revolution*, 208, for information that some guerrilla units were court-martialed for refusing to fight rival guerrilla forces.

³⁰ Fierce battles between the EPLF and the ELF at Zager and Woqi, in Hamasén, were brought to an end in October 1974, through the intervention of the local elders and priests. Mogäs Fassil, 4; and Sherman, *Eritrea*, 82.

³¹ A committee of local representatives established by the Provisional Military Administrative Council which was assigned to contact the insurgents in order to open dialogue between the guerrillas and the government also tried to reconcile the warring guerrilla factions.

³² Interview: Däbäsay.

³³ Ibid.; Pliny, "Eritrean Liberation Front," 39; Sherman, *Eritrea*, 85.

³⁴ *The Guardian*, 15 August 1975.

³⁵ Ibrahim Totil is from the Baria tribe. He had no formal education, but had received military training in Iraq. Täwäldä Bärhé, "Yä Jäbeha Menenätena Wudqät" mimeo., (Asmara, January 1982), 21.

³⁶ Azzein Yassin was born in Ali Gider, near Tässänäy. He was born from a Sudanese woman. His father, Blatta Yassin, was an influential leader of the Answar Isuna sect. Azzein graduated from Khartoum University. His close relation with Idris Osman Qälaydos, also from the same Ali Gider area, earned him important posts in the ELF in the 1960s: Ibid., 15.

[37] No one appeared for this meeting from the EPLF's field leadership. Sabby claimed in this meeting that he was mandated by the field leadership to represent them as well. ELF, *Eritrean Revolution*, 26; Däbäsay, "Yä Jäbeha Tarikawi Anäsas..." 39.

[38] Pliny, "The Eritrean Liberation Front," 39.

[39] David B. Ottaway, "Eritrean Nationalist Group's Sign an Agreement to Merge," *International Herald Tribune*, 20 October 1975.

[40] It was later revealed that Sabby had actually written to the field commanders on August 9, 1975, asking Issayas Afäwärqi, Ramadan Mohammed Nur, and Abu T'iyara, to attend the Khartoum meeting. They responded to Sabby a week later that they would not attend nor abide by its decisions. Sabby allegedly presented a forged document which showed that the EPLF field administrative committee had agreed to be represented by him: ELF, *Eritrean Revolution*, 26.

[41] Ali Seid Abdella had participated in the Hijacking of an Ethiopian Airlines passanger plane in 1969 in Karachi. He was the Foreign Minister of Eritrea from 2000 to his death on August 28, 2005.

[42] Mogäs Fassil, 4; and EPLF, Hafäshawi Polätikawi Temeherti, 55.

[43] Cited in Africa Contemporary Record, 1974-75.

[44] See, for instance, Eritreans for Liberation in North America, Reactionary Clique Forced Out of the EPLF (New York, 1976)

[45] Mogäs Fassil, 4.

[46] Interview: Däbäsay.

[47] Fallul, meaning anarchy, was the name given to the movement by the ELF leadership, signifying its defiance of authority and its tendency to take matters into its own hands and to operate outside of the established organizational structure.

[48] ELF, Eritrean Revolution, 27.

[49] EPLF, Hafäshawi Polätikawi Temherti, Part II, n.d., 42-44.

[50] Pliny, "The Eritrean Liberation Front," 40; ELF, Eritrean Revolution, 27.

[51] See The Economist, 1-7 April 1978; Africa Confidential, XX, 19(12 September 1979); Lloyd Ellingson, "The Origins and Development of the Eritrean Liberation Movement," Proceedings of the Fifth International Conference of Ethiopian Studies (1978), 623.

[52] Sabby's concession was said to have been made on the realization that the two fronts would not be able to reach agreement to form one organization. He could, therefore, create a positive impression among his Arab patrons without at the same time losing anything

[53] Quoted by The Times, 28 April 1978.

[54] Skirmishes between the two fronts were reported during the capture of Elabärät from government hands in April 1977, over the issue of who would control the town. There were also accusations and counter-accusations after the fall of Kärän. ELF forces were said to have refused to accept EPLF help and lost a major base near Adi

Qayeh as a result: Africa Confidential, XVIII, 23(November 18, 1977); Pliny, "The Eritrean Liberation Front," 43-44.

[55] The joint committee for information initially made progress by coordinating joint broadcasts over Omduruman Radio. Partisanship in dissemination of information, however, soon made joint work difficult. The committee broke down in September 1978 following disagreements over the handling of news coming from the field. See for instance, Impact International, VIII, 24(London, December 22, 1978 - January 11, 1979).

[56] The EPLF held a series of talks with the Ethiopian government in Berlin from the end of 1977 to June 1978.

[57] The highly coordinated attack on the ELF was carried out by Task Forces 501, 502 and 507 of the government army: Ethiopia, Ministry of Defense, Political Department of the Northern Command, a mimeographed account of the 1978 offensive.

[58] Hussien Khalifa, interview, September 29, 1978, in ELF, Eritrean Revolution, 55-56.

[59] EPLF, leaflet distributed in Adi Quala (Särayé) in May 1982; interview, Däbäsay.

[60] Cited in a statement of the ELF's Executive Committee on 3 November 1978, in ELF, Eritrean Revolution, 8.

[61] Interview: Re'esom and Däbäsay.

[62] Africa Confidential, XX, 19(September 12, 1979).

[63] Quoted in Africa Research Bulletin, October 1979, 5438-9.

[64] Interview: Täwäldä, Däbäsay, and Re'esom.

[65] After its first organizational congress in 1971, the ELF had divided the areas in which it operated into twelve administrative units: Gash, Sätit, Kunama and Bariya region, upper Barka, lower Barka, southern Sänhit, northern and eastern Sänhit, Sahel, Sämhar, Hamasén, Särayé, Akälä Guzay, northern Danakil and southern Danakil. The administrative units were further subdivided into smaller area committees. ELF forces were distributed throughout these administrative units. Although they had evacuated most areas after the 1978 government offensive, they still maintained presence in the Gash, Barka, Danakil, and Särayé areas, and also kept small pockets of forces in the rest.

[66] Mogäs Fassil, 11; see also ELF, Awot, no. 6, December 28, 1980, which accuses the EPLF of starting the war "to break its isolation from the masses."

[67] Interview: Re'esom and Däbäsay.

[68] Interview: Ibid., and Täwäldä. See Africa Research Bulletin, October 1980, 5830, for similar statements by ex-ELF members living abroad. See also Tesfatsion Medhane, Eritrea: Dynamics of a National Question (Amsterdam: B.R. Grunner, 1986), for the kind of sympathetic attitude towards the Ethiopian Revolution which was developing among ELF members.

[69] Täwäldä Bärhé, "Yä Jäbeha Menenätena Wudqät," 38; interview: Däbäsay, Re'esom, and Téwodros.

[70] Mogäs Fassil, 11; see also EPLF, Fes'amétat, September 15-November 15, 1980, for an EPLF accusation that the ELF was conducting secret negotiations with the Ethiopian government to attack it.

[71] This organization also known as the "Ajib's Group" broke away from Sabby at the end of 1979. It was led by Osman Ajib and Ali Mohammad Barhatu. Both were known to have been pro-Iraqi Ba'athists. They drew their support exclusively from Iraq. Osman Ajib was assassinated in Khartoum in November 1980: See Africa Research Bulletin, 1981, 5993; and Täwäldä, "Yä Jäbeha Menenätena Wudqät," 5; Täwäldä, 35-36; Africa Confidential, XX, 19, September 12, 1979, and XXI, 24, November 26, 1980.

[72] Mogäs Fassil, 30; interview: Re'esom, Däbäsay, and Täwäldä.

[73] Ibid.; Täwäldä Bärhé, "Yä Jäbeha Menenätena Wudqät," p. 37.

EPILOGUE

The implosion of the regime of Colonel Mengistu Hailämaryam and the dramatic disintegration of the Ethiopian army in the spring of 1991 marked a decisive phase in the history of the three decades of armed insurgency in Eritrea. It also marked the climax of the severe crisis and paralysis which had bedeviled Ethiopian politics for over three decades.

Notwithstanding his immense international prestige and the reverence shown to him by many of his subjects, Emperor Haile Selassie left Ethiopia in the doldrums. Although he fathered most of the reforms which shaped the modern Ethiopian state, he was unable and in most instances unwilling to go the extra mile required to give substance to many of these reforms.

The emperor's penchant for undermining traditional institutions was not matched by a willingness to create new ones. He virtually destroyed all rival bases of power and left only himself as arbiter of the country's destiny. The Ethiopian state became synonymous with the person of the emperor.[1] His obsession with personal power led him to favor loyalty over competence and to cripple initiative in his regime.

The emperor was not willing to delegate authority even after he had reached an advanced age bordering on senility. Those who opposed him were thrown into oblivion and those who chose to work for him were reduced to the status of mere puppets. With the old generation politically emasculated and the younger ones profoundly alienated, Ethiopia found herself in the 1960s on the edge of a political precipice.

Nowhere was the cost of the emperor's policy and the paralysis of his regime more evident as it was in Eritrea. In its quest to destroy any semblance of independent political activity, the government suppressed not only the opposition parties, but also its own allies. It dismantled the Unionist Party, the bulwark of the Ethio-Eritrean union. By so doing it tore down its single most important base of support inside Eritrea.[2]

The activists of the Unionist Party were made to fade into obscurity at the very time when Ethiopia's hostile neighbors were busy sponsoring opposition forces to facilitate the secession of Eritrea. The haphazard and grossly incompetent measures which the central government took to deal with the insurgency resulted in the further erosion of its position in Eritrea.

The rebellion in Eritrea, together with the widening disenchantment of the Ethiopian intelligentsia, and the growing urban discontent, contributed greatly in hastening the collapse of Haile Selassie's regime in 1974. The demise of the old regime, however, did not, as many had hoped, inaugurate an era of progress and stability. If at all, societal cleavages which were pushed under the rug throughout the long reign of the emperor, resurfaced, and threw the Ethiopian polity into a state of profound political disarray. Its politically naive, and yet ideologically contentious youth, engaged itself in fratricidal struggle.

The polarization of political differences and the ruthlessness with which these differences, were played out in post-1974 Ethiopia, left in the political arena only the extremist elements - those that did not hesitate to use any means to achieve their goals. In Addis Ababa, state power which was initially held by the rather nebulous, though democratically inclined committee of young officers (the Därg), was eventually hijacked by the most ruthless of them all, Mengistu Hailämaryam.

Among the many contending guerrilla forces which were swarming the Ethiopian countryside in the 1970s and 1980s, only the most rigidly organized Tegray People's Liberation Front, which idolized Stalin, managed to survive and prosper.

In Eritrea, too, those groups that were relatively open and organizationally decentralized were swept away by the determined onslaught of the highly regimented forces of the EPLF. The latter was also able to benefit greatly from the folly of the military junta in Addis Ababa which ended up in alienating a broad section of the Eritrean society. The radical political rhetoric and socialistic economic measures of the new regime antagonized a good deal of the urban businessmen and the gentry in the countryside. The junta's inept handling of the Eritrean problem, and the brutal repression it subsequently launched in the towns, drove thousands of the youth into the arms of the insurgents. This phenomenon escalated the conflict tremendously and aggravated the scale of disaffection in the province.

Having squandered what little support it had generated in the early years of the revolution, and paralyzed by the ferocious purges it had carried out within its own ranks, the embattled military regime continued to blunder its way into disaster. The massive, but poorly led and disorderly, military campaigns it undertook in Eritrea, and elsewhere in the country, ended up only in feeding its enemies with much needed armament. Its excessive demands on the countryside drove the peasantry into desparation and made it attentive to insurgent propaganda.

This progressive loss of political and military initiative, and the complete erosion of its credibility, eventually led Colonel Mengistu's regime into a state of total paralysis. The manner in which it collapsed in the middle of 1991 is testimony to the scope of its impotence and the severity of the crisis which surrounded it.

The collapse of Mengistu's regime and the disintegration of the Ethiopian army, left the EPLF, which had smashed all other rival groups in Eritrea through two decades of bitter civil war, as the sole power in the province. It soon established itself as a provisional government of Eritrea, and earnestly embarked legitimizing the creation of an independent Eritrean state.

Addressing a conference that met in Addis Ababa in June 1991, to draw a charter for a transitional government for Ethiopia, the EPLF Secretary General, Issayas Afäwärqi, said: "Forget history. Men make history, and we have made an independent Eritrea."[3] It is one of the greatest ironies of history that a movement which originated from the predominantly Christian highlands of Eritrea - the core region of the historic Ethiopian polity and the bastion of the Ethiopian irredentist movement in the political struggles of the 1940s and 1950s - should preside over the liquidation of the Ethio-Eritrean union. Only four decades back, the Eritrean youth from the Christian highland region, rallied solidly behind Andinät, the militant irredentist youth organization. Hundreds of young men from the city of Asmara and the surrounding Hamasén district had fled into the bush to fight anti-unionist forces. Their famous slogan then was, "Mother Ethiopia or Death." The fact that the EPLF succeeded in mobilizing the youth from this same region to destroy this hard-won union, is an indication of the sea change which had occurred in that region over the last three decades.

This irony assumed a particulary sharp edge, when a large delegation of Eritreans from the Moslem areas of the western lowland, the birth place of the secessionist movement, arrived in Addis Ababa in 1989 to express their willingess to abandon secessionist demands in return for guaranteed internal autonomy.

Another surprising historical twist which showed the extent of the changes which had occurred in perceptions of self-identification in that region was the stubborn resistance of the Kunama community to secessionist demands. The Kunama, whose past connections with historic Ethiopia were rather checkered, stood on the side of the Ethiopian army and waged a determined war against secessionist armies untila massive EPLF victory broke their resistance in 1984.

Equally ironic was the substantial and unreserved assistance provided to Eritrean secessionism by the Tegray People's Liberation Front. Considering the very close historical, cultural, linguistic and economic affinities between Tegray and the Tegreñña-speaking parts of Eritrea, the rather enthusiastic support rendered by the Tegréan political elite in the TPLF, for the secession of Eritrea, is hard to explain. The measure was a complete reversal of the traditional position of the power elite in Tegray which had considered the highland provinces of Eritrea as unambiguouly a part of the Tegray domain. Nor had any of the political movements of the 1940s in the Christian highlands of Eritrea envisaged an arrangement which would result in a separation of the Tegreñña-speaking communities on both sides of the Märäb river.

Considering the current flux in the state of affairs in the Horn of Africa, it would be futile to try to explain these historical paradoxes subject as they are to still further transformations. But they certainly reflect the massive socio-political fissure, aggravated by deepening misery, which has gripped that part of the world.

Notes

[1] On the nature of Haile Selassie's personal rule, see Clapham, *Haile-Selassie's Government*; and Bahru Zewde, *A History of Modern Ethiopia*, 1855-1974 (London: James Currey, 1991), p. 201f.

[2] John W. Harbeson argues: "in ending Eritrean federation in favor of central imperial rule , Haile Selassie placed the consolidation of his personal regime above the evolving basis of the Ethiopian state, with injurious consequences for its future:" *The Ethiopian Transformation: The Quest for the Post-Imperial State* (Boulder: Westview Press, 1988), p. 220.

[3] *Time*, July 15, 1991.

BIBLIOGRAPHY

I. Unpublished Materials

A. Archives

Addis Ababa University. Library of the Institute of Ethiopian Studies, Manuscript Section.

Ethiopian government. Eritrean Province Archive [E.P.A.]

_____. Archives of Ghinda Wäräda Administration (Eritrea).

_____. Archives of Red Sea Awraja Administration (Massawa).

Great Britain. Public Record Office, Foreign Office papers. Kew Gardens, London.

_____. Bodleian Library, Oxford. Trevaskis's Papers.

Italian Government. Archivio storico del Ministero degli Affari Esteri (ASMAE). Rome.

_____. Archivio storico del Ministero dell'Africa Italiana (ASMAI). Rome.

Archivio dello stato (PCM). Rome.

United States. National Archives. Department of State papers.

B. Documents and Manuscripts

Amdämikaél Dässaläñ. *Yä Ityoppya Liyézon Offisär Mastawäsha* [Amharic]. (The Ethiopian Liaison Officer's notebook). Asmara, 1952.

Anonymous. "Reserved Areas, and Somaliland: An American Critic's Observation," n.d.

Anonymous. *Eritrea Bä Tarik Yä Ityoppya Akal Selämähonwa* [Amharic]. (The historical evidence about Eritrea being an integral part of Ethiopia). n.d.

Däbäsay Bäyänä. *Yä Jäbeha Tarikawi Anäsasena Bäyägizéw Yakahédachäw Tarikawi Kenewunoch* [Amharic]. (The history of the rise of the ELF and its activities). Asmara, 1982.

Imperial Ethiopian government. Governorate General of Eritrea. *Kä 1941 Amätä Mehrät Wädih Yä Eretra Yä Polätika Hunétawoch* [Amharic]. (Political conditions in Eritrea since 1948). [1960s?], Asmara.

_____. *Kä 1956 Amätä Mehrät Eskä 1961 Amätä Meherät Deräs Yätäfäs'ämutena Bämät'änat Lay Yaluten Gudayoch Baçeru Yämiyasay Mist'irawi Mäs'ehét* [Amharic]. (A confidential booklet showing the works accomplished between 1963 and 1969 and those under study). Asmara, September 1969.

_____. *Bä 1962 Amätä Meherät Yätäfäs'ämutenena Bämät'änat Lay Yalutin Yäsera Gudayoch Baçeru Yämiyasay Mist'irawi Mäs'ehét* [Amharic]. (A confidential booklet showing the works accomplished and those under study in 1969). Asmara, September 1970.

_____. *Survey of Counter-Insurgency Operations in Eritrea and Draft Proposals* [Project Adwa]. 1968.

_____. *Yä Eretra Hezbena Yä Mist'er Derejet* [Amharic]. (Underground organizations and the Eritrean people). n.d.

Ethiopian government. *Yä Qeññ Gezat Astädadär Bä Eretra, 1941-1952* [Amharic], (a compilation of selected documents from the archives of the former Ministry of the Pen).

_____. *Federation, 1952-1962* [Amharic]. (A compilation of selected documents from the archives of the former Ministry of the Pen).

_____. *Eretra Keflä Hagär Bä Feudo-Bourgeoisie Astädadär Wäqt, 1962-1974* [Amharic]. (A collection of documents selected from various government archives).

Fessehayé Täsfamikaél. *Alla Adehanänä Emkulu Ekuy As'ene Walteha Tehtäl Sälameha* [Tegreñña]. Asmara, 1947.

_____. *Hezbi Mätahet Käränen, Aqurdaten, Baräntun, Be'arbaetä Abäyiti Mängestat Le'ukan Kämzetmärämärä Zegäles'* [Tegreñña]. (A description of the investigation by the Four Powers Commission of the peoples of the lowland, Kärän, Aqordät, Bäräntu). November 1947.

Great Britain, Foreign Office Research Department. *Eritrea and Italian Somaliland*. February 1944.

"The Hamasien: A Social Survey," 1944, in Trevaskis Papers, Rhodes Library, MSS Brit. Emp. S 367, Box 1.

Ibrahim Sultan. *Statement of Eritrean People: An Appeal to the Second Arab Summit Conference*. August 31, 1964.

L' Associazione Italo-Eritrei. *Situazione Degli Italo-Eritrei Nel Futuro Della Eritrea*. Asmara, February 1947.

Longrigg, S. *Some Problems of Administration in Eritrea*. March 1944.

_____. *Ethiopian Irredentism in Eritrea*, 25 March 1943.

_____. *Mischief-making in Eritrea*, n.d.

Mahbär Feqri Hagär. *Minutes of the Meetings of the Central Committee of the Mahbar Feqri Hagär* [Tegreñña]. Asmara, 1951-52.

Mezhiet [pen name]. "Relazione Approssimativa dei Partiti Politici - Attuali Affiliati al Partito Centrale (Mahber Fekri' Hagher)." Asmara, March 1947.

Mogäs Fassil. No Title. (An account of the organizational character of the EPLF by a former member)

Mohammed Omar Qadi, *Promemoria Della Lega Musulmana Indipendente Dell'Eritrea, Con Sede A Massaua.* 1947.

Moslem League of Eritrea. *To the United Nation Commission for Eritrea.* Asmara, 1950.

Nägga Hayläsellasé. *Yä Hagär Feqir Yä Wäqetu Hunéta* [Amharic]. (The present conditions of the Hagär Feqir). Asmara, May 1946.

_____. *Selä T'alyanoch* [Amharic]. (About the Italians). Asmara, 1947.

_____. *Yä T'alyanoch Polätika Bä Eretra* [Amharic]. (Italian politics in Eritrea). Asmara, March 1947.

_____. *Yä Eretra Polätika Hunéta* [Amharic]. (political conditions in Eritrea). Asmara, 1949.

Ostini, F. *Il `Comitato' e la sua azione politica.* Asmara, June 1947.

Partito Liberale Unionista. *Perche Si Chiede L'Union Condizionati.* Asmara, February 28, 1950.

Simret Habte. *Background to the Dilemma of the Eritrean Liberation Fronts.* Stockholm, February 1978.

Tädla Bairu. *The British Military Administration in Eritrea and Some Aspects of its Political Activities in this Territory.* Asmara, 1947.

Täklähaymanot Abära. *Yä Gel Mastawäsha* [Amharic]. (private notebook). Massawa, 1981.

Täklay Gäbrämaryam, *Interview to Ethiopian News Agency,* Addis Ababa, n.d.

Täsfamikaél Georgio. *Yä Sha'ebiya Amäsärarätena Yalächebät Hunéta* [Amharic]. (On the formation of the EPLF and its present situation). January 1982.

Täwäldä Bärhé. *Yä Jäbeha Menenätena Wudqät* [Amharic]. (What the ELF is and the reasons for its failure). Asmara. January 1982.

_____. no title. [Amharic]. (An account of developments within the insurgent movements by an ex-director of the ELF Cadre School). Asmara, 1981.

Trevaskis, G.K.N. *The Former Italian Colony of Eritrea.*

U.S., Department of State. "The Reserved Area and Somaliland." 10.7.1945.

Wäldä'ab Wäldämaryam. *The Liquidation of Eritrea?* 1947.

_____. *The Truth About Eritrea: Lecture Delivered by Mr. Woldeab Woldemariam, Head of the Eritrean Liberation Movement's Delegation Abroad.* Khartoum, 20 January 1965.

_____. *An Open Letter to Brothers Idris Mohammed Adem, Taha Nur, Idris Kelaydos, Sayed Mohammed and Muhammed Salih.* 8.3.1969.

Worqu Mäkonen (Colonel). *Abiy Riport Lä Germawi Negusä Nägäst* [Amharic]. (An Important Report to His Imperial Majesty). 12 November 1970.

C. Theses

Amare Tekle. "The Creation of the Ethio-Eritrean Federation: A Case Study in Post-War International Relations (1945-1950)" Ph.D., University of Denver, 1964.

Araia Tseggai, "The Economic Viability of an Independent Eritrea" Ph.D., Lincoln, Nebraska, 1981.

Ellingson, Lloyd. "Eritrea: Separatism and Irredentism, 1941-1985." Ph.D., Michigan State University, 1986.

Gebru Tareke. "Rural Protest in Ethiopia, 1941-1970: A Study of Three Rebellions." Ph.D., Syracuse University, 1977.

Giorgulli, Mauro. "Origini E Vicende Della Federazione Etiopica - Eritrea, 1947-1962." Tesi di Laura, Universita di Roma, 1982/2.

Kidanemariam Mengesteab. "The Careers of the Masazgi Brothers: Banditry in 1941-1951 Eritrea." B.A., Addis Ababa University, 1976.

Medhane Tadesse. "The History of Geza Abba Shaul (Asmara) up to 1974." B.A. Thesis, Addis Ababa University, 1988.

Merid W. Aregay. "The Settlement of the Status of Eritrea, 1941-52." M.A. Thesis, University of Chicago, August 1959.

Mesfin Araya, "Eritrea, 1941-52, the failure of the emergence of the nation state: Towards a clarification of the Eritrean question in Ethiopia." Ph.d., City University of New York, 1988.

II. Published Materials

A. Official Publications

Great Britain. Ministry of Information. *The First to be Freed: The Records of the British Military Administration in Eritrea and Somalia, 1941-1943*. London: His Majesty's Stationary Office, 1944.

_____. *House of Commons, Sessional Papers* (1952-3). Vol. 30, Cmd. 8690.

_____. *Report of the Government of the United Kingdom of Great Britain and Northern Ireland to the General Assembly Concerning the Administration of Eritrea (for the period December 1950 to September 1952)*. 8 November 1952.

Four Power Commission of Investigation for the Former Italian Colonies. *Report on Eritrea*. 1948.

Government of Egypt. *Memorandum Submitted by the Egyptian Government to the Paris Peace Conference*. August 1946.

Governo Dell'Eritrea. *Elenco dei capie e notabili indigeni stipendiati e del personale indigeno in servizio dell' Aministrazione civile dell'Eritrea*. Asmara, 1917.

Imperial Ethiopian government. *Memorandum Presented by the Imperial Ethiopian government to the Council of Foreign Ministers in London,* September 1945. London: St. Clements Press, 1946.

_____. State Bank of Ethiopia. *Report on Economic Conditions and Market Trends.* Addis Ababa, December 1963.

Government of Italy, Istituto Agricolo Coloniale. *Some Data on Italian Activity in the Colonies.* Firenze: Istituto Agricolo Coloniale, 1945.

_____. L' agricoltura nella colonia *Eritrea, e l' opera dell' Italia.* Firenze: Istituto Agricolo Coloniale, 1946.

_____. *Some Photographic Representations of Italy's Actions in Ethiopia.* 1946.

_____. *Main Features of Italy's Actions in Ethiopia, 1936-1941.* n.d.

_____. *Note aggiutive a Memorandum su i territori Italiani in Africa.* 1946.

_____. *Memorandum Sulla situazione economica e finanzieria dei territori in Africa.* Firenze: Istituto Agricolo Coloniale, 1947.

United Nations. *Official Records. 314th Meeting, First Committee.* New York, 1949.

_____. *Official Records of the Third Session of the General Assembly, 217th Plenary Meeting.* Part II. New York, 1949.

_____. *Official Records of the Fourth Session of the General Assembly, Plenary Meetings.* New York, 1950.

_____. *Report of the United Nations Commission for Eritrea. General Assembly Official Records, Fifth Session, Supplement No. 8 (A/1285).* New York, 1950.

_____. *Official Records of the Fifth Session, Ad Hoc Political Committee.* New York, 1950.

_____. *Progress Report of the United Nations Commissioner in Eritrea During the Year 1951* (A/1959). 16 November 1951.

_____. *Final Report of the United Nations Commissioner in Eritrea, General Assembly Official Records, Seventh Session, Supplement No. 15* (A.2188). 1952.

United States. Department of Commerce. *International Reference Service.* No. 12, May 1947.

_____. Department of State. *Foreign Relations of the United States.* Vol. V, 1947.

_____. Office of Intelligence Report. *Affinities of the Western Province of Eritrea with Adjacent Areas.* OIR no. 4996, September 1949.

_____. Office of Intelligence Report. *The Ethiopia - Eritrea Federation: A Progress Report.* OIR no. 7130, 8 February 1956.

_____. Office of Naval Intelligence. *Opportunities for Communist Penetration of Ethiopia and the Horn of Africa.* 1958.

B. Insurgent Publications

Association of Eritrean Students in North America. *Reactionary Clique Forced Out of the EPLF.* New York, 1976.

_____. *In Defence of the Eritrean Revolution Against Ethiopian Social Chauvinists.* New York, 1978.

Eritreans for Liberation in North America. *Harinet* (Liberation). Vol. II, no. 3, March 1973.

Eritrean Liberation Front (ELF). *Awot.* No. 6, December 28, 1980.

_____. *The Eritrean People's Cause* [Arabic]. 1963.

_____. *Eritrean Revolution.* Beirut, 1979.

_____. *Political Programme of the ELF.* Beirut: ELF Foreign Information Center, 1975.

_____. *Statement of the ELF Executive Committee concerning the war with the EPLF.* September 26, 1981.

Eritrean Liberation Front - People's Liberation Forces (ELF/PLF). *Eritrean Review.* August 1977, February 1980, June 1980, December 1980.

Eritrean People's Liberation Front (EPLF). *Fes'amétat* [Tegreñña]. Vol. III, September-November, 1980.

_____. *Hafäshawi Polätikawi Temeherti Netägadälti.* 2 vols. n.d.

_____. *Memorandum.* August 1978.

_____. *Vanguard.* January 1975, August, 1977.

Research and Information Center on Eritrea. *Revolution in Eritrea: Eyewitness Reports.* 1980.

_____. *The Eritrean Case: Proceedings of the Permanent People's Tribunal.* Rome, 1982.

C. Articles

Bahru Zewde, "The Concept of Japanization in the Intellectual History of Modern Ethiopia." *Proceedings of the Fifth Seminar of the Department of History* (Addis Ababa: Addis Ababa University, 1990).

Bell, J. B. "Bab El Mandab, Strategic Trouble Spot." *Orbis* XVI, 14(1972-3).

_____. "Endemic Insurgency and International Order: The Eritrean Experience." *Orbis* XVIII, 2(Summer 1974).

Campbell, John F. "Background to the Eritrean Conflict: Differed Results of Colonial Map-Making, Geopolitics and Religion." *Africa Report,* May 1971.

Caulk, Richard A. "Ethiopia and the Horn," in A. Roberts (ed.), *The Cambridge History of Africa,* Vol. VII

Clapham, Christopher. "The Structure of Regional Conflict in Northern Ethiopia." *Henok: Journal of Historical and Philosophical Thought I* (August 1990).

Connell, Dan. "The Birth of an Eritrean Nation." *Horn of Africa* III, 1(1980).

Cumming, Cameron Duncan. "The Disposal of Eritrea." *The Middle East Journal* VII, 1(Winter 1953).

Ellingson, Lloyd. "The Origins and Development of the Eritrean Liberation Movement." *Proceedings of the Fifth International Conference of Ethiopian Studies* 1978.

Erlich, Haggai. "Tigrean Nationalism, British Involvement and Haile Selassie's Emerging Absolutism in Northern Ethiopia." *Asian and African Studies* XV (1981).

———. "Ras Alula, Ras Seyum, Tigre and Ethiopia's Integrity." *Eighth International Conference of Ethiopian Studies*, Addis Ababa, 1984.

———. "Tigre in Modern Ethiopian History." *A Paper Presented at the Seventh International Conference of Ethiopian Studies*. Lund, 1982.

Gamst, Frederick C. "The Horn of Africa as a Problem Area in Anthropological Perspective." *XIth International Congress of Anthropological and Ethnological Sciences.* Harrison Hot Springs, British Columbia, August 1983.

Haines, Grove C. "The Problem of the Italian Colonies." *Middle East Journal* I(October 1945).

Halliday, Fred. "The Fighting in Eritrea." *New Left Review* 67 (May-June 1971).

Longrigg, S.H. "Italy's Colonies." *The Spectator* July 27, 1945.

———. "Disposal of Italian Africa." *International Affairs* XXI(July 1945).

———. "The Future Administration of Eritrea." *East Africa and Rhodesia* July 20, 1946.

———. "Eritrea: Present and Future." *United Empire* September 1946.

McCann, James C. "A Dura Revolution and Frontier Agriculture in Northwest Ethiopia, 1898-1920." *Journal of African History* 31 (1990).

Moreno, M. Martino. "La politica di razza e la politica coloniale Italiana," *Gli annali dell'Africa Italiana* 2:2 (1939).

Morrison, Godfrey. "Eritrea and the Southern Sudan: Aspects of Some Wider African Problems." *The Minority Rights Group Report* no. 5, London, 1976.

Nadel, S.F. "Notes on Beni-Amer Society." *Sudan Notes and Records* XXVI, 1(1945).

Pliny [pen name]. "Eclectic Notes on the Eritrean Liberation Front, E Pluribus unum?" *Ethiopianist Notes*. Michigan State University, 1978.

Shumet Sishagne. "When Guerilla's Become Gevernment: The Political Tradition in the Eritrean Peoples Liberation Front and the Tigray Peoples Liberation Front and Its Connection with the Recent Ethio-Eritrean Conflict," *International Third World Studies Journal & Review,* Vol. 12, 2001.

_____. "The Genesis of the Differences in the Eritrean Secessionist Movement," *Proceeding of the Eighth International Conference of Ethiopian Studies,* vol II, 1988.

_____. "Notes on the Backround to the Eritrean Problem," *Proceedings of the Second Annual Seminar of the Department of History, Addis Ababa University,* Addis Ababa, 1984.

_____. "Yä Eretra Hezboch Yä Andenät Tegel," Dialogue, 3rd Series, Vol.1 no. 2 Addis Ababa 1992.

Taye Geremew. "Rebellion in Eritrea - Who is Behind it? What are its Aims?" *New Middle East* 31(April 1971).

Taylor, Graham. "Ethiopia's Rebellion." *Africa Report* December 1969.

D. Books

Addis Hiwet. *Ethiopia: From Autocracy to Revolution.* London: Review of African Political Economy, 1975.

Alazar Tesfa Michael. *Eritrea Today: Fascist Occupation Under the Nose of British Military.* Essex: New Times Book Department, n.d.

Anderson, Benedict. *Imagined Communities: Reflections on the Origin and Spread of Nationalism.* London: Verso, 1983.

Badoglio, Pietro (Marshal). *The War in Abyssinia.* New York: G.P. Putnam's Sons, 1937.

Baker, J.A. *Eritrea, 1941.* London: Faber and Faber, 1966.

Bahru Zewde. *A History of Modern Ethiopia, 1855-1991* London: James Currey, 2002.

Bereket Habte Selassie. *Conflict and Intervention in the Horn of Africa.* New York: Monthly Review Press, 1980.

_____. *Eritrea and the United Nations.* Trenton, N.J.: The Red Sea Press, 1989.

Byrnes, James F. *Speaking Frankly.* New York: Harper & Brothers, 1947.

Cabral, Amilcar. *Revolution in Guinea.* London: Stage One, 1969.

Cahsai Berhane and Williamson, E.C. *Érythrée: Un peuple en marche.* Paris: L'Harmattan, 1985.

Clapham, Christopher. *Transformation and Continuity in Revolutionary Ethiopia.* Cambridge: Cambridge University Press, 1988.

_____. *Haile-Selassie's Government.* New York: Praeger, 1969.

Davidson, Basil; Cliffe, Lionel; and Bereket Habte Selassie (eds.). *Behind the War in Eritrea.* Nottingham: Spokesman Press, 1980.

De Bono, Emilio. *Anno XIIII: The Conquest of an Empire*. London: Cressent Press, 1937.

Del Boca, Angelo. *Gli Italiani in Africa Orientale*, Nostalgia delle Colonie. Bari: Laterza, 1984.

Deutsch, K. *Nationalism and Social Communication*, 2nd revised edition. Cambridge, Mass.: M.I.T. Press, 1966.

Firebrace, J., and Holland, S. *Eritrea Never Kneel Down*. Trenton, N.J.: The Red Sea Press, 1985.

Gellner, Ernest. *Thought and Change*. Chicago: Chicago University Press, 1965.

Gray, J.C., Silberman, L. and an Observer in Eritrea. *The Fate of Italy's Colonies: A Report to the Fabian Colonial Bureau*. London: Fabian Publication Ltd., 1948.

Haile Selassie [Emperor]. *Feré Känafer*, Part I. Berhanena Sälam Printing Press, 1944 [E.C.].

Harbeson, John W. *The Ethiopian Transformation: The Quest for the Post-Imperial State*. Boulder, Colo.: Westview Press, 1988.

Henderson, K.D.D. *The Making of the Modern Sudan: The Life and Letters of Sir Douglas Newbold, K.B.E*. London: Faber and Faber, 1953.

Heywot Hedaru. *Yachi Qän Täräsach: Kätemehert Bét Wädä Qonsela Sera, 1925-1933 E.C*. Addis Ababa: Berhanena Sälam Printing Press, 1967 [E.C.].

Hobsbawm, Eric. *Bandits* (New York, Pantheon Books, 1981.

Houtart, François. *Social Aspects of the Eritrean Revolution*. Louvain-La-Neuve Belgium, 1979.

Iyob, Ruth. *The Eritrean Struggle for Independence: Domination, Resistance, Nationalism, 1942 - 1993*. Cambridge: Cambridge University Press, 1995.

Jordan Gebre-Medhin. *Peasants and Nationalism in Eritrea*. Trenton, N.J.: The Red Sea Press, 1989.

Käbädä Täsämma. *Yätarik Mastawäsha*. Addis Ababa: Artistic Printing Press, 1962 [E.C.].

Kohn, Hans. *Nationalism: Its Meaning and History*. Princeton, N.J.: D. Van Nostrand Co., 1955.

Longrigg, Stephen H.A *Short History of Eritrea*. Oxford: Clarendon Press, 1945.

Magri, Giacomo. *La Politica Estera Etiopica E Le Questioni Eritrea E Somalia (1941-1960)*. Milano: A. Giuffre, 1980.

Makereth, G. *Economic Conditions in Ethiopia*. Department of Overseas Trade, No. 507, 1932.

Mamo Wudeneh, *Yä Eretra Tarik Bä Acher Yätäwut'at'a*.

Mangano, Vedovato-Moreno. *The Question of the Administration of Italian Colonies in Africa Under Trusteeship*. Firenze: 1947.

Marcus, Harold G. *Ethiopia, Great Britain, and the United States, 1941-1974: The Politics of Empire.* Berkeley: University of California Press, 1983.

Markakis, John. *National and Class Conflict in the Horn of Africa.* Cambridge: Cambridge University Press, 1987.

Mitchell, Sir Philip. *African Afterthoughts.* London: Hutchinson, 1954.

Mockler, Anthony. *Haile Selassie's War: The Italian-Ethiopian Campaign, 1935-1941.* New York: Random House, 1984.

Okbazghi Yohannes. *Eritrea, a Pawn in World Politics.* Gainesville: University of Florida Press, 1991.

Ottaway, Marina and David. Ethiopia: *Empire in Revolution.* New York: Africana Publishing Co., 1978.

Pankhurst, Sylvia. *British Policy in Eritrea and Northern Ethiopia.* Woodford Green, Essex: 1945.

_____. *Eritrea on the Eve.* Woodford Green, Essex: New Times and Ethiopian News, Book Department, 1952.

_____, and Pankhurst, Richard. Ethiopia and Eritrea, *The Last Phase of the Reunion Struggle, 1941-52.* Woodford Green, Essex: Lalibela House, 1953.

Perham, Margery. *The Government of Ethiopia.* London: Faber and Faber, 1947.

Plamenatz, John Petrov. *On Alien Rule and Self-Government.* London: Longmans, 1960.

Pool, David. *Eritrea: Africa's Longest War.* London: Anti-Slavery Society, 1980.

Poscia, Stefano. *Eritrea Colonia Tradita.* Roma: Edizioni Associate, 1989.

Puglisi, Giuseppe. *Chi E'? dell'Eritrea.* Asmara: Agenzia Regina, 1952.

Rampone, Oscar. *Avvenne in Eritrea.* Milano: Nuovi Autori, 1985.

Ranger, Terence O. *The Invention of Tradition.* Cambridgeshire: Cambridge, 1983.

Rodd, Lord Rennell. *British Military Administration of Occupied Territories in Africa During the Years 1941-1947.* London: His Majesty's Stationary Office, 1948.

Rossi, Gianluigi. *L'Africa Italiana Verso L'Independenza, 1941-194*9. Milano: Giuffre, 1980.

Seton-Watson, Hugh. *Nations and States: An Inquiry Into the Origins of Nations and the Politics of Nationalism.* Boulder, Colo: Westview Press, 1977.

Sforza, Carlo. *Cinque Anni a Palazzo Chiggi, La Politica Estera Italiana dal 1947 al 1951.* Roma: Atlante, 1952.

Shafer, Boyd C. *Faces of Nationalism: New Realities and Old Myths.* New York: Harcourt Brace Jovanonich, 1972.

Sherman, Richard. *Eritrea: The Unfinished Revolution.* New York: Praeger, 1980.

Spencer, John H. *Ethiopia at Bay: A Personal Account of the Haile Selassie Years.* Hollywood, California: Tsehai Publishers and Distributors, 2006.

_____. *Ethiopia and the Horn of Africa: Hearings before the Subcommittee on African Affairs of the Committee on Foreign Relations. United States Senate,* August 4, 5, and 6, 1976.

Steer, G.L. *Sealed and Delivered: A Book on the Abyssinian Campaign.* London: Hodder and Stoughton, 1942.

Sykes, Christopher. *Orde Wingate: A Biography.* Cleveland: The World Publishing Company, 1959.

Tadässä Méça. *Tequr Anbässa Bä Me'erab Ethiopia.* Asmara: n.d.

Taddesse Tamrat. *Church and State in Ethiopia, 1270-1527.* Oxford: Clarendon Press, 1972.

Taddia, Irma. *L'Eritrea - Colonia 1890-1952: Paesaggi, Strutture, Uomini del colonialismo.* Milano: Franco Angeli, 1986.

Talbot, David A. *Haile Selassie I: Silver Jubilee.* Rotterdam: W.P. Van Stockum & Zoon Publishers, 1955.

Tekeste Negash. *Italian Colonialism in Eritrea, 1882-1941: Policies, Praxis and Impact.* Uppsala: Acta Universitatis Upsaliensis, 1987.

_____. *No Medicine for the Bite of a White Snake: Notes on Nationalism and Resistance in Eritrea, 1890-1940.* Uppsala: University of Uppsala, 1986.

_____. and Kjetil Tronvoll. *Brothers at War: Making Sense of the Etirean-Ethiopian War.* Oxford: James Currey, 20000.

Tesfatsion Medhane. *Eritrea: Dynamics of a National Question.* Amsterdam: B.R. Grunner, 1986.

Thesiger, Wilfred. *The Life of My Choice.* Glasgow: Collins, 1987.

Trevaskis, G.K.N. *Eritrea, A Colony in Transition: 1941-52.* London: Oxford University Press, 1960.

Ullendorff, Edward. *The Two Zions: Reminiscences of Jerusalem and Ethiopia.* Oxford: Oxford University Press, 1988.

Universita Degli Studi di Firenze, Centro di Studi Coloniali. *Amministrazione fiduciaria all'Italia in Africa.* Firenze: 1947.

World Dominion Press. *Light and Darkness in East Africa: A Missionary Survey of Uganda, Anglo-Egyptian Sudan, Abyssinia, Eritrea, and the Three Somalilands.* London: Dominion World Press, 1927.

Zewde Gebre Sellassie. *Eritrea and Ethiopia in the Context of the Red Sea and Africa.* Washington, D.C.: Woodrow Wilson International Center for Scholars, 1976.

Zewde Retta. *Yä Eretra Guday* (1941-1963). Addis Ababa, 1999.

E. Periodicals

Africa Confidential
Africa Contemporary Record
Africa Research Bulletin
Impact International
International Affairs
New Times and Ethiopia News
The Spectator
Time

F. Newspapers

Addis Zämän
Christian Science Monitor
Daily Telegraph
The Economist
Eritrea Daily News
Eritrea Nuova
Nay Eretra Sämunawi Gazét'a
The Eritrean Gazette
Ethiopia (Asmara)
Ethiopian Herald
The Guardian (New York)
Yä Hamasén Dems'e (Addis Ababa)
Hebrät (Asmara).
International Herald Tribune
The London Times
Lavoro (Asmara)
Mäbrahati Eretra
IL Messaggero di Roma
Le Monde
La Settimana (Rome)
La Specchio
La Stampa (Rome).
The Sunday Times (London)
Il Tempo (Rome)
The Times (London)
Washington Post

INDEX

Abära Mäkonnen, 169
Abdulkadir Kebire, 43
Abdulkarim Ahmed, 137
Abdullah Idris, 157, 160, 162, 164, 169, 170
Abreha Täsämma, *Däjazmach*, 38, 49, 56, 62, 81, 82, 84, 89, 125
Abreham Negussu, 44
Abreham Täwäldä, 155, 169, 170
Abun, 26, 27
Abu Tiyara, 144, 172
Adam Salih, 155
Ad Täkläsan, 81
Adi Qayeh, 49
Adi Quala, 118, 173
Adi Ugri, 17, 86
Adobha, 140, 165, 167
Adobha Conference, 141, 142, 156
Adulis, 12, 98
Adwa, 81
Adwa, Battle of, 2, 21
Ahmad Adam Omar, 155
Ahmad Nasser, 160, 164
Akälä Guzai, 7, 37-38, 47, 49, 57, 63-64, 114, 121, 137, 149, 154, 171
Aklilu Habtäwäld, 42, 79, 104, 119, 121
Ala River, 64
Ali Ahmad Affendi, 144
Ali Gider, 171
Ali Mohammed Barhatu, 186
Ali Mohammed Idris (Ali Muntaz), 83
Ali Mohammed Mussa Rädai, Sheik, 106, 114-115, 122, 125
Ali Seid Abdella, 172
Alla, 154-155
Alula, *Ras*, 21, 46, 184
Andenät, 52, 111, 124
Aqordat, 43, 54, 59-60, 81, 83, 107, 129, 137, 149, 148, 162, 170, 180
Arab League, 131, 168
Araya Sebhatu, 47
Araya Wassé, *Däjazmach*, 53, 80, 119-120, 125, 147
Asfaha Abreha, *Blatta*, 47
Asfaw Agostino, Inspector, 47

Asfawossän Haile Selassie, Crown Prince, 71
Asfeha Wäldämikael, *Bitwoded*, 49, 115-116, 120, 123-125
Askaris, 11, 19, 22, 28, 41, 86, 136
Asmärom Gäbräegziabhér, 169
Asräsahañ Barakhi, 80
Asratä Kassa, *Ras*, 124, 146, 149
Assäfa Ayana, Lt. General, 76, 89
Assab, 85, 93, 108
Awate Military Conference, 155
Azzein Yassin, 160, 171

Ba'ath Party, 132, 160
Bäni Amer, 58, 83, 87, 169
Bahr Negash, 67
Barahi Negusé, 69
Barakhi Habtä'ezgi, *Azmach*, 41, 47
Baräntu, 40, 43, 54, 59, 143, 180
Barattolo, 17
Barka, 58, 68, 128, 137, 144, 155-156, 161-162, 167-168, 173
Barka Bloc, 140-143, 150
Barre, Siyad, President, 165
Bäyänä Barakhi, *Däjazmach* (later *Ras*), 47, 54, 89, 125
Beirut, 157, 160-161
Belay, Colonel, 41
Beni Amer, 46, 58, 83, 87, 128, 133, 137, 140-141, 143-144, 148, 150, 169-170, 185
Berhanä Keflämaryam, 111
Berhanä Germas'ion, 81
Berhanu Ahmeddin, 56
Bét Giyorgis, 57-58
Bilän, 137
British Military Administration (BMA), vii, x, 11, 15, 17-18, 22-24, 26-27, 29, 33-35, 37, 39, 41-45, 47-48, 52, 59, 71, 74, 82, 87

Cabral, Amilcar, 3, 10
Carbinieri, 16
Casi, Giovanni, 68
Casciani, Filippo, 68

Chapman-Andrews, E.A., Major, 21, 31, 42
Cerrulli, Enrico, 65
Cheesman, R.E., Major, 31-32
Churchill, Winston, 82
Comitato Rappresentativo Degli Italiani (CRIE), 67
Conditionalists, 56-57, 77-79
Crawford, Lt. Col., 43
Cumming, Duncan, Sir, 42, 121
Cunningham, Alan, General, 39

Däbrä Bizän, 5
Damascus, 138-139, 163
Damascus Radio, 132, 145, 148-149, 169
Dämoz, *Däjazmach*, 38
Dämsas Wäldämikael, *Blatta*, 80
Danakil, 46, 85, 118, 137, 153, 156, 168, 173
Däqemehärä, 22, 54
Därg, 176
Dawit Oqbazghi, *Blatta*, 41, 73, 80
De Bono, Emilio, Marshal, 27
De Gasperi, Alcide, 64, 84-85
Demét'ros Gäbrämaryam, *Qés* (later *Nebureid*), 47, 114, 125
Djibouti, 9, 25, 30

Eden, Anthony, 31, 70
Éfrém Täwoldämädhen, *Blatén-Géta*, 41, 79, 90, 99
Egypt, 2, 11, 15, 31-32, 46, 51, 73, 80, 115, 127, 130-132, 136, 144-146, 150
Elabärät, 172
ELF/PLF, 162-165, 168
ELF/PLF - Revolutionary Council, 168
Embayé Habté, *Däjazmach*, 111, 125
Eritrea Nuova, 70, 189
Eritrean Liberation Front (ELF), xi, 1, 9, 72, 115, 128-143, 146-148, 153-169
Eritrean Liberation Movement (ELM), 127-128, 143, 150, 154, 169
Eritrean Peoples Liberation Front (EPLF, Sha'ebia), ix, xi, 1, 10, 12, 143, 157-174, 176-178
Eritrean Popular Liberation Forces, 157
Eritrean Weekly Newspaper, 35, 46
Ertola, Luigi, 68

Fallul, 162, 172
Fasil Oqba'ezghi, *Blatta*, 47
Fessehas'ion Haylé, 125
Fessehayé Tasfamikaél, 43, 80-82

Gäbräegzi Guangul, *Däjazmach*, 79
Gäbräegziabhér Gilamaryam, *Blatta*, 4
Gäbräegziabhér Maharana, Colonel, 170
Gäbrai, *Däjazmach*, 80
Gäbrämikaél Gurmu, *Azazh*, 80-81
Gäbrämäsqäl Habtämaryam, 41, 74, 77, 88
Gäbrämäsqäl Wäldu, *Fitawurari*, 24, 43, 48, 53-54, 56, 81
Gäbrayohannes Täsfamaryam, 111
Gadaref, 132
Galabat, 27
Gäräkidan Täsämma, *Grazmach*, 105
Gäräsellasé Garza, 111, 124
Gash, 58, 128, 137, 139, 144, 156-157, 169, 173
Gasparini, Jacopo, 5, 11
General Command, 141-143, 150, 153-156, 169
Georgio Habtit, *Azmach* (later *Däjazmach*), 47, 56, 80
Giacomo De Ponti, 68
Gilla Germay, 139-140
Gondär, 6, 71, 108
Govanni Casi, 68
Graziani, Rodolfo, 11
Great Britain, 2, 16, 31, 46-47, 51, 65, 70-71, 73, 85, 95-96, 118
Greater Tegray, 30, 32, 36-38
Guido De Rossi, 68
Gura, 26, 40, 107, 122

Häbtäsellasé Gäbrämadhen, 169
Hadendowa, 58, 83
Hadgu Gilagaber, *Fitawurari*, 80, 147
Hagaz, 147, 170
Hagos Gäbré, *Däjazmach*, 47, 80
Hailé Guangul, 140, 147
Hamasén, 7, 17, 19, 21, 34, 37, 40, 44, 47, 49, 54, 63, 84, 88-89, 112, 114, 123, 144, 171, 173, 177
Hamed Idris Awate, 128, 143-144
Hamid Faraj, 115
Harägot Abbai, *Däjazmach*, 80,125

Haraka Tahrir, 127-128
Hassen Ali, *Däjazmach*, 56
Haylämäläkot Wäldämikaél, *Däjazmach*, 87
Haile Selassie, Emperor, 9, 12, 15, 25-26, 31, 39, 41, 43-44, 46, 55, 72-74, 76, 80, 82-86, 88-89, 130, 133, 147, 169, 175-176, 178
Hayläsellasé Gugsa, Däjazmach, 38, 49
Hebrät, 150
Heruy Tädla Bairu, 156, 170
Hididam, 139
Holäta, 21
Hussien Khalifa, 164, 173

Ibrahim Affa, 164
Ibrahim Sultan Ali, 130, 135-136, 144-145, 147-148, 154
Ibrahim Totil, 160, 164, 171
Idris Mohammed Adum, 144-149, 154, 156
Idris Osman Qälaydos, 129, 136, 139, 144, 148, 171
Iraq, 130, 132, 171, 174
Issayas Afäwarqi, 146, 154, 157-158, 161, 164, 169, 171-172, 177
Istituto Agricolo Coloniale di Firenze, 65, 85
Italo-Eritreans Association, 68-69, 86
Iyasu Täsämma, 124

Kärän, 11, 20, 26, 43, 54, 59, 60, 63, 69, 81, 110-111, 118, 123-125, 128, 136-137, 139, 144, 147, 160, 172
Kagnew Station, 154, 169-170
Kassala, 138-142, 148-150, 168-169
Kennedy-Cooke, Brian, *Brigadier*, 24
Khartoum, 15, 45, 70, 129, 131-132, 143, 145, 160-161, 163-165, 171-172, 174
Khatmiya Brotherhood, 61
Kidanämaryam, *Blatta*, 80, 90
Kidanämaryam Gäbrämaäsqäl, *Ras*, 54, 87
Kidané Keflu, 142
Kohayin, 139
Kunama, 58, 143, 169, 173, 177
Kurmuk, 15
Kuwait, 132

Liberal Progressive Party, 61, 62, 64, 67, 82, 84, 98, 102, 113
Libya, 86, 117, 132, 136, 161, 166
Longrigg, Brig. S.H., 25-26, 35-38, 40-41, 43-44, 45, 47-49, 63, 77, 123
Lorénzo Ta'ezaz, Blatén Géta, 41, 73

Mä'ashio Zäwoldi, *Däjazmach*, 64
Mäbraheti Eritrea, 70, 86
Mackereth, Gilbert, 40, 45
Mahbär Eritrea Mes Ethiopia, 52, 54
Mahbär Feqri Hagär, 3, 22, 24-26, 28-29, 34-35, 37, 42-43, 47, 49, 52-55, 60-61, 73-74, 77, 81, 83, 87-88, 120
Mahbär Shäwatä, 127-128, 143
Mälässe Andom, 42
Mängestu Neway, Maj. Gen., 76
Manka, 171
Marinoni, Bishop, 67
Marqos (Abun), 27, 54
Mäsfen Hagos, 169
Massawa, 2, 26, 30, 43, 54, 78, 83, 89, 93, 105, 107-109, 118-119, 121-122, 136, 144-145, 147
Matienzo, Eduardo Anze, 100, 120
Medri Bahr, 67
Mengistu Haile Mariam, President 175-177
Menilek II, Emperor, 4, 11
Michele Pollera, 68
Ministero dell'Africa Italiana, ix, 11, 68-69
Mitchell, Philip, Sir, 16, 18, 40, 45
Mogadishu, 144, 165
Mohammed Ahmad Idris, 144, 155
Mohammed Ahmad Abdu, 140, 150
Mohammed Ali, 2
Mohammed Ali Omaro, 137, 153
Mohammed Dinai, 137, 144, 149
Mohammed Omar Qadi, 43, 56, 63, 81-82, 87, 105, 111, 117
Mohammed Said Nawud, 143, 154
Moreno, Martino, 5
Mulugétta Buli, Maj. Gen., 76, 89
Muslim League of Eritrea (Rabit'a El Islamia), 6, 8, 57, 61, 63, 67, 76, 79, 83, 87, 93, 97, 101-102, 110-111, 114-115, 118, 124, 143, 148

Muslim League of Massawa, 78, 89, 105
Muslim League of the Western Province, 98, 101-102, 105-106, 110, 115, 120, 125, 148
Mussolini, Benito, 11, 15-16, 18, 25

Nägga Hayläsellasé, 49, 74-81, 83-84, 86, 88-90, 117-121, 146-147
Naqfa, 47, 54, 59
Näs'a Hamasén Society, 74
Nasser, Gamal Abdul, 130, 131, 145
Nay Eritrea Semunawi Gazetta, 35, 36, 82
New Times and Ethiopia News, 35, 44, 48, 82, 122
Newbold, Douglas, Sir, 20, 32, 40, 45
Nhenan Elamanan, 154
Numeiri, Jafaar Mohammed, President, 160

Obel Group, 155-156, 161
Occupied Enemy Territory Administration (O.E.T.A), 16-18, 72
Ogaden, 30, 33, 131
Om Hajär, 54, 59
Omar Izaz, 137
Organization of African Unity (OAU), 131
Orthodox Church (Ethiopian), 5, 26, 34, 44, 67, 79, 93
Osman Ajib, 155, 174
Osman Hadad (Kä'ntibai), 47
Osman Salih Sabby, 129, 135-136, 138, 142, 144, 146, 153, 160, 163-164, 167, 169, 172, 174

Pankhurst, Sylvia, 35, 40, 43-44, 47-48, 82
Perham, Margery, 36, 48,
Pét'ros Solomon, 161
Platt, William (General), 31, 45
Pollera, Michele, 68
Popular Liberation Forces, 153, 157
Port Sudan 127, 132
Project Adwa, 146
Provisional Military Administrative Council, 171
Qaddafi, Muammar, 157, 170
Quotidiano Eritreo, 86, 118, 122, 124

Qvale, Erling, 117

Radio Cairo, 127, 131
Ramadan Mohammed Nur, 146, 157, 161, 172
Revolutionary Council, 156, 160, 162, 164, 167, 170
Riyad, 131
Ruba Ansäba, 167

Sahel, 59, 110, 123, 128, 136-137, 144, 147, 156-157, 165-169
Saho, 7, 118-119, 137
Said Abubaker El Morghani, 61
S'ägädé, 64
S'älämt, 64
Salfi Nas'enät, 154, 156, 161
Salih Kekia, 90, 144
Salih T'ét'ow, 161
Samhar, 118, 173
Sänafé, 38, 54
Sandford, D., *Brigadier*, 31
Säraye, 139, 150, 168, 173
Sätit, 58, 137, 139, 149-150, 169, 173
Sebhat Éfrém, 161
Seyum Mä'asho, 62, 79, 84, 119
Seyum Mängäsha, *Ras*, 30, 46, 184
Shifta, 92-93, 97-98, 128-129, 134, 143
Shumagellä, 59
S'ena Dagle, 41
Smuts, Jan, *Field Marshal*, 31
Solomon Wäldämaryam, 155, 161, 169-170
Somalia, 30, 39, 45, 66, 127, 130-131, 165
Somaliland, 15-16, 30, 46, 48, 108, 117
Spencer, John H., 46, 101, 122, 126, 145
Steer, George, 20, 40
Sudan, 1, 7, 9, 11, 15, 20, 30-32, 45-46, 58-59-60, 69, 83, 87-88, 93, 95, 98, 105, 108, 111, 127, 130-132, 142-143, 146, 150, 153, 160, 162-163, 165, 169, 170
Sudanese Communist Party, 127
Sudoha-Ella, 153
Syria, 132, 150, 170

Tädla Bairu, 54, 56, 80-82, 106, 111-115, 117, 123-124, 156, 170

Täfäri Mäkonnen School, 21, 88
T'aha Adam, *Fitawurari*, 56
Täkäzé River, 64
Täkunbia, 139
Täsamma Asbärom, *Ras*, 37-38, 48-49, 56, 61-64, 81, 105, 113
Täsfai Barakhi, *Däjazmach*, 80
Täsfaledät Täklé, 169
Täsfamikaél Georgio, 149, 170-171
Täsfamikaél Worqé, *Grazmach*, 47
Täsfayohannes Bärhé, *Däjazmach*, 125, 170
Tässänäy, 40-41, 59, 135, 147, 171
Täwäldä Iyob, 169
Tegray, 7, 9, 30, 32, 36, 37-38, 49, 62-64, 84, 136, 165, 168, 176, 178
Tegray People's Liberation Front (TPLF), 165, 168, 178
Tegré, 59,125
Tegreñña, 127, 131, 178
Trevaskis, G.K.N., (later Sir Kennedy), 83-84, 92, 118

Wäldä'ab Wäldämaryam, 36, 39, 41, 43, 46, 48, 56, 57, 61, 63, 78, 81-82, 84, 88-90, 105, 113, 121, 127, 131, 136, 143, 147-148, 154, 160

Wäldägiyorgis Wäldäyohannes, *S'ahafi Taezaz*, 79, 90
Wäldämikaél Haylé, 169
Wälday Gedäy, 142, 169
Wälday Kahsay, 138-139, 146, 149-150
Walwal, 98
War Veterans Association, 69, 86, 102
Wavell, Earl, Gen, 16
Wingate, Orde, Lt. Col., 31, 39
Wingate, Reginald, Sir, 31, 46
Wolqayet, 64

Yä Hamasén Dems'e, 34, 88
Yassin, *Blatta*, 171
Yelma Deréssa, 79
Yohannes IV, Emperor, 2, 30, 38, 55, 78
Yoséf Mahs'un, *Grazmach* 139

Zäreom Kiflä, *Azazh*, 53, 80, 111, 120
Zarré Bakit, *Grazmach*, 47
Zoli, Corrado, *Governor*, 5, 11

GIVE THE GIFT OF KNOWLEDGE!

New Books you will love to read!

WWW.TSEHAIPUBLISHERS.COM

GIVE THE GIFT OF KNOWLEDGE!

Our books are the best gifts for all occassion.

So, give the gift of knowledge!

TSEHAI
Publishers & Distributors

We publish the books you love to read!

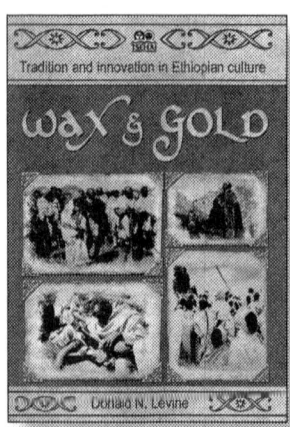

Guess What's Next?

You can place orders at www.tsehaipublishers.com, or to order by mail, send us a check at TP Books, P. O. Box: 1881, Hollywood, CA 90078. For any other question, please send us an email at info@tsehaipublishers.com or call us at 323-732-6685.

W W W . T S E H A I P U B L I S H E R S . C O M

www.tsehaipublishers.com

www.ingramcontent.com/pod-product-compliance
Lightning Source LLC
Chambersburg PA
CBHW071416160426
43195CB00013B/1706